Lucy Dent is a pseudonym – the author wishes to remain anonymous.

www.transworldbooks.co.uk

TURNED ON

Lucy Dent

BLACK SWAN

TRANSWORLD PUBLISHERS
61–63 Uxbridge Road, London W5 5SA
A Random House Group Company
www.transworldbooks.co.uk

TURNED ON
A BLACK SWAN BOOK: 9780552778824

First published in Great Britain
in 2013 by Doubleday
an imprint of Transworld Publishers
Black Swan edition published 2014

Addresses for Random House Group Ltd companies outside the UK
can be found at: www.randomhouse.co.uk
The Random House Group Ltd Reg. No. 954009

The Random House Group Limited supports the Forest Stewardship Council® (FSC®),
the leading international forest-certification organisation. Our books carrying the FSC
label are printed on FSC®-certified paper. FSC is the only forest-certification scheme
supported by the leading environmental organisations, including Greenpeace. Our paper
procurement policy can be found at www.randomhouse.co.uk/environment

Typeset in Adobe Caslon by Falcon Oast Graphic Art Ltd.
Printed and bound by CPI Group (UK) Ltd, Croydon, CR0 4YY.

2 4 6 8 10 9 7 5 3 1

MIX
Paper from
responsible sources
FSC
www.fsc.org   FSC® C016897

For Lummy

Acknowledgements

I would like to thank Patrick Walsh and all at Conville & Walsh, and everyone at Transworld, with special thanks to Michelle Signore, for seeing something in my story, for all her hard work, and for the invaluable advice and guidance along the way.

I wish to express gratitude to my counsellor for his supportive wisdom, and for helping me deal with things I was trying to avoid. Grateful thanks and appreciation also to my long-standing real-life friends (particularly the longest-standing of all, for everything), and the virtual kindred souls I encountered, without whom there would be no book. Love and thanks to my family, extended and surrogate, and to my husband, for his patience, faith, understanding, and for giving me his blessing to share my story.

Prologue

When you marry for love and choose not to have children, you can find yourself with time on your hands, and holes to fill. It was in trying to fill these holes – during our second year of marriage, seven long years since our first date, and with the realization I was about to turn forty – that I inadvertently made my life complicated, and in doing so my husband got hurt. For my actions – the majority of them online but, as any divorce lawyer would point out, not *all* of them – he has yet to forgive me entirely.

I did not expect to be drawn into a brand-new world so comparatively late in life, and neither did I expect to be writing about it here quite so openly. I am doing so, I think, because I know that I am not alone and I want everybody else who considers themselves alone to realize the truth. We are not. Back then, I thought my actions marked me out as odd, strange and perverse in the way only people who find themselves addicted to online activity can be, but in fact I am one of thousands, perhaps even millions. It is a modern condition, a twenty-first-century malaise. Everyone is at it. Look around you right now. On the tube, the train, in the café, the park; anyone staring intently into an open laptop, or else assiduously thumbing at an iPhone, is quite possibly *at it* the way I so incessantly was. Granted, no doubt many are actually doing entirely innocent things –

compiling next week's shopping list, updating photos on Facebook, texting a friend – but then just as many, perhaps more than you would expect, are as likely to be doing something furtive and illicit, a little grubby, and a lot of fun.

We live today in a world of instant communication, our affairs in need of almost perpetual maintenance. To those of us who didn't grow up with social networking as a part of life, it's still a thrilling, addictive novelty. To be stuck on a bus as it negotiates an early-morning jam while instant-messaging a young man you happen to know is still in bed and naked from the waist down can offer more escape than reading a book or magazine ever could. To be able to do likewise during a meeting at work – your colleagues yammering away as a message comes in, vibrating and furtively glanced at – is a pleasure to be savoured. I savoured it repeatedly. It made me feel fifteen again, which, at my age, is as close to time travel as I ever expect to get. But it also made me obsessive and needy, and it greatly compromised my marriage.

Writing all this down will perhaps give me not closure – no; I haven't done enough therapy yet consciously to seek anything quite so American – but perhaps instead the opportunity to draw a fundamental line under things: that was then, this is now. At the curtain-call of my thirties I made mistakes, and I hope I learned from them. I am truly sorry for my actions, and now I need to move on. I hope in putting it all down on paper I am not revealed as evil or malicious, but merely as ordinary and humdrum, just another woman with needs unmet who decided to do something about it.

Until recently, I lived a fairly blameless, uneventful life. I had a decent career and what I believed was a typical private life, falling in love with a succession of boyfriends before either falling out of love with them or having them fall out of love with me, and then starting over again, optimism blindly renewed. I ate well (mostly), exercised regularly, had never been too fat, nor too thin, and I had come to accept my imperfections. I'd like to think I had a competent grasp of fashion and had been told that I was attractive enough, or at the very least not overly unattractive. I was a home-owner, and though my career had recently been downgraded due to the lingering after-effects of the global financial crisis, I had been retained by the company to do the same job, albeit on a part-time basis. Losing the routine of a full working week was not exactly what I was expecting at my time of life, but I was just grateful to have any job at all and I never really had been the ambitious type. Elsewhere, I was relatively sane, reliably monogamous, and any neuroses I was prey to were capably maintained by the women's magazines I helplessly browsed each month, whose articles ensured I remained chocolate-loving, shoe-obsessed and sex mad. I had regular cervical smear tests, I visited my dentist. I no longer fake-tanned, and I kept in touch with my favourite aunt, my cherished cousins, even my mother.

In other words, life was good. It was fine. It could have been worse, and in many ways I was lucky. But over the past couple of years, boredom of a very unanticipated kind had begun to seep into my days. I had married a man I loved, and still mostly did, but I came to feel increasingly stifled in the suffocating state of what fairy tales would have us believe is wedded bliss. Our sex life had stuttered to a halt in favour of evenings in front of the TV. Age perhaps played a part in this, but circumstance too. My husband was four years past his fortieth birthday and mired in a job he increasingly disliked. It made him tired and he needed recuperative sleep. He snored terribly, so for several months now we had slept in separate rooms.

And though there has never been any rule that states married couples must make love only at bedtime and in their bedroom, my husband and I never were the kind of couple to do it on the living-room floor, the washing-machine top, the bath or the kitchen table. Especially not the kitchen table: it was Japanese, made from iroko wood, and it was my husband's pride and joy. We barely dared eat off the thing when it first arrived, much less splay our bare haunches on it.

The only things we did side by side any more were consume food and watch television. But I'd lost my appetite, and my interest in TV as well.

And so, after much prevarication, a lot of initial timidity and successive waves of guilt, I did what so many of us in marriage seem to do, if statistics are to be believed: I sought destruction. With the benefit of hindsight, I can say now that I wish I never had. I wish that I had opted for the quiet life. But whoever really wants a quiet life once they have one?

What started out as a whim to pass the time, then became habit; and it soon became what I suppose I have to define as an *addiction*. I got hooked on online flirting, virtual affairs, and in doing so stumbled across a great many like-minded souls whose postings littered the message boards like so much confetti, maintaining an endless thread of chat in which they divulged not merely their fantasies but also their personal problems with a frankness they could never do with their partners, their families, their best friends even. Online, everybody is there for everybody else, and so none of us need suffer in silence again. The virtual shoulder to cry on is now available to us all, twenty-four hours a day, seven days a week, 365 days a year. Christmas Day especially, I can now state with some authority, fields an awful lot of online traffic – the loneliest time of the year, the busiest time for chatrooms. In cyberspace nobody sleeps, somebody somewhere is always there, just getting up, refusing to go to bed, keeping up a marathon session fuelled only by Mars bars and gin, reluctant for their own entirely individual reasons to close down, to switch off and re-enter the real world.

Illicit affairs used to be conducted in private, hidden away from partners, furtively concealed from prying eyes. Not any more. Now that we can use our thumbs to update it, inappropriate behaviour has become the norm. Where once I wouldn't have dared flirt with anyone in front of my husband, I now did so all the time. Infidelity had become easier: my online lovers were always just a click of a mouse away, or else waiting for a response to their latest text, which I could type out during dinner even, while my husband sat opposite me pouring more wine. I didn't always respond immediately, but I could have done. And mostly I did.

But even in an instant world it was nice sometimes to make them wait, to tease, to stretch out the moment the way we stretched out moments at Christmas as kids, keeping the biggest and the best present in full view but unwrapped until, unbearably twitchy, we could take the anticipation no more.

Our modest terraced house – in one of those parts of the city that seemed to be unendingly gentrifying itself shop by shop, French-inspired delicatessens one week, artisan butchers with Facebook accounts the next, the streets crammed with self-aware creative types in designer specs and sockless sandals whatever the weather – was nicer on the inside than its smog-stained Victorian bricks suggested. When we bought it, it was unmodernized and tired, in dire need of what the estate agent called TLC. But it's remarkable what £100,000, twelve months of exhausting renovation and a near nervous breakdown can do for a place.

It was arranged over two and a half floors, with three bedrooms, the two on the first floor along with a large bathroom, and then another one, which we called the den, up in the loft. For the first few months of our marriage we shared the marital bed, kept the spare as a spare and the den crammed full with boxes of rubbish neither of us had the strength to throw out. But after our marriage Andrew's drinking increased, and with it his snoring worsened. Andrew had always snored, but lightly and almost, at least to my lovestruck ears, melodiously. Now, through beer and wine (and time), it had become deeper, heavier, and no longer quite so tuneful. By the time I'd banished him to the spare room, I was half mad with sleep deprivation. I'd invested in earplugs.

He seemed quite happy to move into the spare room – a fact that upset me at first. But then in sleep he was territorial about his space, wanting to claim as much of it for himself as he could, and so the lack of a wife beside him gave him ample room to do just that. He once used to sleep curled neatly on his side, but this brought pain to his upper arms now and so he stopped. He ended most nights flat on his back, in a pose that rendered him faintly cadaverous: arms and legs spread, mouth agape. Only the snores confirmed that he was still alive, and they were sometimes so loud you could practically see them disturbing the air around him.

I thought I'd be lonely in bed all by myself, and I was, ultimately, but I also came to love my personal space. The room had a lovely soft carpet underfoot and a huge built-in cupboard. I'd bought a chest of drawers to go alongside it and a brand-new make-up table which I set in front of the window, allowing me to look out on to the quiet road with its cats and cars and, at night, its furtive foxes. I felt protected in there, and with my earplugs in I began to sleep better than I had in years.

The room was my sole domain, my sacred cocoon. And it became, in time, my place of separate, solo pleasure.

Now, before retiring for the night, I went to feed Rummy, our hamster, in his cage in a corner of our living room. Rummy had belonged to a neighbour of ours who asked us to look after him while they were off on holiday. But they had returned months ago and had never come to claim him. He was ours now, Andrew doting on the thing in a way that spoke of hidden depths, and, just perhaps, secret paternal longings. I poured some seeds into his bowl and waited for him to emerge from his red plastic house. I called his name a couple of times, quietly, but Rummy stayed where he was, hidden beneath a bed of straw.

Switching the light off, I climbed the stairs, went to the toilet, brushed my teeth and then my hair. I walked past Andrew's room, he already dead to the world and noisily letting the world know about it, and into mine, where I changed into my pyjamas, inserted my earplugs, got into bed, and eagerly angled the laptop open.

A couple of messages were awaiting me, both from the man who had come to dominate my life of late, Paranoidandroid. My breath caught in my throat as I opened them. As I read the messages I knew that it would be another sleepless night.

Paranoidandroid: I'm here . . . and thinking of you, in case you need distracting, now or later . . .

Paranoidandroid: And in turn I hope you're there thinking of me, because I *need* distracting, both now and later . . .

A warmth filled me. I smiled, and started typing.

Lucy: Hello. I'm here – now, later, and for all the bits in between. So tell me, what exactly did you have in mind . . . ?

Paranoidandroid: hey, you're there! Well I'm open to suggestions, as ever . . .

Lucy: You're open to lots of things from what I gather ;)

Paranoidandroid: yes, well (blushes) . . .

Paranoidandroid: but right at this moment in time I'd just love

7

to slide next to you, wherever you may be . . .

Paranoidandroid: where are you, incidentally?

Lucy: I'm under the sheets.

Paranoidandroid: naked?

Lucy: let me check. Yes.

Paranoidandroid: perfect.

Lucy: And then what would you do? I'm all ears.

And once again I was lost to the words on my screen as they scrolled quickly by, consuming my nighttime hours and keeping me so blissfully occupied.

Paranoidandroid: I miss you when I'm not *with* you.

Lucy: *With* me?

Paranoidandroid: here, online, typing. Talking.

Lucy: it's nice to be missed, to be noticed.

Paranoidandroid: your husband doesn't notice you?

Lucy: He's usually tired. It's usually been a long day. He wants to unwind, to kill a bottle of wine in front of the television. He knows I'm there, that I'm next to him on the sofa . . . But, no, he doesn't *notice* me.

Lucy: not like you do ;)

Paranoidandroid: he's a fool! If I had you next to me on the sofa . . .

Lucy: yes . . . ?

Paranoidandroid: . . . Well, I'd notice you. I wouldn't take you for granted. *Ever*.

Lucy: it's what happens when you grow up, I'm afraid. It's called marriage.

Paranoidandroid: you're sounding very cynical.

Lucy: you find me at a low point, I'm afraid. I apologize.

Paranoidandroid: a marital spat?

Lucy: one of many. It's how we communicate these days, through

8

marital spats.

Paranoidandroid: ☹

What was I doing? This was not the direction I wanted to be heading in tonight. I changed the subject.

Lucy: Anyway. You've asked me what I'm wearing, but what about you?

Paranoidandroid: let me check . . .

Paranoidandroid: nothing. Naked, except for socks.

Lucy: socks???

Paranoidandroid: It's cold in here!

Lucy: I have a request.

Paranoidandroid: do tell.

Lucy: I'd like you sockless.

Paranoidandroid: both of them?

Lucy: both of them.

Paranoidandroid: okay, done. Naked as the day they were born. As naked as you.

Lucy: you have nice feet, soft, tender, fragrant :P

Paranoidandroid: careful. You're revealing yourself as kinky. Are you a foot fetishist?

Lucy: not normally, no, but you have the strangest effect on me. With you, everything appeals.

Paranoidandroid: Wow.

Paranoidandroid: you make my heart beat faster, you know, Lucy? When we start doing . . . these things, I feel at first full of lust, but then halfway through, you say something amazing, and the lust suddenly transforms into something else, something deeper. I don't want to spoil the moment here . . .

Lucy: No, please. Do go on!

Paranoidandroid: well, you make me feel . . . you make me feel . . .

9

I waited for him to complete the sentence, but you can be as tongue-tied on a keyboard as you can in verbal conversation. I blushed into the silence, and felt the same deeper emotions too. There was something nice about them remaining, for now, unspoken. I could wait. For Paranoidandroid, I would always wait.

Paranoidandroid: so anyway, what are you wearing?
Paranoidandroid: Oops! You've told me that already! Sorry, I got nervous! May I do something to you?
Lucy: yes please.
Paranoidandroid: if I put my finger *here*, and trace it all the way to *here*, what does that do for you?

Ridiculous as it sounds to suggest it now, I could feel his finger as it moved across me, my body raised in anticipation to his all-too-real touch.

Lucy: it feels good. Don't stop. Please don't stop.

The sun was up when I eventually closed my laptop, lowered my eye mask and pulled the duvet up to my chin. I was wide awake, my neurons alert to every sound and sensation around me. I could feel the pulse beating in my temples and in the tendons behind my knees. The snoring from next door suddenly fell silent.

Some minutes passed. From outside I heard car doors, engines starting. From the bathroom I heard the sound of peeing, the splashback from which, I knew, would be summarily ignored by my husband, who never noticed such things. Next I heard a rush of water, the buzz of an electric toothbrush. A sustained fart, the rush of the shower.

I drifted, until the softest of knocks at my door and Andrew peeking his head around its frame.

'It's seven o'clock, darling. Time to get up.'

I sat up, lifted the mask from my eyes and the plugs from my ears, and made a show of only just waking up. He smiled, a cup of coffee for me in his hand, my sweet and kindly, un-complicated husband, at times so annoying to me in so many ways and yet in other ways so nice to have around and in my life.

'Sleep well? I can give you a lift today if you like?'

He came over and sat on my bed. I peered into his small brown eyes and saw the perpetual thumbprint smudges on both lenses of his glasses. He gently squeezed the flesh of my cheek in a manner that was almost paternal, *too* paternal, his expression one of unambiguous warmth, undemanding, ever-ready, mine all mine.

Guilt pierced me as it so frequently did these days, and I felt my heart tighten. I looked shyly away from him and told him I was fine, that I would make my own arrangements. The guilt lingered after he left, but I knew that I would not attempt to lessen it by giving up on my addiction. By this stage I was beyond such a consideration, too far into it all to back away now.

I heard the front door close behind him and reached again, helplessly, for my laptop.

One

It is important, I believe, to state here and now that Andrew was the best thing that ever happened to me. Before meeting him, my relationships were mostly disastrous, but Andrew was in many ways a wonderful man, voluble and doting and gregarious. Four years my senior, he was generous and patient and protective of me in a way no man – no boyfriend – had ever been before. It was not a mistake that I married him; it just sometimes felt that way.

We met eight years ago, in a bar that had recently opened on the high street, a place which just the month before had been an old-man pub with peeling paint and a mostly cancerous clientele but which was now all shiny and new. Andrew, I would come to learn, had been in the neighbourhood for several years by this point, the kind of man who had been perfectly happy in the old-man pubs. He was in his mid to late thirties, and we found much in common, both victims of a string of unhappy relationships, both now carrying wounds and wary of getting more. He was, like me I suppose, a serial monogamist who could never quite work out why each relationship had failed. I would in time find out that he was divorced, though he didn't want to talk about it much then, and never really would. At that still-precious, early stage in a relationship when couples can spend hours over a single bottle of wine *just talking*, he would admit to me that all

12

he wanted from life was peace and quiet, contentment, few fire-works, no drama, and, ideally, an uncomplicated and lasting love. 'Is that really too much to ask?' What he essentially wanted was not to have to endure the pain of romantic death again, which seemed fair enough to me, because neither did I. And when we reached the stage of declarative love – which invariably required *two* bottles of wine – he'd make heroic promises. 'I'll give you everything you ever wanted, anything you demand.' The first time he said this to me he was drunk, but in a nice way. He re-iterated it the morning after in a way that made me believe him.

He should have known such an offer would eventually lead to trouble.

I suppose I would never have met him had Jane not called that night, the first real contact I'd had from her in months.

She was a mess, and demanded tearfully that we meet for a drink and a catch-up. Three years older than me, Jane was one of my oldest friends, though in truth it had been years since we had been really close. These days we were more intermittent crutches for one another whenever either of us had come to the end of yet another relationship. At other times we could go months without speaking. I missed her, but her relationships were of the all-consuming kind. They required her full focus.

Her last relationship had just ended. Initially, she'd believed she had finally met someone who could possibly fulfil the role of father to her sons. At that time they needed both father *and* mother, because Jane was so obsessed with her new man that her boys, aged eleven and nine, were spending more time with their grandmother than they were with her. This latest boyfriend was an investment banker, profligate with his expense account. He had taken her to every fancy restaurant in town and also on business trips to Rome and Paris and Dubai. A text I received from Jane out of the blue a month earlier read: I'VE JUST

13

HAD THE BEST SEX OF MY LIFE IN THE WORST HOTEL!! I'd later find out that, though he could well afford five-star luxury, the boyfriend liked nothing more than low-rent rooms in which to live out his more lurid fantasies. But it proved to be a rollercoaster relationship, the kind in which Jane unfortunately excelled. He frequently omitted to call, standing her up in favour of returning rashly to his ex, before having a panicked rethink, confessing all and begging forgiveness, Jane allowing them each time to pick up where they had so abruptly left off.

She had never had an easy temperament, predisposed, it seemed, to scupper any and all chances she had of long-term happiness, but I was fond of her. She was tall and bright and sadly pretty, and it was the sadness you picked up on first, a general sense about her that clung like lightly applied perfume. If her boyfriends weren't the ones treating her badly, then *she* would treat *them* badly – a helpless affliction orchestrated to keep her in a perennial state of distress, her default setting. She loved the tears, the turbulence, just as she also loved the sudden upswing that such drama invariably brought with it: the highs, the incredible sex. Jane was not one of those women who ever yearned for a quiet life.

We met on a Friday night and started early: a quick bite in a vegan restaurant (Jane was on a diet, watching her food intake if not her drink), then to the first of many bars for alcohol and chat. We ended up in a wine bar, where we sat in the corner catching up, Jane lighting one Marlboro after another. The place was crammed and loud, and I gathered as much of what she was telling me by reading her expressive lips as I did from her raised voice. Her face as she talked twisted with anger, but there was an enthusiasm there as well that betrayed a woman in her element. She ranted and raved, and was heartbreaking and funny. She made me laugh.

She raked over the coals of her relationship, now quite dead, for several hours, wordlessly grateful for my attention, until finally, after at least a couple of bottles of wine, she asked how I was. The fact that I was in the position to chime in with tales of my own relationship cul-de-sacs and emotional car crashes brought an unambiguous smile of sisterhood to her face. I spent much of the evening reminding her I no longer smoked, and hadn't for years, but she kept offering until further resistance was futile. The Marlboro burned deliciously in my throat.

It was eleven o'clock when Andrew and his friend, whose name I have made myself forget, stumbled in from the pub across the road, whose doors had already closed for the night. They were to us just another couple of drunken suits, halfway to hangovers already. They were the kind of men we would have crossed the road to avoid, and yet their presence in the bar killed our conversation stone dead. We sat and watched, helplessly amused, shamefully aroused.

The friend's wallet came out, bulging with cash and receipts and credit cards, several of which he scattered across the bar now, saying to the barmaid, who was younger than us and more beautiful (and, consequently, fundamentally less available), 'Take your pick, darling.' He ordered two large whiskies, then, injured by the barmaid's pointed derision, swung around to face away from her. Elbows sprawling on the bar behind him, he scanned the room, Andrew by his side, and soon spied us in the corner, returning his gaze.

We were maybe twenty, thirty feet away from him. When he spoke to us, in a leery accent I couldn't quite place, he had to shout over the hubbub: 'Ladies, what'll it be?'

Jane, out of the corner of her mouth, whispered to me, 'This could be fun.' Then she stood up and, swaying slightly, shouted back, 'Vodka! Bottle of!'

He spun back around, reopened his wallet and with a flourish ordered one. Even from this distance I had the full measure of the man, whose every emotion was writ large on his face. A bottle of vodka purchased at this late hour at the request of a woman meant only one thing: he would end the night with an orgasm that he himself hadn't knocked out. In other words, *result*.

Moments later, he and Andrew came striding over to our small table, the friend with the bottle, Andrew with four shot glasses. They sat down and made their introductions. The friend was sarcastic and obnoxious, louder than Andrew and more conventionally handsome. Something in his repellent nature attracted something base and animal within me.

The vodka went down like water, and the rest of the evening became a blur.

I awoke the morning after in my own bed to learn that, actually, it was afternoon. The hangover was just beginning, but I already felt dreadful. I lay very still in my bed, aware that the headache was not confined merely to my head but had spread to the rest of my body. I padded into the kitchen for one, then two, glasses of water. The flat was silent; I was alone. In the bathroom I felt between my legs and realized, with relief, that I had not been molested the night before, had not had sex. I saw ink on my hand, a telephone number beginning with 07804. The friend, obviously. Perhaps I had played hard to get, or perhaps *he* had played hard to get with *me*. I couldn't for the life of me unscramble the confusion in my brain, and didn't, frankly, want to. I put my phone on silent in case Jane called for an update. I was in no mood to talk to anyone.

For the remainder of the afternoon I sat in front of the television and watched a daytime movie. I drank a lot of water, and intermittently slept. By evening the hangover was at last in remission, replaced with that familiar feeling of emptiness – a Saturday evening that found me all by myself again, unloved and alone, in no mood to keep to any kind of resolve. I called the

16

friend. Even as his phone began to ring and I felt that I should hang up now, immediately, I knew that I wouldn't. I couldn't. The pursuit of unsuitable men was, it seemed, my perpetual destiny.

He must have been expecting my call, because he recognized my voice immediately. He even knew my name. He took immediate control of the conversation, requiring me only to agree, to giggle, to say yes. He asked if I fancied meeting for a drink later that night (he, too, clearly alone and unloved on a Saturday night). It turned out that we were near neighbours, just a few streets away from one another. I was in no state to go, but I said yes.

A long time ago now – I must have been nine or ten – I heard one of the mothers at the school gate describe my mother as *damaged goods*. I bristled protectively, of course, but it nevertheless rang uncomfortably true. You could argue, and she doubtless did, that being a single parent didn't help – a single parent with no money and living in a rough part of town with a daughter she'd never really wanted in the first place; but then you'd need to account for far more than that to explain away *all* her anger.

She was a force of nature, quick to fury, her mouth perenni-ally puckered as if she had just sucked on a lemon. She was actually a capable woman who worked two jobs, but everything was an ordeal for her, each drama a hair-tearing crisis. Life was never dull in her company. If she wasn't crying, she was scream-ing. I would catch her doing this in front of the bathroom mirror, watching her make-up create inky black spiders down her cheeks. I would often fall asleep to the sound of her tears, and would lie awake the morning after reluctant to get out of bed for fear of how the miserable day would play itself out. Though she could function in depression, it sometimes got so bad that she would retreat to her bed, often for days.

17

Her depression had first descended, she later told me, mere hours after I was born, though it was never officially pronounced as a post-natal condition. As she wailed uncontrollably at the very sight of me from her hospital bed, I was placed in an incubator while the nurses waited for her to calm down, and when she didn't, a full week later, I was handed over to Aunty Jean – not a real aunt at all, but a close friend of the family who became my surrogate mother, on and off, for some years. She remained an important figure in my life until her death shortly after I had turned twenty.

If my mother's depression mellowed out (assisted by Valium), it nevertheless remained prone to regular flare-ups. At nine years old I was regularly doing the shopping alone – she couldn't face the crowds – to buy food, and Tampax, and cigarettes; to all intents and purposes looking after her when all my friends at school told me that it should have been her looking after me.

It was my mother who first warned me off men, who told me that they were all wasters who would use me for one thing and one thing only. I was ten years old when she told me this for the first time, and I had no idea what that one thing could be. 'Just look at your father,' she told me. This was a figure of speech, because my father was not around for me to look at. He had left before I was two and dipped back into my life only infrequently, perhaps once every couple of years, and never for more than a few hours at a time. I have vague memories of being eight or nine, and a milkshake spill at Wimpy's; or grazed knees at the playground, the man whose hand was holding mine as much a stranger to me as I must have been to him. On those occasions when he did reappear, always unannounced but with an armful of presents, my mother raged, at me mostly, and then took to bed. She would invariably land herself a new boyfriend after his subsequent departure, someone skinny and mousey and leaking nicotine sweat, who sprawled proprietorially on our living-room couch and unnerved me; but he would never last for long. And when these relationships ended, which of course they did, her depressions would turn to furious despair. She needed to vent on somebody, and I was all she had. I was regularly blamed for my father having left her ('We were happy until you came along,' said with an Elvis sneer), and she would chase me round the kitchen with a wooden spoon, landing as many blows to my head as she could. I became good at ducking these lunges, but not always. Other times, she would make me kneel on my bare knees on the front doormat, the word WELCOME scratching painfully into my skin. Here I had to remain not only until I had apologized for whichever transgression she believed me guilty of, but until she felt me truly repentant.

In my teenage years she saw me, rightly, as chaste and awkward behind thick National Health glasses, and mocked me for it. But she still somehow convinced herself I was the school slut who would be pregnant by fourteen and bring shame to the family name.

'And don't think you'll get any help from me,' she'd say. 'I'm too young to be a grandmother, so don't you dare, don't you *bloody* dare.'

I would be married before I turned twenty, she predicted, and divorced by twenty-two, a single, miserable mother, damaged goods. 'Just like me.' What she didn't realize – perhaps what she *couldn't* realize – was that I would do everything in my powers never to be in any way remotely like her.

On the eve of my fortieth birthday, it was entirely likely that I was, in some ways at least, my mother's daughter, but I'd never fulfilled her prophecy and I'd triumphed where she had predicted disaster. It had been a battle to do so, but I'd done it. I wasn't an easy girlfriend; I knew that. As did many of my previous boyfriends.

This was something I was trying to remedy.

It wasn't, of course, the friend. It was Andrew. I tried to conceal my surprise the moment I saw him in the bar, but as I walked towards him, aware of the shape of my hips beneath my skirt, I realized that my surprise was tinged with relief, and gratitude. My hangover would have returned with a vengeance had it been his odious friend, irrespective of my purely physical feelings towards him. Andrew, in his own come-down state, was a softer and more gentle proposition. Boyishly handsome, with friendly, unthreatening eyes. He was sipping a Guinness. 'Hair of the dog,' was the first thing he said to me, smiling. He had a foam moustache which, rather forwardly of me, I wiped off with my forefinger. He blushed – and that was it, really. He blushed, and I fell for him.

A month later, both of us enjoying the process of having taken it slow, and we finished a date – curry, two bottles of bring-your-own – in bed back at my place. He was eager but nervous, passionate but tender – more tender, perhaps, than I would have expected. In his arms afterwards, I realized that here was a man I might just be able to fall in love with. I fell asleep shortly after he did, his light snoring sending me into a blissful unconsciousness. I'd imagined we'd have a light sleep before waking, then him making awkward excuses about why he had to return to his place, but instead we slept until morning.

We both called in sick for work, Andrew insisting he take me for a long, lingering breakfast. We went to a newly opened café round the corner, where we were comfortable in each other's company in a way that normally took me months to achieve with other men. He'd popped into a newsagent beforehand and bought himself a *Racing Post* and me the *Guardian*, and we sat at our large table eating and reading in companionable silence. From time to time I looked over at him and felt myself strangely content. He had egg on his lip, and his glasses were slightly crooked and smudged. He caught me staring and grinned. I could feel the people at the next table watching us, his hand finding mine, our fingers lacing together, me glowing with the pride of ownership. He was mine already, and I was his.

Because of prior bad experiences on both sides, we felt little need to move in with one another too quickly or to make any grand public statement of our love. We lived a gentle fifteen-minute stroll from each other's front door, a walk bisected by the high street upon which our social life unwound nightly. Though I knew by now that Jane had gone home that first night with the odious friend, and spent several subsequent weeks with him (it had been an expensive bottle of vodka), this was something Andrew and I never discussed, as if perhaps both slightly embarrassed about how we had met, a secret shared wish that the circumstances that brought us together had been more romantic. By the time Jane met Andrew with me, well over a year later, the odious friend was such distant history that I wasn't the only one unable to recall his name.

I myself had no real desire to move in with Andrew, not at first. But then I was never going to relinquish my own flat quite so easily. It was the first thing I had ever properly owned in my life, and I didn't want to give it up. Even my mother grudgingly admired it, and what it suggested of me. I lived on the top of a once grand Victorian semi, now carved up into three decent and surprisingly spacious flats. A young professional couple lived on the floor below, while on the ground floor was a middle-aged woman with an impressive windowsill display of flowers and tomato plants from which, several times each year, she would leave new pickings outside my door. It was that kind of house, and that kind of newly evolving neighbourhood: everybody looked out for one another in our self-consciously metropolitan way. You knew when autumn was on its way in our street when

21

all the wind chimes hanging from all the windows began to sing in harmony.

I felt more at home in my little haven than I ever had anywhere else. I had fallen in love in this flat, and had also realized here how easy it was to fall *out* of love and how living alone might just become my ideal state. I had had parties in this flat, had never been happier, and had cried a lot of tears. But it felt like a proper home to me, which is more than I could ever have felt about Andrew's place.

Andrew's flat, he told me early on, was actually an *apartment*. 'That's what it said in the brochure, anyway.' It was situated on the first floor of a new-build apartment block that appeared to cater exclusively to people under forty, and was a gleaming monument to bachelor living (and also, twice a week, Polish cleaning). When his marriage to the rarely mentioned Alice ended after six years, he ploughed what remained of his savings into this place, a functional but never beautiful one-bedroom that would remain perpetually under-furnished, his only prize possessions a leather sofa, a vast fridge that remained mostly empty, a plasma-screen TV and an Xbox. It was now worth twice what he had paid for it, but it still looked like it did in the original brochure. Walking into the kitchen was like walking into a kitchen-showroom display, with its shining electric hob, built-in microwave, chrome toaster and the espresso-maker. The most used item in here was the bottle-opener, which was not as practical as it was artful, full of curling chrome steel, hanging on proud display next to the fridge.

Both the bedroom and the living room were generously proportioned but basic, with windows overlooking the communal car park below. Only his wardrobe revealed the true essence of the owner, stuffed with expensive suits and ties and, beneath them, sensible shoes and a couple of pairs of trainers. Every time I opened its doors, an undeniably male smell reached my nostrils.

Staying overnight at Andrew's place, as I did many times over the next few years, was like staying in a hotel, especially on Tuesdays and Fridays when, while we were still lounging in bed, carelessly late for work, Kasia would let herself in, reach immediately for the Hoover in the hall closet and start cleaning.

Andrew liked his clothes, and dressed like a grown-up befitting his age. I would rarely see him in a pair of jeans. Instead, he wore suits during the week and mostly comfortable slacks at the weekend. He went for labels, high-end department store ones, and he wore them well. I was used to boyfriends looking like overgrown students; Andrew never looked anything less than a man.

Over the first few months of our relationship I met few of his friends and he met few of mine. Neither of us, perhaps tellingly, ever really orchestrated this; instead, we bumped into respective acquaintances in local bars and restaurants, dragging tables together and requesting more chairs, and enjoying amiable enough conversations but never such that we then suggested double dating, or going round to one another's houses for dinner parties. I sensed, though I never liked to ask, that Andrew was happy with this. Like many men I had known before, Andrew tended not to mix his friends. He had those he went to football with, and those he got drunk with. His oldest and closest friends remained those he'd gone to school with. Most of them had never moved from their home town, another couple were in Canada and one was in New Zealand. They were all married with children, or, increasingly, divorced with children. Two were dead, one from suicide, several in AA and NA. I had always thought my friends to be a little on the dramatic side until I met Andrew's.

But we became, for one another, a good fit. I felt profoundly in love and showered him with attention, kisses, little presents. I'd leave work early, rush to his flat and prepare him meals that, in those early days of our passion, we wouldn't always finish. I trusted him, and he proved tirelessly patient of me, growing accustomed to my emotional upheavals, my mood swings, my PMT; I in turn learned not to draw attention to his own fleeting depressions, those weeks when his mood would suddenly turn, when he would drink more and wake the morning after in a cold sweat and with heart palpitations, somewhere concealed deep within him an incipient fear of – of what, exactly?

We waited six full months before either of us decided it was time to meet respective parents. Both of us were reluctant, each for our own private reasons.

'You first,' I insisted.

'But *your* mother is closer,' he countered. 'If we got in the car now,' he continued, 'we could be at her door in half an hour.'

'She might not be in,' I said.

Perhaps I shouldn't have been so fearful. Half a year in, we had had all the important conversations any relationship needs to negotiate if it stands a chance of lasting the course. I found I wanted to meet his family, to see where, and from whom, he had come, but found I could live quite happily if my mother remained to him nothing more than a scurrilous rumour, the punchline to a sour joke. But he would not be put off, convinced he could charm her, unearth a softer side. He thought she sounded funny and amusing, a TV sitcom character come to my life, but it was clear he was much more taken by the sound of my late father.

What I had told him about my father I had pieced together via bitter recollections from my mother, some of my own and whatever I could recall of what he had told me himself down the years. If my mother was sitcom, my father was Ken Loach territory, a restless ne'er-do-well convinced he'd missed his calling as a British country and western legend. Stifled by a series of day jobs – hospital porter, funeral-home assistant, school cook – and the occasional brush with the law, he saved up all his money – money my mother felt should by rights be coming to us – got his first passport at the age of thirty-seven and bought a plane ticket to Los Angeles. There he hired a car and spent several weeks driving through America's backwaters before shoring up in Nashville, where he bought himself a guitar and began to busk on street corners. He passed the next couple of months living on his wits, playing every bar that would have him. They loved his accent, he later told me, his unusual pronunciation of those staple words for any C&W lament – love, divorce, Ruby – and his endless wise-cracking between songs. My father was in many ways perfect for Nashville, a frequently drunk dreamer waiting for his cards to fall favourably at last. He made friends, and even saw a future for himself there as a permanent busking barfly. America was full of them, after all; surely they had room for one more? But a ninety-day visitor's visa only ever lasted three months, even for my father, and on the occasion that he was stopped by a cop for jaywalking, a bottle of Jack Daniel's dangling visibly from his hand, he was hauled to the local police station where his transgression was dis-covered. He was driven to the nearest airport and instructed to get the hell out of there.

The memory of Nashville would sustain him for the next twenty years, in lieu of any other major incident to spark his days up out of the ordinary.

I only properly reconnected with my father much later in life, at the very end of his own. He was almost sixty and dying from cancer when he finally found me again, his by now thirty-year-old daughter. The memory I had of him didn't fit at all with the man I went to visit in the hospital. He was tiny, and hairless, a pale imitation of the few photographs that had survived my mother's scissors, in which he was cast very much as a man of his era, with his permed hair, handlebar moustache, shirt open to

25

the naval to reveal what Tom Jones must have seen in the mirror – thick, matted hair, gold medallion – and, to shield the focal point of his carefully constructed enigmatic shtick, a pair of heavy-framed tinted sunglasses.

I had to ask one of the nurses to point him out; he could have been any one of these dying men. The first thing he said to me, with a smile in his eyes that didn't quite reach his lips, was, 'You haven't got any cigarettes, have you? I'm gasping.'

He died two weeks later. I'd gone in to visit him every day, during which time he talked and talked, told and retold tales of his life, which may have been true, or exaggerated, or entirely false, his hopes and dreams mistaken for reality. He asked me little about myself, but I was simply glad to be there by his side, experiencing a deep and present love for the man I had never fully got to know. I vowed to myself that that was where I would remain – by his side – until at last he died. One morning he awoke and told me that he had a sudden craving for fruit. 'I'd kill for a tangerine, girl,' were the last words he said to me. By the time I got back from the shop, with six in a brown paper bag, he was gone.

My mother never found out that it was he who had got in touch with me from the hospital, nor that I went every day to visit him. An hour after he died I called her with the news. She dropped the phone to the floor, but I could still hear her cries, loud and dreadfully shocking. She did not accompany me to the funeral.

She bounced back, of course. My mother always did. He may well have been the love of her life, the one who broke her irreparably, but they'd been apart almost as long as I had been alive. The fresh pain from his death soon faded.

Over the years, I had introduced her to very few boyfriends, and usually only at the boyfriend's insistence. I always felt embarrassed by her and her blunt ways. Prospective husbands would meet her and, I feared, see me in thirty years' time. And then they would turn and run.

My mother was sixty-eight years old now, but age had not dimmed her. She remained in many ways a formidable woman. I was still young when she admitted to me that she had never been cut out for children, but she raised me in her own contrary, bare-knuckled way. She was not the kind of pensioner you could readily take advantage of. Cold-calling insurance companies quickly struck her off their lists; plumbers were cowed by her; in the streets, even burdened with heavy shopping, she seemed unmuggable. I can see now that this harshness was a form of self-protection. Not showing even the slightest flicker of vulnerability was her solitary defence against the world.

For the past ten years she had been living with Clive, a sweet and gentle man she had met at the bingo, a widower of sixty-five who liked gardening and cricket and bridge, *The Archers*, *Antiques Roadshow*. He had once been an occasional ballroom dancer, and liked these days to buy and sell stocks and shares over the internet. A retired accountant, he had sensibly put away enough over the years to ensure that they would live comfortably, but his online investments were shrewd ones and he spent his windfalls taking my mother on cruises, often whether she liked it or not. These days, he would tell me, he wanted to see the world in comfort and at a slow pace: 'From the prow of a ship would suit me fine.'

They lived together in a house in the green belt. My mother was officially a lady of leisure these days, in permanent thrall to daytime TV, while Clive volunteered a couple of days a week in a charity shop and at weekends played in the local elderlies' cricket league.

He was the best thing that had ever happened to her, and whenever I visited them it was with him I bonded most. It was obvious just how much he had enriched my mother's life, but I

27

couldn't help wonder what it was, aside from staving off loneliness, that she brought to his.

I was fond of him and knew Andrew would be too. My mother, I was regrettably fairly sure, would terrify him.

Andrew was very good at making a first impression. He could be gregarious and enthusiastic, a little overpowering, perhaps, but an ice-breaker certainly, and as we pulled into my mother's quiet, tree-lined street I felt confident that she would be helplessly charmed by him the way I had been. Previous boyfriends had been cowed by her; Andrew, I hoped, would be anything but.

Clive answered the door with hugs and kisses, a firm handshake and an exhortation to come through into the living room and get comfortable. My mother was still just upstairs getting ready. She'd be down soon.

My original intention had been to make introductions, but Andrew beat me to it, standing up on her arrival, taking her hand and pulling it towards him in an impromptu hug into which she pointedly did not melt. We sat down again and Andrew immediately began talking, his words tumbling into one another, repeated salutations, an unrequested explanation of his work, tales of home, an edited version of how we had met, the beauty of racehorses and precisely how to tell a merely decent bottle of wine from a good one.

My mother, habitually deadpan: 'Sorry, and you are . . . ?'

Andrew didn't catch the sarcasm. 'Oh, sorry, didn't I say? Andrew. I'm Andrew. Pleased to meet you, Mrs Dent.'

My mother, smiling at her little verbal victory, sat perched on the sofa, which I knew she would have hoovered moments before our arrival. A frown now creased her forehead and her mouth puckered reliably. Andrew noted the sour expression, which made him gabble even more. I silently thanked Clive for the steady, benevolent smile he beamed at Andrew as if he,

Andrew, were a sun lamp, with Clive soaking up everything he said, interjecting only to offer up encouragement.

'Fascinating, just fascinating. And there I was thinking it was all much of a muchness. The size of the grape, you say? *Fascinating.*'

Andrew now turned inquisitor, bringing my mother unwillingly into the spotlight. He was as eager in his questions as he was in everything else, and I placed a possessive palm on his thigh to quieten him a little, to slow him down. But he was too far gone and failed to register my touch.

'Anyway . . . anyway, what I really want to know from you, Mrs Dent – or may I call you Ava? It's a beautiful name, Ava – what I really want to know from you, *Ava*, is this: what is the best place, the best city, or country – your choice, Ava, your choice – you've ever been to? Lucy tells me you both like cruises and that you've been to – where was it? – all over Europe, down the Bosporus, up the Danube, the Seine, of course . . . See, Ava, Lucy laughs – she says I'm old before my time, and perhaps I am, but I'd love to go on a cruise myself! Instead of you going on holiday, the holiday comes to you. Fantastic! And all that entertainment laid on! All that all-you-can-eat buffet! I tell you, Ava,' and now he placed his hands on his stomach, 'I'd get fat; I'd get *enormous*!'

('He's certainly lively,' my mother would say to me in the kitchen later, offering an opinion on my boyfriend I had quite determinedly not sought. 'I'll give you that: he's lively.'

'You say it like it's a bad thing,' I responded, by which time I could no longer remember why I was in the kitchen with my mother at all, when I wanted to be back there in the living room.)

'Malta,' Clive offered now. 'We liked Malta.'

'Yes, well, of course,' my mother began, 'we can't compete with your sorts of holidays, can we?' Her lips pursed. 'I've heard all about your . . . your *adventures*. Lucy has told me all about them. Though, frankly, why anybody would want to go to Cambodia is beyond me.'

We had timed our visit to coincide with afternoon tea, which I believed would minimize things: a couple of cuppas, a slice of cake, then make our excuses and scuttle home to safety. But Andrew, getting carried away in a manner I would come to know so well, suggested dinner 'someplace nice'. He checked his watch. 'An early dinner. *Early-bird dinner*, like they have in America. My treat. What do you think, Ava?'

In spite of herself, my mother smiled.

Any hopes that the smile indicated the improbable – that my mother actually approved of my taste in men at last – soon dwindled during the meal. The fault, said the tacit expression on her face, was Andrew's.

'Who actually likes *fusion* food?' she wondered aloud, more than once.

'You can move the chilli to one side, dear,' suggested Clive, though he too was struggling with the exoticness of his dish, his cheeks flushed red, beads of sweat dotting his brow. Andrew, oblivious to their suffering, was regaling them now with stories of the places he had gone to before we had met – Vietnam, Cambodia, the Seychelles.

When my mother went to the toilet, Clive insisted to us that the restaurant was wonderful and that, spice aside, the food was quite marvellous. He had drunk so much beer to quell its fire that he was now well past tipsy.

'Shall we go?' My mother was now back at the table and already reaching for her coat.

'What about dessert?' Clive asked hopefully.

'"Green Tea Ice Cream" is *not* a dessert.'

We drove them back to their house, where Andrew attempted to embrace my mother in farewell. But she was too quick for him, leaning back sharply. He didn't even flinch. 'Ava,' he said, grabbing her hand instead, 'it's been a real pleasure. You must come to visit us next, and soon.'

In the car, he opened all the windows and, as I watched him at last unclench, I became aware that the day had exerted much the same toll on him as it had on me. He just hid it better.

'I have never met a woman with such a terrifying eyebrow arch,' he said. 'She could kill with one stare.'

We began to laugh, maniacally, our laughter trailing in the car's slipstream.

He placed a hand on my knee, and squeezed. 'You obviously take more after your father.'

It was the kindest thing he ever said to me.

I'd never been on an adventurous holiday. Before Andrew, Europe had always suited me fine. I figured that it was a pretty big continent, with plenty of countries to visit. Why go further afield? With earlier boyfriends I'd been on a succession of romantic city breaks – Paris, Amsterdam, Rome and Prague – and I was just as fond of Devon and Cornwall.

But Andrew broadened my horizons. He had travelled a lot in the previous ten years, mostly with Alice, his former wife. They had been to places I considered properly adventurous, *Rough Guide* countries like Cambodia and Malaysia, a pre-developed Dubai and war-torn Lebanon, which Andrew reported was actually cool and cosmopolitan, and fantastic on a Saturday night. He would regale me endlessly with travellers' tales, always carefully edited for my benefit, referring only ever to 'I' and never to 'we', as if he had visited these places alone and not with the woman who would one day divorce him. He found it amusing at first, then perplexing, that I had never made proper use of my passport. And despite my vague assertion that I was afraid of flying – the flight to Prague had been bumpy and panicked me in a way I hadn't forgotten – he was determined to do something about it.

As I would come to learn, he loved to perform unexpected grand gestures – the kind I invariably loved to receive – and so, his first big present to me was a holiday for two to Vietnam, flying into Hanoi in the north and departing from Saigon, with nineteen days in between to travel by train and bus and motorbike from one end of the country to the other. The only luggage I had ever previously owned was a suitcase on wheels with an extendable handle; now I was a backpacker roughing it alongside my backpacking boyfriend. Our nights were spent on the Reunification Express, an appealingly slow train that never left on time and arrived later still, sharing ad hoc dinners we'd purchased on the platform moments before with our fellow travellers, Westerners and Vietnamese alike, before sleeping surprisingly well on the pull-down couchettes, rocked into dreams by the clackety rhythms coming up from the tracks.

I fell in love with Andrew afresh every morning, drinking sugary tea with him in the dining compartment and gazing over miles of lush green paddy fields that stretched out on either side of our train. We stopped in Halong Bay, Hoi An and Hue, in Dalat and Nha Trang, a seaside resort where I fell for a nine-year-old boy called Long, who offered his services each morning as tour guide, shoe-shiner and general fixer. On our last day there, before leaving for Saigon, we bought him pens and books for class, and a new school uniform – something I had never done for anybody in Devon or Cornwall.

By the time of our homebound flight we were ready instead to take a slow boat into Cambodia and never return home at all. I could retrain as a yoga teacher, Andrew could set up his own tour-guide agency for visiting Westerners. We were by then brown and thin, in love with the local diet and the gentle way of life. And, like all travellers, I suppose, we became convinced we'd found a new way of life that rendered our old one meaningless and obsolete.

It was Andrew who had opened my eyes and shown me a world beyond my own in the first place, who made my re-entry on to British soil manageable, who was there to keep me company back at home, in the rain, after work and late at night. I had met my soulmate, my saviour, and after our first holiday together I was convinced that I would follow him anywhere.

Where next I followed him was to his parents' house, in the same small town in which he had been born and raised. Because we both had time to spare, we elected to drive.

It took us seven hours, door-to-door. Seven hours in such close confines would probably kill us now, but back then, still in the honeymoon period of our relationship, we laughed and snacked and sang to each other all the way. Twice we pulled over for sex in the back seat. We declared our love for each other so much I thought I might burst with happiness.

His parents, Thomas and Deirdre, stood huddled together in the driveway of their modest semi as we arrived. They were, on first impression, everything my mother and Clive weren't – a jointly beaming, radiant couple, and genuinely overjoyed to see us both. They hugged me as if I were the returning daughter rather than a stranger, and within moments of being ushered into their small front room, a room stuffed with pictures and trinkets and dozens of potted plants, Thomas was popping open a bottle of champagne, pouring out three glasses, an orange juice for himself, and toasting us.

'To Andrew and . . . and . . .'

'It's *Lucy*, Dad.'

'I know, son, I know. I was milking the moment, is all.' He turned, winked at me, and laughed. 'To Andrew and *Lucy*.'

I wondered what it was Andrew had told them about me to be the recipient of such immediate sweetness. I had met several prospective in-laws by this stage in my life, but never had I felt more welcome, more swiftly accepted, and even loved. I watched as Thomas downed his orange juice in one, and then, while his wife and Andrew drifted off towards the kitchen for a plate of mini sausage rolls and a bowl of spicy Mexican crisps, he winked at me again, poured some more juice into his glass and topped it up with champagne.

'Just a snifter,' he said, and laughed in a way that made me complicit.

Thomas had a big, ruddy face, and a drinker's nose that exploded across his cheeks like a cabbage. His eyes were a bright dancing blue, almost translucent, and rendered him younger than his sixty-seven years. He was retired now, but had once been a publican. He had been locally famous, a bon viveur well known to everyone who passed through the pub's doors and much loved by the clientele. He had retired last year on doctor's orders – too much drinking, too many cigars, a thousand late nights. He was on the wagon now, but frequently fell off. Retirement didn't suit him. Their marriage, Andrew had told me, had been a tempestuous one: a lot of arguments, a lot of broken crockery, countless temporary separations. 'But,' Andrew said, 'they can't survive without one another.'

Deirdre was big and bosomy, heavily made-up and dressed in loud colours. Andrew once told me of her that she laughed to hide her pain. She was laughing now, coming back from the kitchen and spying Thomas topping up his glass with champagne. She approached me, steered me to a chair and sat me down.

'Take the weight off you. Now, young lady, tell me all about yourself. Andrew has told us many wonderful things already. Says you're a keeper.'

I looked up at Andrew, who was blushing deeply, and seemed younger somehow.

'Where are the girls?' he asked.

'Kathleen's on her way.'

'And Joyce?'

'Christ, don't get me started on that one.'

'On another bender,' said his father, still drinking. 'Less said, the better.'

Our heads turned as one to the sound of keys rattling in the door. A loud singsong '*Hellooo*' preceded her arrival into the living room, and then there was Kathleen, her mother's double, only younger, painted and glamorous, an unprompted laugh already rising in her throat.

'And you must be Lucy,' she said. I stood, and immediately felt her appraising me as we kissed cheeks, her small eyes travelling the length of my body, taking in my face, my clothes, the shape of my legs, the breadth of my hips. Alongside her, I could only look frowzy and old before my time, black and white to her dazzling colour.

'You've lovely colouring yourself,' she told me later over dinner – beef stroganoff and quiche Lorraine, improbably Deirdre's speciality. 'Where did you say you are from?'

To her, I was exotic fruit, a career girl from the city. Though I knew little about Alice, I did know that she had been from the north of the country, and by the time dessert was served – a quivering lemon meringue pie – her father whispered to Kathleen, so loud it was impossible not to overhear, that he was relieved Andrew was not going to marry the same woman twice.

'Scrawny bitch,' Kathleen whispered back. She patted my hand, and said, 'You're much nicer. Fuller figure.'

'She'll keep Andrew on his toes, this one,' Thomas said. Then, turning to me, he asked, 'Ever been married?'

'No, no.'

'Then don't!' he boomed, roaring with laughter.

We were drinking coffee in the living room when Joyce arrived. Joyce, I knew, was married (but wouldn't be for much longer), with one son. She lived on the other side of town and worked, like her father before her, in a pub, as assistant manager. 'Not a bad place,' Thomas had said earlier, 'all told.' She let herself in, but hung back. We could hear keys jostling and something else rustling, but she did not immediately emerge. We were all silent now, and expectant. From Deirdre's eyes came hope. From Andrew's, a pre-emptive resignation.

'Joyce? In here, girl,' her father called out.

'I *know*!'

She appeared now, tall and thin and nothing like her siblings, with accusing eyes, a sharp nose and a thin, doubting smile. She was wearing a short skirt and a tight blouse through which intricate lace could be seen. I could tell that she had been pretty once, but was not any more.

'Who's this, then?' she said, addressing me, but looking at her father.

'Joyce, love, you know perfectly well who this is. I told you earlier.' Deirdre, sitting next to me, put her coffee cup down and took my hand in hers. 'This is Lucy.'

'Calm down, Mum. I'm only messing.' She strode towards me and I stood, quickly, to meet her face to face and shake her hand. She towered over me. 'Lucy, is it?'

Much as her sister had done, she took me in with hungry eyes and didn't seem overly impressed with what she saw. Her mother, nervous now, also stood, and offered to cook a little late dinner for her.

'I've eaten. But I'd murder a drink.' Deirdre looked at Thomas, who looked at Kathleen, who looked back at her mother. Joyce laughed. 'Don't worry, I'll get it myself.'

I felt awkward, still standing there, a small coffee cup in my hand. Andrew called out to me, quietly, and I went to sit next to him on the sofa. Joyce poured herself a glass of red wine, full, to the brim, and then another one, which she brought over to me. As she handed me the glass, she looked for the first time at her brother.

'Andrew.'

'Joyce.'

'How are you?'

'Good. Yourself?'

'She's nothing like Alice.' Then, turning quickly to me, she added: 'And that's a compliment.'

Andrew blushed. Joyce sat down in between us. 'Has he told you much about Alice? I expect not.'

'*Joyce.*'

In many ways, I was relieved. If you come from an imperfect family yourself, then it can be inhibiting to learn that your boyfriend's is faultless. That his was just as dysfunctional as mine could never have been anything but a blessing. We were equals, still.

'He's told me everything about her,' I said, taking his hand in mine.

Joyce looked taken aback. But she was quickly laughing again.

'Could you tell us, then! He was always very tight-lipped about that one, was our Andrew . . .'

Deirdre and Thomas went up to bed shortly after eleven, Deirdre helping her husband up the stairs, giggling forcibly as he tripped up one step and then the next. Joyce called a cab and asked if I was pregnant yet, then laughed out loud – a private joke, I guessed, designed to soar over my head. Kathleen made me promise that I would let her take me shopping the following day, to her favourite make-up and nail parlour. She said she knew precisely how to help lift my complexion, that it would do me the world of good. 'You'll see.' Her enthusiasm was infectious. I liked her. Then she too called a cab.

Alone now in the living room, a large glass of brandy in hand, Andrew let out a long, low groan, like air slowly escaping from a tyre. He looked at me with a worried expression on his face.

'Still love me?' he asked.

'More.'

They say that if you can survive your partner's family, you can survive anything. I did, and although I didn't go on to become his fiancée for several more years, it nevertheless seemed like a foregone conclusion to us both. We were good together, and I felt that we could continue to be good together, a conviction I had never before experienced about a man. I'd grown up surrounded by divorce, both directly and all around me, and so marriage always seemed to me an outmoded convention that could lead only to misery. It was something I myself would side-step, or so at least I'd thought. But the longer I spent with Andrew, the more I wanted to mark our union with ceremony. I wanted, increasingly I realized, to stand in front of somebody official and say 'I do.'

When we finally announced our engagement, a full five years later, Andrew's mother was overjoyed. Deirdre said she needed some good news. Thomas was back on the drink and the cigarettes, and Joyce, a single mother now, was in a bad way. 'A good wedding is just what this family needs,' she said.

My own mother was less effusive.

'Marriage? *You?*' she kept saying, and not in a good way. But when Andrew insisted on taking me, her and Clive out for a celebratory dinner, she was suddenly all airs and graces, drinking more than I'd ever seen her drink, and laughing, too. My mother, laughing.

'Thank you for taking her off my hands at last!' she cried. 'I can't tell you the worry she's been.'

38

Clive gave me a warm paternal hug – the man I still thought of as my mother's partner rather than my stepfather, but whom I loved dearly none the less.

'So,' my mother wanted to know, 'your family will be coming here for the wedding, will they?'

This quickly cast such a pall on the rest of the evening that we forwent the pleasure of dessert. We hadn't thought about the wedding yet; we were still immersed in the pleasures of the proposal itself. It had come in a fit of impetuosity, Andrew falling to one knee on our penultimate day on holiday in Sri Lanka, and me saying yes not merely because it was my fervent wish but also because I thought it would give me something to focus on other than the impending flight home.

'Actually, we haven't decided where to have it yet,' Andrew admitted.

My mother's voice was loud in the restaurant, an Italian with few other diners in it. It carried over several neighbouring tables. 'What's to think about?' she demanded. 'Of course you're to have it here. Where else *would* you have it?'

The answer to this question would prove divisive.

As with everything in Italy, wedding ceremonies must necessarily pass through an unaccountable amount of bureaucratic red tape in order to be legally binding. It's a wonder a bride has any strength left to get 'I do' out at the end of it. Still, it was a small price to pay: we were getting married beside Lake Garda.

Our translator was an Englishwoman who had settled in the region three decades earlier in pursuit, she told me later, of what turned out to be a fickle Italian boyfriend who left her when she was five months pregnant. The baby, a boy, Stefano, was born there, and she stayed. She now ran her own small olive farm, which she admitted was making steady losses year on year. 'I may have to return home soon,' she lamented. But there was a glimmer of optimism in her otherwise rather bleak life, and the presence of Andrew and I were part of it. 'Lots of Brits are now coming over here to get married,' she said, 'which is good news for me, I suppose.'

She stood a little to my left during the service itself, where I imagine my father would have stood had he lived to see the day. The non-denominational officiator stood dead centre, a stout man in middle age, as wide as he was tall, and with a voice that you imagined would sound good bashing out opera in coliseums. A booming tenor, it seemed to rise from his shoes, which were black, with stacked heels. Though a civil ceremony, the hall nevertheless *felt* religious, and was far more beautiful than any we had seen in England – an imposing but crumbling edifice that, like so much else in Italy, had been standing for hundreds of years. The sun blasted through its large windows to produce columns of weightless dust that spiralled in slow-motion tornadoes as Andrew and I stood to patient attention.

It was a hot May day and I was sweltering in my dress, which I had bought just the week before from Ben de Lisi, following the most determined diet of my life. I had opted for subtle understatement rather than a pantomime of virginal white: swathes of pale blue silk clung tightly to the hips, generous and forgiving where it most needed to be. Kathleen couldn't look at me without welling up, not so much out of pride as distress over the fact that her fashion tips had fallen on such conspicuously deaf ears. Beside me, Andrew was bright red in his black morning suit, smiling and handsome. I couldn't wait to become his wife.

For the kind of reasons that befall all weddings – complicated familial ones mired in unnecessary misery and misunderstanding – we had decided not to get married in England. Our first proposed location, France, was taken as such a slight to my mother that she refused, point-blank, to attend, and refused also to speak to me until I relented. My prospective in-laws were reluctant to travel as well, many of them still incredulous that Andrew had settled in our shared city two decades before. 'Besides,' Joyce told me, 'it's where he honeymooned with Alice. Bad karma.' We needed, then, some kind of compromise, a middle ground, and after a week's driving tour of Europe we happened upon Garda, a picture-book town set around the most beautiful lake I had ever seen, and fell instantly in love. It was a magical place, serene and peaceful and, thanks to certain low-cost airlines, cheap enough to get to without causing too much offence to our guests. Andrew, in a fit of flamboyance, offered to cover the cost of accommodation for immediate family, while everyone else seemed happy simply to get a cheap holiday out of it.

We found, and promptly booked out, a beautiful boutique hotel in one of the region's lovely little villages, and the whole wedding party would spend the night of the wedding itself in the hotel as our guests.

The Italian bureaucracy revealed itself in intriguing increments that would eventually span months, but we coped on a wave of determination compounded by the genuine joy that we were going to marry one another. We travelled there several times in the run-up, and then installed ourselves a week and a half before the ceremony to smooth out any lingering hiccups. We found hotels and apartments for friends, and booked a beautiful cottage each for our prospective in-laws, a safe mile apart. My mother and Clive's was my personal favourite, at the very end of its own winding road in the middle of a nearby lemon grove – perfect for her, I knew, because my mother never did like crowds.

She hated it. 'Too remote,' she complained upon arrival.

When she subsequently learned that her sister, my aunt, was staying in the hotel with us, she accused me of favouritism and spent much of her first evening in Garda locked inside the cottage's bathroom, refusing to come out. Clive and I sat in the living room playing Sudoku. 'She'll come out,' Clive assured us, after our banging on the bathroom door and my tearful pleadings got us nowhere. 'She's just emotional, is all,' he insisted. 'Her baby girl is all grown up.'

Andrew had his own trials, his parents bickering incessantly, Joyce missing the flight. But I left him to his while I got on with mine.

By the time the big day came, we were both emotionally ravaged and vowed never to get married to anybody else again. Too much effort. I felt no nerves as the car came to pick me up, nor as Clive led me into the hall. I was thrilled to be standing in front of my family and friends – if my mother was still smouldering, I said to myself, let her smoulder – and soon we were all back at the hotel for the reception.

All day and for much of the night I was light and airy, smitten with happiness, buoyant with relief. We were sat in the middle of the largest table, my mother and Clive on one side, Thomas and Deirdre on the other. There were five courses and endless bottles of wine. Everyone came up to congratulate us, the hotel staff performed wonders, and I was untouchable, floating above it all, a dazed smile upon my face. My mother moved several places away from me, complaining that all my friends coming to say hello were disturbing her eating, but I didn't care. I didn't care that Joyce had only arrived midway through the service, nor that she spent the rest of the evening becoming aggressively drunk. The children present ran gleefully amok, and I loved them for it, and loved them all the more when, after the band arrived – four moustachioed men in tight-fitting light-blue suits – they were the first on the dance floor. I soon joined them, and waltzed the night away, with my husband, with my friends, and then all by myself, my fairytale wedding now complete with its own fairytale ending: I had survived.

'We're sisters now, you know?' Joyce told me. It was some time after midnight and I was taking a breather on the nearest empty chair. My stockings were cutting into my flesh, my feet exhausted. I had reached for the nearest half-full glass of wine when she came crashing down beside me, her lean, angular frame clad in a sheer cream dress whose elegance was contradicted by the way she sat, like a man, her legs wide apart, elbows resting on knees.

I looked at her, and she looked squarely back. 'I know,' I said, and kissed her gently on the cheek.

The band played on, finishing on this balmy early-summer's night with their own unique version of Bob Marley's 'No Woman No Cry', sung in heavily accented English. Andrew twirled me around the dance floor while those of our guests who were still up applauded from the sidelines.

An hour later most people were in their rooms. Clive was asleep in one of the chairs, head tilted back, mouth open. I shook him gently awake. 'Geraldine?' he said to me, still in dreams, confused, and very quickly turned pink with embarrassment. I helped him towards the lobby and saw him safely up the stairs. Kathleen was crying as I came back down. 'Don't take it personally,' she said to me. 'I always cry at weddings.' I asked her why. 'Because they are so full of optimism,' she said. 'And so much of it misplaced. Goodnight.' Joyce was being violently sick in the bushes, but stood quickly to her full height, a good head taller than me. She nodded once, then walked with unerring steadiness into the hotel lobby. The staircase separated on the sixth step, one way heading left, the other right. I had told her earlier that her room was on the right. She veered aggressively left and kept going.

Andrew and I finally reached our room shortly before four. The honeymoon suite was not a subtle room, its walls a soft

43

pink, the four-poster bed curtained with lace, an ornate bathtub plonked in the middle of the room. I helped my new husband in through the door and over to the bed, where, moments after I removed the glasses from his nose, he fell face first into the pillows, instantly asleep. I looked at his legs dangling off the bed, his new shoes already scuffed and scratched, the laces undone. I slipped them off him. In his socks, he looked childlike, and harmless.

All of a sudden I craved the comfort of a bubble bath, so, after a quarter of an hour spent gently removing my precious dress, my stockings and my stomach-flattening pants, I lowered myself into it and breathed out for what felt like the first time in hours. I began steadily to cry – at first out of happiness, I think, but then, as the first light of a new dawn began to show itself through the window, I was no longer quite so sure why; but I knew that I couldn't stop. Time passed. The bathwater went cold. I pulled the plug, stepped out and wrapped myself in a thick white dressing gown. I curled up on the sofa on the other side of the room and fell quickly into sleep.

The morning seemed to arrive almost immediately and before I was quite aware of what we were doing we were making our puffy-eyed way down to breakfast where everyone had gathered early, despite hangovers, to toast us. Some had to leave early for the airport. Others would stay on for another few days, perhaps a week. Andrew and I would drive to the next village across and check into a hotel there, in need, at last, of some time alone.

'To the happy couple, and to their future,' beamed Clive.

'The happy couple.'

Andrew and I clinked glasses, but clumsily, his too heavy on mine. Mine broke, a clean shard falling away and on to the table, my morning-after outfit (Kathleen-approved) drenched in Buck's Fizz.

A bad omen?

Two

There is nothing quite like a marriage to focus the mind. We arrived home from Italy after a pleasantly uneventful honeymoon, tanned and exhausted but happy to be back, and yet somewhere between closing the door to Andrew's flat and switching on the kettle, I had a plummeting moment of pure clarity: that everything now lay before me, months, years, decades opening up like one monumental yawn. It was up to me to do something meaningful with my life now, and if we weren't going to have children – we'd had The Discussion, and neither of us, for our own reasons, was keen – then at least I would need a plan, a project, a continued reason for getting up in the morning. To date, I only had a job, but that particular thread was about to run conspicuously thin.

I had been working in my job, at a successful media company, for the past fifteen years. It had been my first real job out of university, and I had risen solidly through various departments, a key component amongst countless key components. In my time I'd been assistant researcher, researcher, assistant producer, producer, and now one of two senior producers on our smallish, close-knit team. I had no private office, no company car, but it was challenging work, and fun, and the pension plan would keep me from poverty. I had once thought of my job as a career, and one full of potential, but came steadily to the realization some time back in my mid-twenties that I simply didn't have the necessary aggressive streak, and that I was not prepared to over-look my private life in order to pursue my professional one. Back then, and for all I know still today, the company was full of thrustingly young ambitious types keen to make their mark, many of them terribly clever and terribly pretty, who would clamber over one another in pursuit of any likely promotion going. I just didn't possess that sort of drive, and didn't want to either.

I was by now, nevertheless, part of the furniture, one of the quieter worker bees at one of the more distant desks in a sprawl-ing open-plan area that forever hummed with anxious activity – people screaming about deadlines and bookings, and ways to tame the more hot-headed of our presenters (most of our presenters were hot-headed). Of late, I had been retrained as one of the company's so-called 'Change Evangelists', my purpose to help develop our company's web presence and round-the-clock viewer interactivity, essentially attempting to drag a very twentieth-century way of thinking into the new age.

It was going to be a challenging morning, another inter-departmental meeting which I was to chair in order to mete out company objectives to as many employees as possible. Today my audience would comprise some of the senior editors and pro-ducers across TV with their ambitious assistants. Because of recent cutbacks, many of the company's original interactive teams no longer existed. What this meant was that editors and producers themselves would now, in addition to having to make the programmes, also have to help create and control additional online content, a prospect not everyone welcomed with unparalleled enthusiasm.

I dressed the way I always did for such occasions, soberly, in blacks and greys, sheer tights, moderate heels – anything to help convey the level of seriousness required, and also to help allay my own secret fears that what I had to say would not be taken seriously. If it wasn't, then I would be seen as failing in my new role. This would mean repercussions.

Many of the attendees this morning I would know by face rather than name, a couple of dozen people to whom I would attempt to put a positive spin on what many of them, I knew, would loathe on instinct. 'Webmonkeying', as one had put it.

I was early to my desk, and set about clearing overnight emails that had arrived. Before long, senior producer June arrived and commandeered six of us to come over to the so-called 'hot desk' in the middle of our floor, the newly installed open-plan format within the company having rid us of dividing walls and doors – and, consequently, the possibility of slamming those doors – the better to encourage a statusless, harmonious communality among us all – or so a recent memo on such things suggested. As always, we started by discussing our main competitors' output. Malcolm wryly, if predictably, brought up how well our competitors seemed to be doing, knowing full well that such talk was frowned upon. June, having tolerated Malcolm for over two decades now, rose above it and steered us safely back to our own output, which we were all to critique constructively, but ultimately to praise. The latest work-experience person, never referred to by name but merely as WP, was dispatched to get us all coffee and Rich Tea biscuits. When she got lost, heading for one of the supply cupboards rather than the walk-in kitchen, I went to rescue her. She was a sweet twenty-one-year-old fresh from Cambridge called Jess, who asked me what the chances of meeting somebody famous were.

June was underlining once again the need for full and total compliance from all editors and producers with all the latest editorial policy, stressing that legal issues were absolutely not to be breached, and that defamation, slander or contempt of court must not in any way be provoked, even mildly, as it so carelessly had been just a month previously when X inadvertently slandered Y on Z, which had resulted in an out-of-court settlement that, mercifully, was never leaked to the press.

I checked the wall clock: 10.30. My meeting was due to begin at eleven. June caught me clock-gazing.

'You've got your content meeting this morning, haven't you?' she asked.

I smiled, and wondered how she knew.

She laughed. 'You always power-dress before one of those.'

The WP arrived back with the coffee and biscuits. 'Sorry, I forgot to ask,' she said nervously to the table, 'did anybody want sugar?' Half a dozen voices responded with an impatient *yes*. The WP blushed deeply, then picked up the full tray again and headed back to the kitchen. She stopped halfway and sheepishly retraced her steps.

'Sorry, how many does everybody take?'

Malcolm bridled. 'Oh for goodness' sake, girl. Leave the drinks here and go and fetch the bloody sugar.'

My stomach growled, though not from hunger. I had given similar talks on similar topics for years here, and yet the prospect of standing up in front of a room full of frowning faces – the company nothing if not a hotbed for barely suppressed foment over any procedural changes – always terrified me. For the past half-hour now my stomach had been audible right across the hot desk, churning last night's dinner into this morning's breakfast and sounding like an echo chamber. I placed a palm against my abdomen and pressed, as if this would help silence it.

My fringe, I suddenly realized, was too long, errant strands poking me in the eyes and causing me to blink.

'Hello everyone.' I cleared my throat and started again. 'Hello everyone, and thanks for coming. I know how busy you all are, so I'll keep the waffling to a minimum. Any questions, I'll deal with at the end.'

Twentysomething pairs of eyes appraised me coolly, but I had started now and had quickly found my stride. Already the nerves were beginning to evaporate.

'I'm here this morning to give you a demo of the new content management systems that have been designed to offer more to the viewers, and to make your job, I hope, easier in the process. This meeting is a good opportunity to brainstorm any ideas that any of you may have to help make that happen. We'll be looking at exciting new interactive offerings where we can all help to enhance the viewers' overall experience.'

Several members of the audience groaned, but I was ready for them and continued to spin the message. I explained that this was good news, that it offered us all even more opportunity to exercise our collective creative thought.

'Think of the possibilities,' I told them. 'The website is one, of course, and it's really going from strength to strength – the feedback we've had has been fantastic. Even the boss thinks so. But this is just the tip of the iceberg. We feel we can really improve on our presence, not just via the website, but throughout social networking, and I'm talking here about Facebook, about Twitter . . .'

'Webmonkeying, in other words,' said Malcolm, confidently speaking up for the older producers in the room.

There was a smattering of laughter here, but the younger ones immediately started discussing amongst themselves how they could add additional content and how best to implement it across these various platforms. I honed in on the brightest of them, Catriona, and asked her to share her thoughts with the room.

She reddened. 'Well, we could make use of all the stuff that goes on the cutting-room floor,' she began. 'And we could take pics of popular guests for the website. Anyone can use a digital camera. Even you, Malcolm!' she added, to his pantomime scowl.

She started to expound upon this, referencing possible new interactive functions, which viewers could be encouraged to explore the moment they craved more information on any of our programmes, but was quickly drowned out.

'Yes, yes, but this all sounds like it will take a lot of time, a lot of *extra* time, and whenever did any of us have extra time?' Malcolm wanted to know. 'I don't know about the rest of you, but my day is pretty full as it is. My question to you, Lucy, and to you too, Catriona,' and here she blushed even harder, 'is: when precisely are we supposed to do all of this? On top of our existing jobs? Would it be easier if we all stayed until eight o'clock at night, until ten – without pay, of course . . . ?'

Beside him, Sylvia spoke up. Sylvia was one of our more established producers. She had interviewed me for my job here fifteen years previously and was in the same position today as she had been then.

'How many people ever use the interactive services anyway?' she asked.

'More than you'd expect, actually.' I explained that we had just received the results of a nationwide survey.

'Yes, but who will approve all this extra content we have to come up with?' Malcolm interrupted. 'And what if something goes wrong? And where do we get the training?'

'Well, we can start here, today, Malcolm. Proper training will be scheduled over the next few months, and I'm sure we can find pockets of time during our regular working day, nine to five for some of us, ten to six for others, and our lunch hours will remain ours alone. I can promise you that. You see, Malcolm, it's all part of the ongoing restructuring, and it's what we all have to do if we want to keep the company successful.'

I winced at the clunking phrases I was so robotically trotting out here, but I'd been the recipient of training courses myself and this was the language, I had been instructed, that I was required to use with everybody else.

Groans unfurled slowly around the room.

Catriona leapt to her feet. 'I could help!' she said. Quickly, she turned to me. 'That's if Lucy doesn't mind?'

I assured her I didn't, and made a mental note to tell my boss that Catriona should be considered for promotion the next time one became available.

The meeting ran well over its allotted forty-five minutes as we explored the so very many ways in which we could all help maximize the channel's online reach and help to keep a hold of viewers who were otherwise increasingly abandoning us for other channels, for the internet, for pirated movies on their iPads.

It was June who knocked on the door and interrupted us, who reminded me that she and I had an early lunch appointment with the presenter of one of the channel's flagship programmes who had recently been grumbling about his contract, his agent threatening to take him to another channel. It would be our job, over a lunch of Dover sole and white wine, to coddle and ameliorate, to flatter endlessly, and to flirt if need be.

There would definitely *need be*.

It was a long, exhausting day and I didn't manage to leave my desk until a good couple of hours after Malcolm had left his. The lunch had gone well but not, I feared, successfully. I knew the signs by now, and so did June. The presenter would leave us for, as his agent so euphemistically described it, 'new challenges' soon enough, no matter how much Dover sole we bought him, and June and I would be unofficially blamed – nothing personal, we would be assured, but scapegoats were always required in such situations.

Coming home after a day like that was at first solace; I valued the peace and the quiet, my similarly exhausted husband on the sofa beside me. But the unnamed niggling sensation did not recede. I wanted in some other way now to define myself outside the office, if only to *myself*. If I could manage to land a husband, perhaps there were other things I could manage too.

In other words, we had to move.

Two months after our wedding we took the grown-up, and somewhat belated, step of making our cohabitation official. My flat had lain empty for months now, as I was spending almost all my time in Andrew's. After much personal heartache, I put it on the market and sold it within a week for what I considered an astronomical sum – over three times what I had paid for it nine years earlier. Suddenly, for the first time in my life, I was cash-rich. Then, with plans to put his place on the rental market, we began to look for a house. This proved easier than we could have imagined.

Given that our area was rapidly changing, the neighbourhood was filled with long-term residents suddenly finding themselves sitting on potential fortunes. And, unimpressed by the high street's sudden proliferation of independently owned fashion boutiques, they were happy to sell up at huge profit and move out into the ever-swelling suburbs.

I knew the house was right for us the moment I stepped over its crumbling threshold, despite the evidence in front of me – stained carpets, peeling walls, a rich, and not good, smell. Andrew hated it.

'It's awful,' he said. 'Dark, cramped.' He pointed. 'And look at the wallpaper.'

But I was already looking beyond it, and in my mind's eye I saw nothing but potential. It was perfect. I had my project at last.

A mid-terrace two-up two-down, it belonged to a sweet

elderly Jamaican man who had lived there since the late 1960s. He was selling, he told me, my hand clamped tightly between his, because his wife had died the previous year and he wanted to move further out, to be nearer his daughters and grand-children. He was so pleasantly shocked when, without even requesting a second viewing, we offered the asking price that he threw in the furniture and wouldn't take no for an answer. (The furniture, like so much else of the house's 'original' sixties features, would end up in the skip.) When the day came for him to hand over the keys, he did so personally rather than via the estate agent, and he cried as he clutched us both to his chest, wishing us a beautiful life together and many children.

But this house was to be our only dependant, at least for the time being. Did I know that it would drive me to mental and emotional ruin? No, of course not. Can an expectant mother ever quite understand just how draining her children will grow up to be? No. You go in blind, and you spend the rest of your life foraging wildly in search of that ever-elusive equilibrium.

The house was stuck in a time warp, circa 1968. It had brown walls and orange carpets, now threadbare and, in the corners, fungal. One room had been kept for *best*, with vinyl covering to protect the rug on which the largely under-used dining table sat, and there was a faux-leather sofa in the living room proper, whose cushions had faded and flattened. The kitchen was rudimentary, lots of Formica, lots of rust, and absolutely filthy. The bedrooms upstairs, both of them, were large enough but dark, and both dominated by DIY-assembled cupboards that listed a little because, as the owner had already alerted us, the floorboards sloped. 'I always meant to fix them, but . . .'

Modernizing all this would be a big job, but curiously, despite no prior experience, I felt up to it. Perhaps it was an age thing, a time of life thing, but I had seen all the television programmes and began quickly to read all the glossy magazines as if they were directed specifically at *me*. Renovation now appealed the way gardening had suddenly begun to appeal to my mother a decade earlier. I was somehow brazenly confident that I could transform a sorry old house into a model of urbane twenty-first-century design. And, thrillingly, Andrew and I now had the funds, if carefully managed, to do just that.

But it was to be a slow, torturous work-in-progress. Andrew's flat, which we had originally intended to put up for rental as soon as we could – the money from which would cover our new mortgage repayments and leave us with plenty to spare – would remain our home for another fourteen months. By the time we finally left there for the marital home, I would be frequently dyeing my hair to cover up all the grey that was emerging, and relying upon a prescribed inhaler to quell my panic attacks.

As for Andrew, he seemed perfectly happy to remain in his flat for as long as it took, and saw no particular rush for the house to be finished. 'So long as we've got the money, we'll be fine,' was a mantra I'd hear many times over the slow year.

But then, three months into the project, came the first rumblings of an economic crisis – first other countries, then our own Northern Rock, then everything else. Cuts at work were to be unavoidable, we were told, and it wasn't long before I was called in to see my boss. I prepared myself for the worst, convinced I was about to be made redundant from a company to which I had devoted, or in part devoted, the past fifteen years of my life.

'Lucy, could you come into my office, please?'

My boss was a nice, gentle man with a perpetually confused air about him that belied his many abilities. He smiled at me as I walked in, but forlornly. As I sat down, I was told that my services were valuable and would continue to be so, irrespective of economic chaos. But in order to get the most out of my services in the current climate, I would now be required to come in only three days a week. 'You understand?' How couldn't I? It was plain enough, after all: I would now be required to cram five days' worth of work into three, and for much less money. My boss, terribly apologetic, remained grudgingly positive.

'Look at it this way. I've had to let several others go – Sylvia and Sue, and Malcolm, poor Malcolm. But you, Lucy, I hope to hold on to.' *Hope*. Once the economy recovered, he continued, my lost days would be duly returned. We might even discuss a pay rise. To help keep up efficiency in the department, he told me, a department that required a great many tiny but crucial cogs, a selection of university graduates would be drafted in for the short term. 'I know, I know,' he said, before I had the chance to object. 'But they are keen, and they'll work for peanuts. And peanuts is all we can afford to pay right now. They're clever, and bright, and I'd be terribly grateful to you, Lucy, if you could take them under your wing and train them up accordingly.'

I'd spent long enough there to know precisely how to mask disappointment and dejection. I found the necessary smile, thanked him for his mercy, and returned to my desk. Across the room, I saw Sylvia comforting poor Malcolm and realized that I felt far worse for him than I did myself.

If my three days at work ran me ragged, then the two days at home, during which I oversaw the initial renovations, sapped me of any energy I had left. A few months later and my three days a week were trimmed, again necessarily, to just two. The country was by now in comprehensive economic meltdown. I wanted to be devastated by this, I *felt* I should be, but by now the renovation was becoming an all-consuming obsession, something to fret about day and night to the exclusion of everything else. And so I hardly registered it. Besides, Andrew was making more than enough for both of us, and the money from my flat sale was still steadily pouring into the new house. For the time being, things were fine.

*

The redecoration programmes on television and the features in those bloody monthly magazines had led me into a false sense of security. I thought I knew what I was doing, knew how to avoid calamity before it happened. But I didn't. We made mistakes, *many* mistakes.

Our first builder, for example: a mate of a mate of Andrew's. They'd met at the pub, but not one of the pubs I'd ever frequented.

'Irish lads, good as gold. I'm sure they'll give us a discount,' was Andrew's initial prediction.

I'd married a fool, clearly, but then hindsight can make fools of us all. Andrew brought them to the house one night for a prospective chat. There were two of them, Bill and Bungle. Bill was the mouth and trousers, a wideboy fortysomething of dubious Irish descent, the kind of man with an incorrigible twinkle in his eye that he employed all too regularly, while Bungle was soft and simple, a shapeless youth in his early twenties, football T-shirt tucked into a pair of stained sweatpants, and whose smile revealed large gaps between his teeth. They arrived in a cloud of nicotine, stinking of drink. Andrew offered each a can of Guinness from the fridge, which they greedily accepted, Bill wiping one hand on his ruined Lois jeans and the other across his whiskery mouth before drinking deep. He told me that he was a plasterer by trade but that he could do pretty much anything. 'The original handyman,' he grinned, casting an eye around the place, and nodding and grunting in what was possibly appreciation, or perhaps indigestion. It was difficult to tell. Andrew, meanwhile, gave the briefest outline of what we wanted, in essence, to do: transform 1968 into 2008, while restoring the original Victorian features.

'No problem, no problem,' was Bill's confident reply.

I went into more detail, but for everything I said Bill had the same response: 'No problem, no problem.' When they left, I looked at Andrew and shook my head. No, no. *No*. But Andrew insisted that I was worrying for nothing. 'It'll be fine.'

They turned up a week later, on time, with huge heavy mallets slung over their shoulders. It was a hot, late-August day, and Bungle already had huge great sweat patches under his armpits and across his swollen belly.

'Demolition first,' Bill told me, accepting his first mug of tea and slurping loudly from it. 'Can't put up new walls without pulling down old ones first, right?'

I told him, somewhat panicked, that I didn't want any new walls putting up.

He laughed. 'Figure of speech, darling.'

There was a partition wall separating the best room from the living room, and this was where they started. Standing at a safe distance, I watched as they went about their work, and registered a twinge of guilt; the former owner had been so sweet in his recollections of how it was only ever used when guests came for tea.

'My wife, she loved this room,' he had told me. I had at first felt inclined to keep it as a shrine to the widower, but Andrew reminded me that we had paid a fortune for the place, making the man rich. We would now do exactly as we pleased with it.

Watching such unbridled destruction nevertheless upset me, so I went back to the flat. But being back in the flat made me fear for the house, so I returned, quickly, and arrived to a volcanic cloud of dust pouring through the open front door. I called out an elongated hello, as if to warn them of my arrival.

'Back already?' Bill shouted in reply. 'Perfect timing. Gasping for a cuppa.'

I'd been gone less than half an hour. I walked down the hall and into the kitchen, one flimsy wall separating me from them, and turned the kettle on. Minutes later, I entered the empty living room with the tea to see a room now strewn with broken bricks in a cloud of heavy dust, the dividing wall already gone, rubble. Bill and Bungle pulled down the scarves from their noses and mouths.

'We'll cart the bricks out to the skip in a minute,' Bill told me, before adding, 'You know, you remind me of my second wife.' He looked me up and down the way Kathleen and Joyce once had. 'Same firm build. You carry it well.'

I recoiled, then tried to conceal it. It upset me to register the fact that, in a certain light, Bill was an attractive man and that he wore that incorrigibility of his like a charm bracelet. It upset me more, in the next moment, to learn that I was *that* kind of woman, happily married but so easily flattered by someone else's bullshit. I turned and went back into the kitchen where, for want of anything better to do, I made more tea, which Bungle then pissed away loudly in the toilet upstairs ten minutes later.

'I'll be needing some loo roll up here,' he shouted, the only words I was to hear from him during my brief time as his employer.

And so in this way began my year of hell.

My relationship with Bill and Bungle spiralled rapidly downwards. They would arrive any time between eight and ten in the morning, Bill immediately sparking up a roll-up, then sitting down with a cup of tea and a paper while chatting endlessly away on his mobile phone, Bungle beside him, his ears concealed by a pair of headphones. I would loiter in the kitchen awhile, then burst into the living room, ostensibly to clear away their mugs, but chiefly to prompt them into action. Often when he saw me coming, his mobile still clamped to his ear, Bill would hold an index finger aloft as if warning me not to interrupt. It was only when he clicked off the call that he permitted me to approach, but then neatly avoided the necessity of conversation by pointing to the bricks they'd knocked down, the floorboards they'd ripped up, and the fact that the skip outside the house was already overspilling.

'All under control,' he'd say.

On the days when I was at work, I insisted he call me with any questions and that they should categorically do nothing to the house we hadn't previously agreed on.

'Of course, darling.'

He never did call, and whenever *I* called him, the line was engaged.

Bill had a brother, Trev. A plumber. Bill brought him round one morning, unannounced, and promptly put him on the payroll. We needed a plumber, he explained. I realized this, of course, but as far as I, no expert, was concerned, we wouldn't need one for several months yet. Bill explained that Trev was the best in the business, he was available now, and who knew where he would be several months down the line? Best to get him while we could.

Against my better judgement, and Andrew's infuriating ambivalence, I reneged and started to pay him too, without ever realizing quite what it was he did. In those early days I paid them in cash because cash was what Bill had demanded. 'It's easier.' This, I was later to realize, was a big mistake. Not only did I have no comeback should I be unhappy with their work, but the process itself was wretched, each of them standing anxiously around me on a Friday afternoon while I counted out the £20 notes, still fresh from the cash machine, their clammy hands thrust out towards me. But I made them wait for it, demanding beforehand that they fill me in on everything that had happened during the week. Bill, however, had neither the time nor the patience for this. Any serious discussions on the house, he felt, he would have solely with Andrew, the man, his mate. Serious discussion was clearly beyond me.

I had several times told Trev what I wanted plumbing in, and where, but he paid little or no heed. After he left each night, I would nose around the kitchen and bathroom, the scenes of his particular crimes, make notes, then go home and Google my findings. It transpired that he was plumbing in equipment where equipment shouldn't be plumbed in, and insisted on putting the boiler in the bathroom next to the bath, against plumbing regulations. 'Everybody does it,' he countered when I confronted him. 'Don't worry about it.' I asked him if he'd had any quotes back yet on my request for underfloor heating.

'Haven't bothered, love. It's a waste, trust me.'

'I hope you don't mind me asking,' I said next, the full weight of my Google expertise backing me up, 'but are you Corgi registered?'

He offered me the only smile I was ever to get from him. 'Don't like dogs, do I?' he said.

My incessant worry was making me frantic. They had been at the house now almost four full weeks and had gutted everything that needed to be gutted. Now they seemed to be starting to renovate, which was something we had never agreed upon. I asked more questions, and demanded answers, trying but failing to keep the shrill notes from my voice.

'It's all been agreed,' Bill informed me.

'Not with me, it hasn't.'

Bill, it transpired, had told Andrew that he, Trev and Bungle could pretty much do the bulk of whatever we needed straight away, and Andrew had told them fine, whatever. Tears prickled my eyes. I stormed outside and called Andrew at work. He sounded cowed and sheepish and insistent all at once.

'Come on, Lucy. He's a mate, he's cheap.'

But they were also dangerous, and they were destroying our house. I sat on the wall outside, waiting for them to finish up for the day, and for Andrew to arrive direct from work. Once they'd left, I went back into the house. The evenings were drawing in now and there was a chill in the air. It was eerie in there once they'd vacated it, dark and full of bricks and dust, the pages of tabloid newspapers curling in the corners of the bathroom and kitchen.

Andrew turned up late, tired and smelling conspicuously of Dutch courage, as if I was now a wife he had to fear.

'Follow me,' I snapped.

In my hand I had my laptop, upon it evidence, and as I walked him through the shell of our house I pointed out the work they had done that I hadn't requested, and the work they hadn't done that I had begged and pleaded for. We saw gaping holes every-where, gaps between the window frames and the walls, and what looked suspiciously like fungus growing up the stripped walls, which were now full of wide cracks. We sat on the dusty floor of what would one day become the master bedroom and I opened the laptop. I typed HOUSE RENOVATION WHAT GOES WRONG into the search engine, and together we spent the next hour in increasingly gloomy light in a state of mutual mounting panic. I scrolled through the hundreds, if not thousands, of testimonials on endless sites, all of them concern-ing builders who had wilfully ignored safety standards, thus ruining, often irrevocably, the houses they were supposed to be improving. There was photographic evidence: of caving ceilings, of walls that had been torn down in such a way as to damage the very foundations, and of dry rot. The images of dry rot, I saw now, looked worryingly familiar, and we raced back through the rooms peering into the holes left by Bungle's mallet. I was horrified, and relieved to see that Andrew, nodding beside me, was in agreement – we had dry rot, which was to houses what cancer was to so many people: terminal. I called Bill im-mediately, but he didn't pick up. I considered leaving a message, then realized the futility of it.

'I think we should sack him, Andrew. He's done as much as

he can, and we should never have hired him in the first place. I can't stand him, or his brother. Andrew, I want them gone. Sack them, please.'

In the damp darkness of our dream house, Andrew looked at me aghast. 'Why me?'

We walked defeatedly back to the flat, Andrew brooding. Bill, he said, was a drinking buddy. He didn't want things to get awkward between them. I stopped in my tracks, in the middle of the street, and loudly upbraided him, those shrill notes in my voice again. I screamed about the grand scheme of things, that it was easier to lose a drinking buddy, surely, than a home, than seeing our money wasted, our marriage broken. People stopped to look; a man leaned out of the passenger side of a passing car and cried: 'Let him have it!'

'Okay, fine, fine,' he said, as desperate to mollify as he was to silence me. But then later, in bed, with the lights off, lying next to one another but careful not to touch, he reviewed the situation. 'Couldn't you do it?' he asked, his voice plaintive and pleading. 'You're better at this kind of thing. Besides, it is *your* project . . .'

I arrived at the house early the next morning, 7 a.m. This was the time Bill insisted they always arrived (they had their own keys), but there was of course no sign of them. They eventually turned up at 8.30. I heard their heavy footsteps in the hall, and their trailing laughter. Bungle emerged into the kitchen first, where I was sat at the table nursing my third coffee, and stopped dead in his tracks. He looked terrified, and from this I drew necessary strength. Bill, not looking where he was going, walked straight into him.

'Bungle, what the fu—? Oh,' he said, when he saw me. 'Morning, love. Stick the kettle on, would you?'

'Actually, I wanted a word.' I was nervous, but refused to show it.

'A word?' he repeated as his brother walked around him and

threw his heavy bag of tools on the floor without looking up, without acknowledging me.

'Yes. Look.' I stood. 'I'm not really happy with a lot that has been going on here.' I turned to his brother. 'Trev, some of the things you've been doing have been against building regulations. I don't want whatever happens here to go against building regulations, because when a building inspector comes round to check – and they will – we'll be in trouble, and where will you be then?'

He sighed, the weight of the world on his stooping shoulders. 'I've told you loads of times, love. Everybody does it, everybody cuts corners.'

'Well I don't.'

But Trev had by now disregarded me. He walked around me and switched on the kettle himself. Its tubercular rattle told him it was empty, so he yanked out the plug, took it to the sink and filled it with water, then switched it on again.

'I want you to listen to me,' I said to him, my voice rising.

'*Listen?*'

'Yes, that's right. Or else.' *Or else.* The words were pitifully childlike.

He looked across the room to his brother and Bungle. He laughed. 'Or else what?'

The realization that I was scared, scared to be alone in the house with three burly men who, though I didn't think them necessarily violent, were nevertheless far from friendly either, came to me only later, when I started to shake so much I had to sit down. But I couldn't show that now. I had started this, and I was going to finish it.

'Or else,' I continued, 'I'll have to let you go.'

'Listen to me, darling—'

'*Darling* nothing,' I said, shouting out. 'Just go, okay? Please just go.'

'You're firing me?'

63

A long, drawn-out second passed. 'I'm firing all of you. Go.'

Bill spoke. 'It was Andrew who employed me, love, not you.'

'No, we both did. And *I'm* firing you.'

I held up my index finger and pointed it through the hall towards the door. It was shortly before nine o'clock in the morning. I could hear the postman forcing something through the letterbox, another catalogue for the widower's deceased wife. In the garden, I could hear one bird call out to another. It was going to be a warm day, but it wouldn't properly start for me until these three were gone. Trev shrugged, picked up his bag and stalked out. Bill pushed Bungle to follow him, but turned to address me once more before he left. Behind me, the kettle whistled.

'I'll be having words with Andrew,' he told me.

You do that, I shouted back at him in my head. He stopped immediately and strode back into the kitchen as if he had heard my inner voice.

'Your keys,' he said, placing them gently on the table in front of me. Then he left. I was all alone in my wreck of a house, and now I would have to start all over again. But the pressure I had been feeling against my ribcage for so many days was lifting already. I could breathe again.

I decided not to call Andrew to tell him straight away, but rather to wait until he came home. I spent the day window-shopping in town and drinking coffee in cafés. I felt free.

Andrew noticed a change in me the moment he got in.

'Something's different.' He looked at me quizzically. 'Is it your hair? Have you had it done?'

I sat him down and told him what had happened, and that we were now back at square one. Relief puddled across his face.

'Come here. I'm proud of you,' he said.

That night, we had the best sex we'd had in months.

Three

The house lay empty, and unworked upon, for three weeks. I still visited every day, just to let it know I hadn't forgotten. When I wasn't worrying about it I was scouring for replacement builders, but in a world where estate agents and traffic wardens dwelt at the very bottom of all that is undesirable on Earth, builders, I now learned, occupied the basement. Every prospective firm I read about were the recipients of bad, and sometimes shockingly bad, online reviews. Andrew did his part too, following up several leads, but nothing came of them. Though I was now reduced to only two days' work a week, I began to call in late in order to maintain my unwavering focus. Even once at work, I would still make countless builder-prospecting calls, scurrying out into the corridor for privacy, then back to my desk to follow up with emails. Any half-decent builder was booked for months in advance. One suggested I call him back next year. 'March or April,' he said.

I resolved, somehow, to keep myself busy. I watched even more house-renovation programmes and took copious notes. I tidied the place incessantly, ridding it of all lingering trace of Bill and Bungle, and began to attempt to stem the dry rot myself. I became a frequent customer at B&Q, and ended each day dirty and exhausted, optimistic that I was making a difference when I knew full well I was affixing a tiny sticking plaster to something that needed a bandage.

'Find anyone yet?'

This was the question Andrew asked every evening the very moment he walked in through the door from work.

'No. You?' My recurring answer.

But then I did, just like that: a card in a shop window, hand-written in blue biro. I jotted down the builder's name and number, and put in a call. He answered on the first ring – the only builder ever to do so. He had a heavy accent and it was so difficult to understand him at first that I couldn't possibly realize the man I was talking to would turn out to be the answer to my prayers. That only came later.

His name was Kushtim. He was from Eastern Europe, and an ardent believer in karma.

I liked him instinctively – something I could say about no other builder I had to date come across. And I trusted him, too. He was short but powerful-looking, twenty-six years old, and had been in the UK for three years. Once I had his full name, I Googled him and found to my enormous relief that here was a tradesman who actually had good write-ups.

I showed him the house and outlined my plans in detail. I showed him the diagrams I'd made, the pages of notes. He listened studiously, sometimes in agreement, sometimes challenging my ideas. He made suggestions of his own, and they were good ones. He had a team of good, trustworthy men at his disposal, including a Corgi-registered plumber, and, because another job had just fallen through, he could start on Monday. *Monday*. I hired him.

They would arrive promptly at seven each morning, and I would get there shortly after to make them tea and toast. Because the kitchen was now a shell, I'd crafted a little snack-preparation area in a corner of the living room, under the window next to a plug socket: kettle, toaster, some plates and, in a plastic bag, cutlery, all neatly arranged next to a mini fridge purchased from Argos. I'd pour out the tea and butter the toast, and distribute it to the men whose idiosyncrasies I would come to know well over the next few months: the Spanish roofer, the French-Moroccan architect, the Geordie electrician, the Bulgarian plumber.

Together they worked at a prodigious rate, and individually kept me helplessly entertained. I watched the house change incrementally with each new day. Autumn gradually gave way to winter, bringing with it gusty winds that rattled through the gaps in the windows and the floorboards. It was impossible to set foot in the house now without leaving coated in dust and grime, and without having swallowed great lungfuls. I worried that none of the men was wearing a mask, but they laughed off my concerns.

Kushtim consulted me regularly on everything, and it was *he* who called *me* to check, and double-check, before he spent any money or bought any additional items. I wrote cheques constantly, arranged temporary parking amnesties, and dealt with the neighbours when they began to complain about the skips that sat unmoving outside the house, blocking up parking spaces and spilling debris. I spent weeks trawling kitchen showrooms and bathroom showrooms, and the hell that is IKEA. I obsessed over colour combinations, the benefits of wallpaper over paint, matt over gloss. I developed opinions on doorknobs and light fittings, skirting boards and dado rails, and mused endlessly on screed, tanking, RSJs, lagging, polypipe. Each evening I'd confer with Andrew, who became increasingly bored and uninterested, after a long day at the office wanting only to sit on his sofa in his flat, watch the football on the large-screen TV and sink a few beers.

'Whatever you like, darling,' he'd repeat.

And each night I would lie in bed alongside my already sleeping husband and dream about the project's eventual completion, the dust of my new house crunching between my teeth and itching the folds, creases and crevices of my exhausted body.

I became a different woman during this time, obsessive, mono-maniacal even. I rarely socialized and frequently forgot to call friends back after they'd left messages enquiring whether I was still alive. My intention was not to be rude, or stand-offish, but I simply could not find the headspace a solicitous phone call required. And when I did, all I could talk about was the house, its myriad complications now my entire world.

Besides, kitchen showrooms were stealing my time in a way I would never before have anticipated, and if I wasn't en route to yet another one I had just located online – which would invari-ably be situated miles away in a distant industrial estate – I was liaising with Kushtim and applying for building permits from council officials, or else choosing paint for each room and then changing my mind, as was my prerogative. Or – *or* – I was in a different kind of showroom holding one patterned tile up along-side its competitor, trying to decide which would flatter the bathroom best, iceberg or soft grey, lavender or bluing, marmalade or caramel.

Andrew thought me tedious by now, and started consciously to avoid me, grabbing dinner in the pub and arriving home mildly drunk at closing time. I hardly noticed his absence. Losing focus on everything else was the only way I could keep focus on the one thing that mattered more than anything else. I no longer cared about my appearance, and just as well. A woman covered in a permanent layer of dust had no place in Miss Selfridge, so I merely wore the same set of clothes again and again, comfortable ones that conveniently concealed the fact that I had put on weight. I considered it insulation for the winter.

The weight gain was not merely down to lack of exercise, but also to diet. Making so much toast for the workmen, it was difficult not to subsist on the stuff myself, thick white slices smeared with butter, while at lunchtime, ravenous again, I found myself actively craving comfort food, the fried bacon and fat sausage sandwiches of the greasy spoon cafés that continued to dominate the lower half of the high street.

The kitchen was coming along. The roof was off, but planning permission had at last been granted for a glass replacement, which would, the architect promised excitedly, bathe the kitchen in daylight. The boiler arrived. The bathroom tiles went missing. When the kitchen tiles arrived, half were cracked and had to be sent back. The shop from which I had bought them had run out of stock. Three weeks, I was told. The planning permission for the glass roof had to be reconsidered after a complaint from one of the neighbours. The company that had rented us our latest skip had gone into receivership, so there it sat, overflowing, a permanent presence. I took each of these near-daily setbacks personally, increasingly crippled under their cumulative weight.

But, approaching Christmas, the house really was starting to take shape. Four months since Bungle had first swung his mallet, I could see how it could now soon be habitable. The gangplanks were gone, the staircases finished. The bath was installed, the shower on order, on its way. The bedrooms were now bright and airy, the floorboards no longer sloping. The dry rot had been banished. On a sunny day, despite the dust, it all looked beautiful.

'You move in soon, I think,' was Kushtim's encouraging prognosis.

This was a relief, because we were by now left with little in our savings account. The profit I'd made selling my flat was all but gone, and our joint bank account was running low – a situation exacerbated by the paltry wages two days' work brought me.

On 21 December the team downed tools for the rest of the year. Many were returning home for Christmas and their coach journeys were going to be long ones. I would miss them. That evening, Andrew and I had our first proper meal in the place. We sat huddled around one of Kushtim's work tables in the living room with a Chinese takeaway, a portable heater blowing hot dust around our ankles. We were so cold we opted for brandy instead of wine to accompany the meal.

'Happy?' Andrew asked me.

I looked around the room, which would soon be painted, and into the kitchen, which was wired now and awaiting the arrival of a hob, the fridge, work surfaces and a sink. *Home*, I thought.

'You're not crying, are you?' he asked, bringing a hand to my face.

Burrowing somewhere underneath my relief and my happiness was a gnawing fear that for the time being I chose to ignore. But it was there nevertheless. What would happen if, I thought to myself, when all this was finally finished, I *wasn't* actually happy? Not with the house itself, but rather with my life now that I no longer had a project to fill it?

What then?

Work started up again a week into the New Year: the finishing touches, Kushtim said. There were countless such finishing touches in every room; my builder was a stickler for detail, so he and just three of his men remained in the house until the end of the month. I was happy to have them there. Frankly, I didn't want them to go.

Halfway through the month, the painters arrived. These we'd found via a friend of a friend of Andrew's. But there was a lot less that could go wrong with painting, surely, so I refused to panic. They turned up on a Wednesday mid-morning, both dressed in paint-splattered overalls. Both were called Jim. They were everything Kushtim wasn't: untrustworthy, crafty, cutters of corners. They finished everything a full week early, having given the walls just one coat, though they still charged us for three weeks.

After they left Andrew and I inspected the house once again, as we had done so many times over the previous six months. It looked almost finished, complete, the walls bright and stark, the floorboards gleaming, the carpets plump and new. All it needed now was furniture, and the two of us living in it.

We walked up the stairs, the freshly laid carpet footstepped with the heavy prints of the painters ('It'll hoover off,' Andrew reassured me), to what would become our bedroom, the bigger of the two, which, in its currently empty state, seemed vast, yellow light from the street lamp outside throwing our shadows up on to the walls. Andrew suggested where we could put the bed, and I told him where I thought it should go. 'Whatever you say.' We went upstairs to what would be the third bedroom, which had previously been the cramped attic space.

It was here that we realized they had given everything only one lick of paint; traces of the original colour underneath bled liberally through. I tried to quash a mounting fury, made all the harder by the discovery of cigarette butts on the windowsill and one in the corner of the new carpet, which, when I stooped to remove it, revealed a perfectly round burn hole.

'It looks good, doesn't it?' said Andrew, glancing round the room, oblivious.

And, ultimately, I suppose it did. This third bedroom we would later anoint 'the den', but only much later: though we would dutifully stick a sofa bed in there, we would also pile endless bags and boxes, to all intents and purposes maintaining its previous function: a place for storage.

We drifted back down the stairs to the bathroom, which still needed tiling, still needed the shower fitting. The bath looked nice, though, sat under the unfrosted window that gave on to the back garden, which would look wonderful come spring. Then we went into the second bedroom and saw more of the painters' detritus: the last of their materials, one T-shirt, two toilet rolls and, next to them, a couple of cut-off plastic Evian bottles. One contained what looked like paint and water, the other brimmed with a liquid the colour of turpentine. I approached it warily, its smell at once dispiritingly familiar. It was the smell of a public toilet.

'Andrew, this isn't – you don't think he . . . ?'

'No, surely not,' he chided. But he could smell it too.

My reaction was out of all proportion; I can admit that now. But this indignation was the final straw, the thing that pushed me over the edge. I was tired, really tired of it all, mentally and physically, spiritually. I had no resolve left. I'd spent many months and several hundred days in what I realized now were the very necessary perpetual pitched battles that come with doing up a house. I'd been mocked, taken advantage of, over-charged and undervalued. My dreams had been dashed and delayed, and summarily ignored. Kushtim and his men aside, I had felt nothing but contempt from the people I had paid to do an honest job. And now the last of them, who had scrimped on the painting, had pissed in a bottle and left it as a memento because – because, well, why exactly? What was the hidden meaning here?

'Perhaps he was just desperate,' Andrew offered. 'He couldn't make it to the toilet in time, so . . .'

I burst into howling tears, staggered forward and stumbled. My right foot connected with one of the Evian bottles, my left with the other. I watched, horrified, as diluted paint and decorator piss spread rapidly across the room's beautiful new carpet, sinking into the fabric and staining fast.

I couldn't breathe. My hands clawed my throat, my eyes

bulged. Andrew grabbed hold of me, shouting words at me. He struck my back with the flat of his hand as if trying to dislodge something stuck. He then part-lifted and part-dragged me out of the room, down the stairs and into the car, bound for the nearest hospital.

The car veered sharply away from the kerb in a squeal of tyres, and as it did my eyes pulled briefly into focus: there, on the pavement, was a neighbour, one of the several I had had to apologize to for the state of the skips over the months, an elderly Indian woman with a kindly face. She was carrying bags of shopping. She placed the bags carefully on the pavement and stooped to peer in at me, a look of helpless fascination on her face. As we drove off, she offered a plaintive wave.

Four

I had been feeling ill for several days previously, if not for weeks, months: a persistent breathlessness, an incremental tightness in the chest. And so by the time the doctor diagnosed me with something real – pneumonia – it was almost a relief to learn that my suffering hadn't been purely of my anxiety's making. This was a proper illness, the doctor told me, adding, perhaps unnecessarily, that people used to die of it. He ordered a strict course of bed rest.

'You really must relax. And I mean for several weeks, if not months. Do not excite yourself, and don't allow yourself any stressful situations.'

I'd have found the irony of this hysterical had I the strength to laugh. On the eve of at last being able to move into the house, I was instead forcibly sequestered back at the flat, so near and yet so far.

Andrew took a week off and insisted on babysitting me, making sure I slept as much as I could and bringing me what everyone believes the infirm need – tea and soup, at regular intervals. I wanted only to be alone.

The pneumonia progressed in stages. At first I lay there in bed fretting about the kitchen and the bathroom, both of which required my full attention if they were to be completed anytime soon; but, and this surprised me, all such worry gradually ebbed away as the illness took proper hold. I'd never felt tired like this before, a draining sensation as if a tap at my feet had been opened as far as it would go, my inner strength whooshing out. I slept all the time, but it was fitful sleep, and busy with night-mares: the house an increasing money pit sinking deeper and deeper into the earth; one of the Jims, cock out, pissing in my direction and laughing maniacally, his horse's teeth bursting out of his mouth, his long tongue licking at lips that puckered up as if ready to suck me dry.

But then the illness worsened and I lost sense of myself and my surroundings. I ran such a high fever that I was never truly fully conscious, not really; instead, I sank in and out of restless sleep, hallucinating, dreaming, whimpering. A week went by, then another. I lost track of time, of day from night. My mother came to visit, bringing grapes. Andrew receded to the periphery, the shadow at the door to the bedroom, the heavy footsteps in the rooms beyond.

Time passed. Gradually, my consciousness returned, but it did so haltingly. I felt depleted, adrift in bed and wanting never to leave. But I was awake at least, and sitting up. Andrew was back at work and I was happy to be alone, in the fetid stink of the room, with the door closed and the curtains drawn. I picked unenthusiastically at the dry toast he'd left me and sipped slowly at tepid water. My chest pain remained intense and ceaseless. It still woke me at night. Whatever medication I was on seemed to be doing precious little so far as I could tell, and it felt as if I were breathing through sandpaper. My lips were chapped. It hurt to pee, to empty my bowels, to cry. Sleep, what I craved more than anything else, was now continually denied, and I rarely managed to do so for more than an hour at a time, day or night. I spent much of my day just staring up at the ceiling, at the intricate swirling brushstrokes left by whichever painter had painted it seven years before, when these apartments were built.

I would leave my bed only to visit the toilet, but I was eating so little that there was mostly little to pass. Everything else was sweated out. My footsteps on the floor when I did get up were shuffling and slovenly, like those of an old woman, and seeing different parts of the flat always discomfited me. I couldn't wait to get back to the seclusion of the bed.

It was a novelty suddenly to have such a blank mind. I'd been so frantic for so long that it was odd to think nothing at all now, untroubled by everything that, previously, had made me so manic. I read nothing, no books, no magazines or newspapers. I didn't watch television. I didn't call anybody on the phone. I returned no texts or emails. I just lay there, alone, empty. Even when Andrew came home at night, desperate, I could see, to have his wife come back to him, I barely spoke. I couldn't find the words, or the strength required. I wouldn't have thought the hours could pass under such inactivity, but they did, as did the days and then the weeks.

When the illness finally began to lift, I almost didn't believe it. I had got so used to bed that it felt alien to get out of it. But my appetite returned, in instalments, and I began to crave distraction again. The house was still off-limits to me, and I couldn't even contemplate returning to work – did my job even exist any more? I imagined a fresh-faced Oxbridge graduate had already consigned me to, in every sense, redundancy – and whenever I thought about either, I'd feel the flutter of panic in my throat. *No stressful situations*, the doctor had instructed. I refocused my thoughts elsewhere. I reached for my laptop and decided that this was the only way I would inch myself back out into the world, one keystroke at a time.

I did something then I'd never done before: I looked up old friends on old friends websites, curious to see if I could learn more about them than merely the empty platitudes of their occasional postings. I'd never been interested in this kind of nostalgia before – the present was more than enough for me to deal with without wanting to delve into the complications of the past as well; but now, sequestered in limbo, I found the idea appealing. Suddenly I was desperate to know what had become of them: how many were now rich, successful and content with their lives? How many were bitter and divorced? How many were advertising themselves on dating websites?

I didn't get very far. Those I did manage to locate gave little away. Most were 'happy with the way things are', a standard posting on so many of these websites that revealed nothing and concealed everything. But many were clearly married, putting up photographs of themselves with their husbands and children. One couple, school sweethearts back in the day, had married and divorced, and three had emigrated, one to Australia, one to America, one to Canada. One was a disc jockey on gospel radio, another a martial-arts expert in Milton Keynes. There was plenty of photographic evidence, and this proved fascinating: they had grown up and filled out, and many of those I remembered only as spotty teenagers had become unexpectedly attractive.

Some had become lawyers, journalists. One was nothing less than a record-company mogul. He'd asked me out once. I'd turned him down. For all those who now lived elsewhere in the world, an awful lot lived in the same neighbourhood they'd grown up in. As my investigations progressed, I experienced a mounting sense of melancholy that I was at a loss to explain. After all, I was just as settled as many of them. I had a good job, or at least I used to, and a loving husband. I had no money worries, and I had tried not to let myself go. I had little to complain about, besides the pneumonia. But I was recovering, and would return, I hoped, to full strength. So why did I feel so low?

I told myself it was a symptom of the illness, and that I would feel better when I *was* better.

A defining sensation was coming back to me now, and it took a confusing amount of time to recognize it: boredom. I'd never been ill like this before and, after retreating so comprehensively from the world, I would now need to summon up a certain effort to get back into it.

Every Tuesday and Friday morning, Kasia the cleaner would arrive. She had been given strict instructions by Andrew not to bother me, and she never did. Now, though, I found myself hoping each time she came that she *would* knock on the door and peek her head round, just to see how I was faring, whether I was still alive. But she never did. Of course, I could have been the one to go out to *her*, but I could never quite summon up the courage. And *courage* was precisely what I felt was required here, something I for whatever reason now lacked. She sounded so bright, Kasia, so carefree and vigorous and full of youth. She whistled while she worked. It was always the same song, its tune vaguely familiar. But I could never, not for the life of me, recall its title.

A couple more weeks elapsed and, though I was still wallowing, I *was* moving about the flat with more confidence, retreating only on those mornings Kasia came, when I hid in my room like a coward.

I began gradually to take an active interest in the house once more, which, in my absence, Andrew was overseeing with an apparent no-fuss efficiency. As my strength returned, so too did my paranoia. No part of the house renovation could be completed, I was convinced, in a state of *no-fuss efficiency*, and so even though he insisted that the kitchen furniture was already, or at least partly, installed, and the bathroom shower and tiles ready and waiting, I began to feel an all-too-familiar panic about it. In short, I didn't trust him. The sensation was physical, starting in my stomach and rising upwards like bile. I would feel lightheaded and anxious, and would have to sit down. I had missed the sensation. But then of *course* I had missed it: panic was the one overriding condition that defined me, my comfort blanket.

One night Andrew pulled out of his briefcase one of the many by now dog-eared bathroom catalogues and asked me, casually, to reconfirm again precisely which of the tiles I had chosen for the shower. 'Just to double-check.' In a house renovation project, even the most seemingly insignificant things can take on exaggerated importance. I had had nightmares over these tiles for months, and more than one screaming row on the phone with a particular bathroom fitter. All part of the process.

'By the way,' Andrew added, 'the toilet finally flushes.' He said this jubilantly. He said this like it was *news*. My hackles rose immediately.

'When had it *stopped* flushing?'

And here it came: the delicious throat flutter of anxiety, my fingers curling instinctively into fists. Andrew, such a dutiful husband in so many ways, went into swift retreat mode. He commanded me not to worry, that there had been a mishap, an oversight, tiny, nothing more, but it had been easily rectified now. The tiles, he added, were due in the morning and would be up in place by the weekend. 'It's these ones, right?' he said, pointing to the page I had folded over in the brochure. It was.

If I was feeling up to it, he promised, he would take me over on Saturday to see the results.

'The house has missed you,' he cooed. I nearly burst into tears.

The next morning, Andrew went to work as usual. I got out of bed, gingerly dressed myself and put on, for the first time in weeks, a pair of shoes and my coat. I was going to the house, a decision made secretly the night before and so emphatically that I didn't sleep. I closed the door to the flat behind me, alert to its click, and faced the staircase, which floated in my vision as if taunting my very ability to descend it. It still hurt to breathe a little, and once I'd made it outside into the forecourt, the fresh air felt so thrillingly sharp in my lungs that I almost doubled over.

It was mid-March, and I was out of doors for the first time in over six weeks. Everything looked so very bright and sharp, unreal even, as if the high street were a film set and I had just been granted a walk-on part. It was a ten-minute stroll between the flat and the house. That day, it took me almost half an hour. I was in no hurry. The pavements were bustling with mid-morning shoppers and ambling mothers pushing prams. I was fearful about bumping into someone I knew, not ready for easy chitchat just yet, but it was good to be outdoors. The sun was warm already. The noises from the cars and buses squealed in my ears, a glorious tinnitus, and the light breeze on my cheeks and in my hair was exquisite. I tilted my head to the sky and felt *alive*.

Turning into my road a good while later, I became terrified. A lump rose in my throat, excitement and trepidation combined. I reached the gate and saw that the house was still standing. I found my keys, shuffled up the path, and let myself in.

The tiler, having already seen off Andrew earlier that morning, clearly wasn't expecting any further disturbances. He must have heard me come in, because a moment later I saw him at the top of the stairs, his big workman boots on my brand-new carpet. *Let it go*, I whispered inwardly.

'Hello?' he called out warily.

My voice was weak, but I managed to introduce myself. He met me halfway down the stairs, his boots leaving little clouds of dust as he went, and helped me – an elderly lady, suddenly – back up the stairs to see his work. I glanced fleetingly at the tiles, piled neatly and orderly in one corner of the room. I felt my right arm, lifeless at my side, rise up now as if by itself, and I pointed to them.

'The tiles. They've arrived?' I asked.

'Yes. They came yesterday.'

Now it was my turn to frown. 'You were here *yesterday*?'

'When I started, yes. Your husband gave me keys.' I could see panic in his face now, something revealed that shouldn't have been. 'He told you, right?'

'Of course he did,' I lied, knowing full well Andrew had told me the tiles weren't due to arrive until today. He had my best interests in mind, of course, wanting to minimize my stress, but a control freak rarely likes to be taken out of the situation.

'Lady, why are you crying?'

And it was only now that I realized I was. Tears were streaming silently down my cheeks.

'Listen, shouldn't you be at home, resting? Your husband said you were ill.'

I looked at the pile of tiles, the right tiles, sage green, and realized, quite suddenly, that they were the *wrong* tiles, wrong for this room. The wrong colour, the wrong shade, the wrong finish. This wasn't how I wanted the bathroom to look. With these tiles, it would now look different, and wrong. But they were unpacked now, and unreturnable. I'd have to get used to them. That's what Andrew would tell me, to calm down, that there was nothing really wrong with them at all, that I'd get used to them soon enough. He was right; of course he was. They sat there in their orderly pile, and all I wanted to do was karate-chop every last one of them into pieces.

Instead, it was easier simply to weep.

I turned and went slowly down the stairs. My initial intention was to carry on straight out of the front door, and back to the flat, to bed, but impulsively I turned and headed down into the kitchen. Andrew had led me to believe that it was all but finished in here. It wasn't. The oven still hadn't arrived, nor had the extractor fan or the fridge. Flex and wires were exposed at the walls, power points remained unfastened. The room, as it

81

was, was not yet habitable, and no dinner outside of instant noodles could yet be cooked in it.

I am glad I didn't know then what I would come to know in time, that the two men we employed – and paid handsomely – to make our beautiful kitchen a reality were cowboys of the highest order, cowboys who would botch everything they could possibly botch, and who, several months later, we would feel forced to sue for neglect and damage – and would eventually win the case a full and torturous year later. This was a foresight I would not have been able to handle.

The tiler joined me in the kitchen and helped me back through the hall. He kindly offered to drive me home, which he did, and even accompanied me to the front door. 'You rest,' he said to me, patting my back. 'Feel better.'

I had thought the pneumonia was at last in full remission. I was wrong.

We moved in, quietly and without fanfare, a little exhausted and much relieved, five weeks later. Spring had arrived, and the weather was good. The house was far from finished: the extractor fan had gone missing somewhere on the motorway; the boiler had trouble maintaining hot water; the shutters for the windows in the living room were to be delayed, inexplicably, by another three months; the glass roof in the kitchen would leak in three places whenever it rained, which was often; and we had completely forgotten to buy either doorbell or door knocker. But ostensibly the job was complete, and our dream home was ready for occupation.

A Japanese restaurant had just opened on the high street. We ordered food enough for six people and, with a bottle of champagne, enjoyed our first official dinner on our iroko dining table in the incomplete kitchen, an early-evening sun streaming in through the windows, lighting up my husband as if from within, his eyes lost in the glare from his lenses.

'To us,' Andrew said, raising his glass. Mine clinked his, with exaggerated care, and we drank.

We then spent a lovely evening reviewing the events of the past ten months, hindsight bringing hilarity where, at the time, it had brought only misery. But we had survived, and we were together.

'We can stop obsessing now and just get on with living our lives,' he said.

We can just get on with living our lives. With these nine words he sent a chill that went right down my back. He was right, though. There were no diversions now, no impediments to whatever was to come next. Which was what, exactly?

It was this, I think, that was worrying me most.

Andrew himself had no such worries. With spring now here, the racing calendar could get fully under way. I knew all about the year's racing calendar. Andrew read the *Racing Post* not only every morning over breakfast, but also frequently over dinner as well – even, sometimes, if we ate out. He had always liked the horses, but they had by now become his abiding obsession, his life's true love. He was a betting man, but not the sort to fritter his money away without first doing a lot of groundwork. He had multiple accounts, with outfits like Betfair and Paddy Power and William Hill, and this obsession even encouraged my husband, a man of forty-four, on to Twitter every day where he would check the racing predictions of a variety of 'experts' and would frequently post some of his own. He had 357 followers, a figure that brought him much pride. He read betting blogs obsessively, and was in touch, virally, with literally thousands of like-minded souls around the world.

One of the first photographs he ever showed me of himself was from 1983, a slimline Andrew in a Mr Buyright suit at a greyhound track, intently studying a betting slip. I thought it rather endearing at the time, but this was in fact a true glimpse into the man I would marry. Around him in the photograph are several other people, including a close friend peering curiously over his shoulder. Andrew is oblivious to them all, with eyes only for the slip. A quarter of a century on, nothing had changed.

He would frequently invite me to accompany him to the races, 'something we can enjoy together', he'd say, suggesting that we wouldn't have to focus so much on the races themselves but rather the splendour of the occasion, the track, the champagne, the people, the atmosphere. 'You can meet my racing friends,' he'd say, adding, 'they have wives.' He insisted I would love it if only I gave it the chance. 'Everybody dresses up. It's like fancy dress.' I felt it my wifely duty, even before we had got married, to accompany him to one or two of the bigger races, but I could never fully enjoy myself. I found it crowded and noisy, and rather dispiriting to be surrounded by boisterous middle-aged men, their faces red from drink and pink with excitement, while their bored wives sat in a corner laughing hysterically at what were clearly private conversations and private jokes.

All marriages have their respective interests, and so they should, but his was becoming increasingly time-consuming and could no longer be considered a mere hobby. The most important races seemed to happen at the weekend, taking him all over the country and leaving me awaiting his return, lonely at home. When I was younger, weekends were times to socialize with friends, but as I had got older they had become unspokenly sacrosanct, two special days for a couple to enjoy alone or, after they'd had children, in the alternating chaos and bliss of the family unit. Which meant that, with Andrew gone, I was increasingly solitary.

'So come with me,' he'd say. 'To whichever race you'd like. You pick.'

I was spoiled for choice. There was the Thousand Guineas in May, the Derby in June. Royal Ascot would stretch over five long days in the summer, and we wouldn't be able even to think about going on holiday until it was over. There was the King George VI shortly after, and also Goodwood. August was, mercifully, a quiet month race-wise. In October there was the Arc, the best flat race in the world, in Paris. He'd have to go to Paris, he insisted, and he always did. He took me once, but I was soon forgotten about, Andrew lost in a frenzy of drink and gambling with his new best friends. October would also see the tail end of the flat season, then Champions Day at Newmarket. Christmas offered yet more Ascot entertainment just a couple of days beforehand and then again immediately afterwards. And then it all kicked in again from scratch, in January and February, with big races in Ireland and France and beyond.

That I had stored all this useless information in my head never ceased to surprise or sadden me. I had been convinced I'd never paid it much attention, but it was impossible to avoid his endless daily updates. He would set his watch by races, and rearrange his calendar, no matter how awkward it would render our social life. During his own personal peak seasons, he would stake at least £100 a day on them, frequently more. Winning never seemed particularly important, which was just as well, because he didn't always win. But when he did, he was ecstatic, over the moon, his hairline rising as his face lifted and swelled, his brown eyes bursting with tears of glorious victory.

I tried to show willing, I really did, and I still did go to the odd Ascot or Goodwood. We took some friends occasionally, non-racing friends, but they rarely came twice. I didn't blame them: they were punishingly long days if you didn't understand what was going on, with surprisingly little in the way of incident. Each race required an awful lot of build-up. The whole thing reminded me of sex, and it always astonished me that the crowd had the temperament for it, because they often didn't look like the kind of men who spent any serious amount of time on foreplay. But foreplay was all this was. First came plenty of pre-event strutting and preening, lining up and then inexplicably wandering off and losing interest, before lining up again, this time properly, adjusting and readjusting and jostling, the little tiny jockeys wiggling their tight little bottoms, gripping hold of their whips, and stroking the lustrous manes in front of them. The races themselves were often over in a flash. The shortest could last just fifty-five seconds, the longest a couple of minutes, and all of them accompanied by deafening roars of male grunts and effortful screams. I couldn't help but feel cheated afterwards.

Nevertheless, I opted to accompany Andrew to the first day of the Thousand Guineas meeting at Newmarket. It was an important day for him, a work day. Clients would be there, whom Andrew would have to lavish with attention if he wanted to keep their business. They would all be bringing their wives, he told me, and so he could hardly turn up without his own, now could he?

We took the train. Andrew was dressed smartly, far more smartly than usual, and looked rather handsome, like a man on the way to his own wedding. His black shoes shone, his hair was tamed and side-parted with wax. I myself was wearing something new from Jigsaw. It pinched a little at the waist, but hopefully flattered my rear. The centrepiece were the shoes, black with three-inch heels, purchased specially, and expensively, for the occasion. In them I stood almost nose to nose with my husband, and when I first put them on my elevated height aroused something within him. But after his initial pleasant surprise, he made no subsequent comment, his mind now shifted, exclusively, on to the business of horses.

The train journey lasted almost an hour because of a delay, something to do with signals, my husband lost inside his *Racing*

Post, a small betting-shop-issue blue pen clamped between his teeth. I browsed a free newspaper that had been left on my seat and a small story caught my eye. New research issued by weight management specialists revealed that one in ten British men were unable to see their penises because of their protruding bellies. This was virtually a national pandemic: millions of adult males were unable to appraise their own genitals when standing up, and could do so only if they consulted, humblingly, a mirror. A distressing 16 per cent of these confessed that they couldn't remember the last time they'd seen theirs at all.

I couldn't help myself. I looked up and over at Andrew, and the swell that now sat prominently above his belt. He had put on weight recently, and I wondered whether he fitted into that statistic. I knew instinctively that his clients would; most of the men Andrew now socialized with were over forty and in helpless thrall to corpulent exercise regimes (golf, darts) and heart-attack diets.

I tried to remember the last time *I'd* seen his penis. The fact that I had to think at all betrayed that it had been a significant while. What with the pneumonia and the slow recovery, I hadn't felt sexual for some time, and Andrew had surprised me by not pressing the matter. Because I still had trouble sleeping, and because his snoring had become inexpressibly annoying of late, we'd made a temporary arrangement of sleeping in separate rooms that was now threatening to become permanent.

I recalled seeing him in the bathroom a week previously, naked but for Y-fronts and a pair of socks. A pale expanse of belly wobbled precariously above the elasticated waistband of his underpants. He caught me looking and grinned, as if proud. 'This,' he said, clutching at it and making it wobble all the more, 'is the sign of a happily married man.'

Ninety minutes later, we were ensconced in the members' enclosure at Newmarket, a thickly carpeted bar room with several TV monitors all screening race preparation, which, right now, involved a lot of grooming and shit-shovelling. The noise was volcanic, the queue at the bar three-deep. Andrew had greeted his clients as if they were close and much-loved friends. There must have been ten of them, gruff and masculine, well turned out and ruddy with it, their faces stretched like sausage skin, and with a collective propensity towards laughter. They communicated with one another exclusively by cracking crude jokes, usually at each other's expense. I stood meekly next to Andrew, who eventually remembered to introduce me, referring to me, with an irony he believed post-modern, as 'the wife'. One of the men responded, 'I've got one of those!' and the rest roared with laughter. They then laughed all the harder when I failed to join in, which presumably confirmed to them that, as a general rule, women simply don't *get* humour.

I wondered where the wives were. Hadn't Andrew told me that the wives' presence was paramount today, hence my own? I moved to ask him, but was too slow. The race was off, and, as one, he and the rest of them surged forward for a better view.

It was at this moment that I felt a couple of fingers touch my shoulder. I turned around to see a lady, in her late forties perhaps, heavily made-up, a vision in pink and taffeta ruffles.

'You're new,' she said to me. It wasn't a question. 'I can tell.'

'Can you?'

She pointed a finger in the general direction of the scrum, Andrew hanging on for dear life at its fringes. 'That yours?' I nodded. She smiled. 'Thought so. I'm Sally, Derek's wife.' She pointed again. 'That's Derek.' We shook hands, and her wrist rattled with thin gold bangles. She looked like a curious mixture of cheap and expensive all at once, but she radiated warmth. 'Your Andrew,' she said. 'I've met him a few times before at these things. He can be quite the life and soul, can't he? Anyway, come and join us.'

I followed in her perfume trail to a corner table situated as far from the race action as it was possible to get in there. It was already full of the other wives, all of them talking animatedly amongst themselves. They looked like guests at the Queen's garden party, in fancy dress with plunging necklines, jewellery dripping from ears and fingers, their faces painted in all the colours of the rainbow. As I drew nearer, their collective smell began to tickle my nostrils, a heady fragrance of lavender and rosewater and vanilla – sweet, sweeter, sweetest. Sally introduced me around, but I caught only a couple of the names – a Kay, a Jean, possibly a Sandra – and space was made for me to sit.

'A glass of champagne for the new arrival!' said one.

'Are you new?' asked another, squinting through her glasses.

Up close, they were elegant and poised and well put together, shiny Christmas presents under the tree of life, and each of a certain age for which the maintenance of outward appearance was everything. But once they had a drink inside them, deportment was cast quickly aside for cheeky abandon. As with the men, everything they said was accompanied by peals of hysterical laughter, and I felt helpless but to laugh along.

They were a collective, Sally explained: the Racing Widows, women from all over the country who would meet up a few times each year at some of the more important races and, as a Sandra put it, 'drink their profits', indicating the husbands, all still screaming and exhorting the horses they'd backed to win.

I confessed my comprehensive lack of interest in racing and they laughed.

'That's exactly why we're sat over *here*,' Sandra said. 'Trust me, you can actually have a lot of fun at these things, so long as you avoid them lot and stick with us.'

'We're lovely,' another told me. I didn't doubt it.

I sat and laughed and drank and bemoaned right along with the Racing Widows for seven hours that day. I have no idea how many races took place in that time, or how much money our husbands might have won or lost, but the champagne kept coming, all of it spilling into empty stomachs lined only with grabbed handfuls of crinkled crisps. Our conversations became increasingly intimate, and I sat back and listened as they told me about their holiday homes in Italy, France and Somerset, their mostly grown children, their accumulating ISAs, their gardens and their rippling gardeners. Almost all of them appeared to be having affairs, if not with their gardeners then with their physiotherapists, their plumbers, or occasionally complete strangers, people they had met online.

'It's rather a new thing to us, all this online business,' a handsome woman called Jane told me. 'But it's terribly efficient. By the time you meet them, it's like you're on your third date already. I can't recommend it enough!'

They asked me to recount my affairs, and seemed shocked when I confessed I hadn't had any.

'How long have you been married, dear?'

I checked my watch, which got a laugh, and then told them: 'A year, a year and a half.'

'Oh, well, no wonder. You're still in your honeymoon period.'

When I explained that Andrew and I had actually been together for seven years, they recoiled in a collective sharp intake of breath, which all too obviously passed as mockery. Were they laughing at me?

'*Seven* years? Well then, welcome to the club, my dear. The itch shall soon be upon you.'

Though only perhaps half a dozen years younger than many of them, I felt helpless and naïve in their company, a mere babe. On offer here was an education of sorts, should I wish to learn. 'Really?' I asked.

They certainly treated me like a babe, explaining that monogamous marriages didn't exist any more, that they very likely didn't in our parents' time, but that they certainly don't in ours. But whereas our parents hid it all away, we were more open about it, at least in certain circles.

'So all of you . . . ?'

'Pretty much, yes,' said one.

'Not all the time, no . . .' This was Sally. 'But some of the time, absolutely!'

'Do your husbands know?'

They answered as one. 'No! Of course not!' Sally continued. 'At least not in so many words. But then we don't know about their *dalliances* in so many words either.' She smiled tartly. 'The bliss of ignorance.'

I closed my mouth, because I sensed it hanging open. 'And you don't mind?'

'Of course we mind! We mind very fucking much, actually.' This was Lorraine. I hadn't yet been properly introduced to Lorraine, sat as she was at the far end of the table and mostly keeping her own counsel. 'But what are we going to do about it?'

'Leave them?'

Her eyes became uncomfortably wide. 'At *our* ages?' She told me that no woman wanted to be left on the scrapheap in her late forties, much less beyond that. 'If you confront your husband with what you know, or what you think you know, then it's effectively the beginning of the unravelling of everything you hold dear – and I'm not talking about your husband here, I'm talking about everything else: your children, your house, your entire lifestyle. No.' She shook her head, with vehemence. 'But if you let them do what they feel they need to do every once in a while, and you do the same, then, well, nobody needs rock the boat. Does that make sense?'

Lorraine took my hand in hers, a warm hand. 'The boys,' she said in reference to our apparently philandering husbands, 'are going to Paris for one of their races in a few weeks' time –

Andrew too, I'm sure. What do you think will happen once all the racing is over, and they are let loose, drunk, on the streets of the ninth arrondissement late at night?'

Andrew had been on the Paris trip every year since I'd met him. I had never suspected anything, chiefly because he had never given me cause to. I now tried hastily to review his mood and temperament after he'd returned from them. Had he been any more loving? Had he been unaccountably doting, his guilt prompting acts of sudden generosity? I recalled, with a shameful shiver, that he would always go down on me shortly after his return, something he didn't seem particularly interested in doing at any other time of the year, offering it up as a kind of homecoming gift. Or else to assuage his guilt. I felt suddenly sick.

'There are lots of women who attend these things specifically to find themselves a sugar daddy,' Kay told me, scanning the crowd. 'There are all the women they meet in bars, in clubs. And then there are the escorts.'

'*Escorts?* You mean prostitutes?'

'If that's the name you want to give them, fine.' Lorraine took in my shock with a glee she failed to disguise. 'Don't worry, dear. They never get attached. It's just three minutes of meaningless fumblings, and I'm sure they all wear condoms these days.'

'But *prostitutes?*' This continued public display of my own naïvety was making me a laughing stock, a gullible ingenue, but I couldn't help myself. Did Andrew really frequent prostitutes? And would it really bother me, I pondered, if he did?

'*Escorts*, dear. Escorts. And what's wrong with that?' said Lorraine, as if offended.

Later, Sally took me to one side. 'Lorraine sees one herself, you see? An escort. It's a regular arrangement. Lovely chap, beautiful body by all accounts. From Australia. All of thirty. He takes her to dinner once a month, or rather she permits him to, and she *always* gets her dessert . . .'

At some point in the evening, the last race run, the men began to drift back over towards us. As they did, the tension in our conversation melted promptly into nothing and we began giggling as frivolously as we had earlier in the afternoon. The men were in good spirits, and Andrew was holding a fistful of £20 notes in his right hand, pure giddy jubilance on his face.

He sat squarely on my lap, heavy, clumsy and drunk.

'Having fun?' he asked.

'It's been an education,' Sally told him, smiling.

'Glad to hear it, glad to hear it.'

We moved on to a nearby bar, and even with the races over we remained separated by gender lines, the women gathering around a large corner table, the men congregating at the bar. Picking up our earlier theme, I asked them what happened if one of their affairs led to love. What then?

Lorraine laughed, but with little humour. 'No woman who ever screws my Roger is ever going to fall in love with him, trust me. It's hard enough for *me* to love him most of the time. And anyway, our husbands aren't looking for love. All they are looking for is a little renewed lust to remind them of the youth that is now behind them.'

'I'm pretty sure *my* husband is simply looking for another hole, most of the time,' Sandra said. Everybody laughed.

What I meant, I said, was what if one of *their* affairs led to love. 'Don't you ever fall for one of your . . . your *escorts*?'

With sudden sobriety, Lorraine told me that they were all mostly too old to fall in love, 'at least realistically, anyway. Life is comfortable as it is. Anything else is a leap into an unknown most of us are not prepared to take any more. It'd be exhausting, and we're no longer twenty-one. No, we have our husbands, our children, and our little bit of fun on the side. This way, no one gets hurt.'

Despite the warmth of the spring day, it was cold now in the late evening, and as we huddled together in the car park while our husbands commandeered taxis, a courtesy extended by Andrew's company, our bare arms turned to goose flesh. I bade them all goodbye, one by one. Sally came and kissed my cheeks.

'Don't let us worry you too much with our talk,' she said. 'We get this way, especially with a little bubbly inside us. Also, you have to remember that most of us never get to talk about these kinds of things except when we are all together, which is pretty rare these days. What I'm trying to say is, we can get carried away, we can generalize. But it's good for us. It lets everything *in* out.'

I smiled at her with genuine fondness.

'And you never know, you and Andrew might just be one of the lucky ones, the exceptions. He seems a lovely man, and I'm sure he doesn't do anything untoward in Paris, or anywhere else for that matter. Not all of them do, you know.'

Her husband, bow-tie undone, shirt-tails flapping, hollered at her to get into the 'blasted cab', whose door he was holding wide open.

'See you at Goodwood, perhaps,' Sally said, and left.

I wouldn't see the Racing Widows for another two years, but I wouldn't forget them.

It was a relief finally to get into the taxi. I asked the driver if he could put on the heating and began slowly to warm up. Beside me, Andrew looked spent but happy. He was drunk enough, I knew, to bring on a murderous hangover in the morning, but right now he was still in the moment, and wanted to remain in it. He draped an arm over me, his fingers tiptoeing down my chest towards my breast, which he scooped up as if it were a ball and gave it a sharp squeeze.

'*Andrew!*' I hissed, so loud that the driver checked, and double-checked, his rear-view mirror. 'That hurt!'

He leaned further in towards me, pressing his lips to my ear. 'I thought maybe when we got home, we could . . . ?'

The drive back took another couple of hours, much of it passing in silence, Andrew now fast asleep, his head thrown back on the top of the seat at an angle of almost 180 degrees. Alcohol fumes poured out of him. Despite the cold, I opened the window.

It took me, and the driver, several minutes to rouse him, and after we'd helped him up the path and in through the front door, he staggered up the stairs on all fours, losing one shoe on the second step, the other on the fifth.

I went into the kitchen, where I drank three glasses of tap-water in big, greedy gulps, then went upstairs to the bathroom to wash the make-up from my face. In the bedroom I found him fast asleep on his back. I removed his glasses, his trousers and socks, and wrapped the duvet around him, asleep and content and safe in the house that he and I had built together. He began, abruptly, to snore with the volume of a brass section. The idea of ever sharing a bed with him again held little appeal.

I picked up my laptop from the side table, then turned the light off and went into the spare room. I was exhausted and a little drunk myself, but nowhere near sleep. I got into bed, opened my laptop, typed the word 'escort' into the search engine, then hit enter: 0.12 seconds later, 264,000,000 results became available to me. I browsed just a few of them, and then a few more, intrigued and bewildered, and increasingly titillated by what I found.

It wasn't until the milk float passed outside my window, its electric hum alerting me to the fact that I should have been asleep ages ago, that I realized quite how many hours had flown by.

I felt powerfully awake, and somehow mobilized.

Five

I woke the morning after feeling teenage – that sensation children get when they have happened upon something illicit and cannot wait to get their parents out of the way in order to return feverishly to it.

I don't think back then I had any real inkling of the breadth of its appeal, this previously unknown world that I would regrettably come to prefer to the real one. This only became obvious to me a few weeks later, after our first lunch party at the new house, which Andrew had insisted would be fun but which left me feeling lonelier than I could ever remember.

'We should have a party,' he told me one night.

We were sat in front of the television, as we always were these days, our glazed expressions falling upon something of little consequence on BBC1. Summer was on its way; you could feel it on the blissful breeze that drifted in through the open garden door and up into our living room. In years gone by we would rarely have been home on evenings like these, choosing instead to drink the night away with friends in bars. Now we rarely left the couch.

'A party? Why?'

Because we had just spent an awful year doing up the house, he said, and because it was worth showing off. We hadn't seen anyone properly since the wedding. We needed to reconnect.

And specifically, it would do me the world of good, provide me with something to focus on now that my days were so tauntingly empty. He was right about that; they were. Though my job had still been waiting for me after my pneumonia faded, I was increasingly humbled there, the Oxbridge influx proving excruciatingly efficient and endlessly enthusiastic. My continued presence in the office felt positively anachronistic.

'We could invite people,' he suggested. 'You know, friends.'

My mind raced. I panicked. I wasn't sure I knew how to be amongst friends any more – whatever would I talk about? But reason prevailed. It would give me an excuse to crack the spine of all those hardback cookbooks that now sat so proudly in my new kitchen, and it would allow me to re-enter the social world.

Andrew nudged me in my ribs. 'Come on, let's do it.'

I found myself nodding.

'All right. Why not?'

Lunch for ten people, cooked by me. It had never happened before; it might never again. They arrived on a Sunday afternoon, Ark-like, in twos, faces I hadn't seen in such a long time, each smiling and cooing as they stepped over the threshold, making encouraging vowel sounds upon first sight of the house that had, in many cases, claimed me from them.

'Ooh, look at this,' said Jane archly, running a hand across the living-room mantelpiece, while Lydia, Lindsay and her boyfriend John grinned and giggled – at what, I couldn't be sure. Andrew beamed back at them, happy to play maître d' in his own home. 'Champagne?'

I felt feline in the company of Jane, Lydia and Lindsay, an instinctive prickling of my fur, claws primed, a low growl in the back of my throat. These were my oldest friends. We'd seen each other through multiple heartaches, two divorces and three births. I'd been with Jane the night I had met Andrew, but by settling with him I had somehow spurned her. We'd stopped socializing properly long before the house project, and by settling down and marrying I had opted out of their single ladies' club. I'd once been in the inner circle; now I was denied membership.

'You never come out with us any more,' she'd complained once, about six months into my relationship with him. 'You can't just pick up where we left off once he's walked out on you, you know? It's not cool to forget your friends.'

Something, of course, Jane had routinely done to me. She herself had not been in a serious relationship for several years now. The very fact of my continued happiness seemed to hurt her, and she could not hide it.

We used to speak daily, and meet up with Lydia and Lindsay all the time, our Friday nights climaxing together, destroyed and hysterical at the corner tables of local bars. But we had spoken only sparingly since the wedding, and the more involved I had become in the house, the less I had seen of all of them. Confronted with the three of them now, all together, I couldn't help but wonder how much gossip had gone on behind my back.

Andrew took John into the kitchen for a glass of something, while I took my friends on a tour of the house. By the time we reached the bathroom, Jane was applauding loudly.

'Lady of the manor!' she cried. 'Who'd have thought it?'

Her eyes were red. 'Are you drunk, Jane?'

She reeled back, affecting a look of insulted shock. 'Hark at her,' she said, before laughing and pulling a bottle of red wine from the voluminous handbag that hung heavily from her shoulder, presenting it to me as a housewarming gift. 'Not yet,' she smirked.

We went back downstairs to the dining room, where Andrew was already opening a bottle of champagne.

'Beautiful table,' said Lydia, with feeling.

'It's iroko,' I said, regretting it immediately.

Jane giggled. 'Bless you!'

The doorbell went, and it was a relief to leave them to it. On the doorstep stood Elliot, his French wife Estelle, and their two daughters, one hiding behind her father's legs, the other just waking up in a pushchair. Elliot held out a bottle of wine, Estelle a beautiful bunch of flowers.

'Come in, come in.'

I had known Elliot since university. He was, in many ways, Jane's male counterpart, a peripheral constant in my life. I had seen increasingly less of him since he and Estelle had moved with their children to the suburbs, in search of a bigger garden and better schools, then even less again since the wedding. I recalled now that he had left several messages for me over the past few months, messages to which I had consistently failed to respond in my pneumonia fog. As a result, we hadn't talked properly in months. All sorts of things had happened to him in life and work to which I would remain oblivious. And it was all my fault.

He smiled and embraced me, and complimented me on the house. After the exchange of pleasantries, my mind went blank. I had no idea what to say to him. That hadn't happened before.

Martin arrived next, the former colleague who had been rather unceremoniously kicked out despite his many years of devotion to the job. He was with his wife of eleven months – a beautiful, doll-like Czech woman called Illeana, the cause of much office gossip at the time after he'd met and married her in a whirlwind three months before she could even speak English properly. They had a baby daughter now, tiny in her buggy and utterly serene in sleep.

I ushered everybody into the dining room and the capable hands of my husband, while I disappeared into the too-hot kitchen, where four saucepans were now boiling at once, but none as boiling as me. I had exerted a lot of sweat and effort over the previous five hours, and my cookbooks were now dog-eared and smeared liberally with grease. Lamb shanks looked easier on the page than they were in the flesh, the persistently pink and bloody flesh. Estelle came to offer help, and her children ran between my legs, then out into the garden. Andrew bustled in for more champagne and, moments later, Lindsay emerged at my shoulder to tell me, sweetly, that the house looked wonderful and that I had done a terrific job. I blew hair from my eyes and thanked her profusely, inexplicably close to tears.

The door went again – a couple of Andrew's friends from work, loud and already preprandially half drunk. My anxiety levels reached 9. I breathed in through my nose and out through my mouth, meditatively, plated the meat and dressed it. It now all looked much as it did on page 314, and relief swam through me in exhausted ripples. I tried to keep the shrill notes from my voice as I shouted for my husband to come and help serve. He arrived immediately and proved gratifyingly obedient. Lunch was served.

I experienced an undeniably sheepish stab of pride the moment I sat at the head of our dining table, which quickly mingled with doubt, as if what I really expected was my mother to come bustling along and ask for her seat back. But here I was, surrounded by people talking and laughing, spooning up vegetables and helping themselves to more drink. I made noises about things perhaps being a little too *al dente* or possibly overdone, but my timid cautions were drowned out in the general hubbub of excitable conversation, the lunch party now aloft on its own momentum. Estelle and Illeana, seated next to one another, fell into companionable conversation about babies and nappies and sore nipples, while Elliot and Martin did the male variant of the same subject. Andrew's friends, who had quickly abandoned the champagne as a 'girls' drink' in favour of Guinness, were much taken with Jane, who was well on the way to being outrageously drunk and flirting with them outlandishly. Then she spilled her red wine across the tablecloth. 'Oops! Red doesn't stain, does it?'

I was complimented on the food, but otherwise felt rather invisible, incapable of joining in conversations about topics – work, babies, Jane's love life – that I knew nothing about. I had become a spectator at my own event.

'What's for afters?' asked Francesca, Elliot's four-year-old.

Estelle admonished her with a prideful smile and told her to be patient, but Andrew, as if hit by a cattle prod, jumped to his feet, announced it a fantastic idea and encouraged us all out into the garden where we could enjoy our strawberries and cream, our boxes of chocolates, more wine and perhaps some coffee to follow, under the warm afternoon sun.

As everybody dutifully filed out, I began to clear the plates.

Andrew lunged for my arm. '*Leave them!*' he whispered urgently, then immediately softened and smiled. 'Go and attend to your guests.'

It was a beautiful June day and my little lunch party was now getting raucous, the children chasing one another through the flower beds, Jane cackling witchily at everything Andrew's friends said, her voice carrying far beyond the garden wall.

'Hellooo?'

I looked over and saw the face of our neighbour, Patricia, her head just visible over the ivy. I put my strawberries to one side and approached, ready with an apology, because surely we had woken her daughter from her afternoon nap. I was used to saying sorry to Patricia by now, though she had proved terribly patient during the months of renovation work. We'd actually seen very little of each other to date, Patricia working long hours in a graphics company and never in her house when I was in mine. Then, suddenly, she was around every day and had with her a small child, three years old.

'Hi, Patricia – look, I'm so s—'

'Is that children in your house?' she asked hopefully.

In her arms, she held her daughter, Poppy, a cute child with Bambi eyes and dark, lustrous curls. She also had a fierce temper on her. Since moving in properly, Andrew and I would frequently hear her through the walls as she stomped from room to room in a tantrum, her mother trailing after, pleading tearfully before losing resolve and screaming back.

'Yes, they're my friends. We're having a . . . I hope we didn't disturb—'

But Patricia was busy looking over my shoulder and pointing out Francesca to Poppy. Andrew approached now, far quicker on the uptake than I.

'Would you like to join us?' he asked.

Her face opened like an envelope. 'Love to!' she said, turning to her daughter. 'Would you like to play with the children, Poppy?'

She came round, said hello to everyone and gratefully accepted a glass of wine. It was the first time I had properly talked to her. She was an attractive woman in her mid-forties, and single. She told us, in a bizarrely singsong voice, that she had just been made redundant. 'But that's okay. I'll have more time to spend at home with this little one.' She beamed, drained her glass and asked for a top-up. 'You must be so pleased the house is finally finished?' she said.

Andrew laughed. 'Not as glad as you, I'm sure!'

'Would you like to have a tour?' I asked her, grateful suddenly to have something that I alone could perform. I took her from room to room, each of which she greeted with a sharp intake of breath and a showy proclamation of beauty and perfection and wonder. 'And all *so* much nicer than my tatty old place!' When I showed her the third bedroom, our den, she smiled.

'Ah, and this will be the nursery one day, will it?'

She looked so hopeful that I couldn't face the idea of disappointing her. 'Perhaps,' I said.

Back in the garden, I quickly lost her to Estelle, the pair of them chatting like old friends. Martin and Illeana left, and Jane was busy exhorting Andrew's friends to accompany her to a nearby wine bar. Half an hour later, she air-kissed me goodbye, trailing five of our remaining guests with her. The rest of us lounged in the garden, enjoying the last of the sun and a little peace, the girls having moved into the living room to watch television – and smear cream cheese on the sofa (though I would only find this out later).

By nine o'clock the house was empty. I was glad to see the last of them go, and eager now to set about the kitchen. But Andrew, red wine staining his lips, commandeered the room for himself and banished me to the sofa. 'Put your feet up,' he said. Exhausted, I gratefully complied, and went to sit in front of the TV, still screening a kids' cartoon. I was unable to change the channels because I couldn't find the remote and was too tired to get up to do so manually. It was now that I saw the cream cheese, spreading a deliberate semicircle across the cushions, a white rainbow studded with tiny particles of chopped chives.

I wondered when I would next see Jane, and whether Patricia, my neighbour, was actively longing for me to fall pregnant so that we could be mothers together, our children friends. Elliot felt lost to me now, our lives on such separate paths, and Martin, who had been furiously tight-lipped all day, still smarting over his redundancy and what was becoming an enduring bout of unemployment, was somewhere I could no longer reach. On the television screen a cat was chasing a mouse with a frying pan in its grip, its eyes full of malevolent intent.

'That was fun, wasn't it?' Andrew joined me now, two full glasses of wine in his hands, the last thing either of us needed.

'We should do it more often.' He laughed, recollecting something. 'Jane was on form, wasn't she?'

'I thought you hated Jane?' I said, suddenly wanting him to admit that he did so that I wouldn't feel quite so alone in the emotion.

But all he did was grin. 'She has her moments.'

We sat in companionable silence, and it wasn't until he went up to bed that I headed into the kitchen, expecting to find he'd done a poor, drunken job of the cleaning up. But the room was gleaming, everything washed and tidied and put back in its rightful place, my husband beyond reproach. Damn.

I went upstairs towards my room and noticed on the landing that the light in the den was on. I went up into it and saw, on the floor, the remote control, bearing traces of cream cheese and chives, which had now dried and hardened. The room was full of boxes and carrier bags and unwanted items of small furniture, about as far in atmosphere from a baby's nursery as a room could get. But Patricia, for one, thought it perfect. I switched off the light and went back down to my room.

Reaching for my laptop in the glow of the bedside lamp felt like instant solace, this little rectangle of metal and plastic and gadgetry a portal into a more comforting universe. Prompted perhaps by all the talk of children, I browsed one of the many online forums for mothers, and watched with mild surprise the endless stream of traffic, posts updated on a minute-by-minute basis, even now, at eleven o'clock on a Sunday night. The postings were frank and funny and full of the kind of opinions you'd expect more from right-leaning politicians. I was drunk, tired and emotional, and I wasn't thinking straight. I created a profile and a username, then began to type. I was a woman in my late thirties, I wrote, and actively didn't want children, seemingly immune to peer pressure and biological requirements. I posed the question: is there anything wrong with me?

It was quiet in the house, with only Andrew's muffled snores – his nose deep in his pillow – breaking the silence. The responses came back almost immediately. My life was empty, one read. What on earth was wrong with me? queried another. How dare I take my womb for granted when so many of those online right now had gone through such endless heartache, and so many thousands of pounds, in order to get themselves pregnant. I was a disgrace to my gender, a self-centred woman who thought only about herself.

'If yr not a mother, then why the hell are you on this site?' one demanded.

'Perhaps she was looking for a swingers' site instead? ☺' someone else wrote.

The last one I read before hurriedly clicking off: 'You can go now. Stop gawping. Bye bye.'

Fleeing the mothers' forum before I could get mortally stung, I spent the next hour surfing porn. I'd not really surfed porn before, convinced it was the preserve of little boys with limited outlets at their disposal. Previous boyfriends had never discussed their pornographic habits with me, and neither, really, had Andrew. I had always considered myself a feminist, convinced that such images would offend me – the endless degradation of women for the benefit of sad men. But now I found myself less offended than I did aroused. Odd. Perhaps having been starved of sex for so long I'd become hyper-aware that it was still going on all around me, and that by abstaining I was missing out, denying myself. What other explanation for the mounting thrill now of all the online submissiveness, the cream pies, the proliferation of MILFs, the older men with younger women, the younger men with older women, the women-on-women, the copious displays of bared flesh? I scrolled through the pages, my antivirus protection pulsing protectively on the toolbar throughout, with such academic fascination of what I was watching that I forgot all about touching myself.

I moved next into the world of webcams. For someone who would only ever pose for Polaroid shots for boyfriends when I was really very drunk indeed, these came as a shock. I'd had no idea that women these days were so intent on revealing quite so much to so many. Porn I could understand. Porn was business, the revealing of flesh in return for money. That made sense. But what sense did webcams make? Why did so many film themselves naked before the camera, masturbating, grabbing their breasts and squirming up their features at the point of (real?) orgasm? What did it do for them that I couldn't imagine it doing for me?

Watching men wank themselves silly was far more straightforward, and somehow more comprehensible. Men always were, in my experience, inexplicably proud of their penises. Lust could transform even the smallest appendage, to its owner at least, into a totem of admirable masculine power that every woman must surely covet. The lone masturbators on these webcams were fat and pale and, in their way, rather sad, displaying themselves on a Sunday night in the hope of awakening something animal inside me. I grew quickly bored, and moved on.

A couple of years before, Jane had told me she had become fascinated with chatrooms, where she could have virtual affairs without, she claimed, 'any proper messy human interaction – unless I really, really want to.' She suggested I come round one night and have a bit of fun with her on one, but I was in the midst of my wedding preparations and the very idea had seemed desperate, and melancholic. I declined.

I Googled chatrooms. There were millions to choose from. I clicked first on the one at the top of the page, then moved steadily down the list. They were amusing and puerile, arousing and moronic, and most filled with seemingly illiterate men looking for women who were UP4IT, and in need of A GOOD

SHAGGIN. The women, too, gave as good as they got – MY C*NT SCREEMING 4 U!!! – and a certain rhythm built up between them, all conversing together, each going at their keyboards hammer and tongs. I WANNA FUCK U. IM GONNA CUM. SPRAY MY TITS. MY GASH FOR YOUR TRASH!!

My gash for your trash was a new one on me.

One of the books that made the biggest impression on me as a teenager was *The Story of O*. I had never read a so bluntly sexual book in my life, and haven't since. I loved that it was written by Anonymous, and initially resolved to read everything that Anonymous had written until somebody explained what it meant. I loved its black cover, its sinister gloss. I felt little attraction in becoming a sex slave myself, but something about O's sense of willing abandon excited me. I'd bought it for a boyfriend, Joe. It was my way of telling him, I suppose, that not all girls were like his rather uptight ex-girlfriend in the bedroom. Some of us had more imagination, a greater sense of daring.

The book did not have quite the effect on him that I'd hoped. I turned up at his house one night, a week after giving it to him. Reluctantly, he invited me into the living room, while his mother kept herself busy in the kitchen. I asked him if he'd read it. Warily, he nodded. 'And?' I asked.

'I . . .' Blood filled his cheeks. 'Look. Um. This is difficult, but . . .'

I waited.

'It's Emily,' he said eventually. His old girlfriend. 'We've been . . . We met up again. And we talked. I think we're going to give it . . . we're going to give it another shot. I'm so sorry. I really am. I hope you can forgive me. I'd love it if we could stay – you know, friends.'

This taught me a valuable lesson: that a willingness for certain depravity in the bedroom is something you shouldn't reveal in a relationship too soon. Joe's mother returned the book to me by post a couple of weeks afterwards (*I'm open to everything, my darling Joe*, I had written on the flyleaf. *Not with my son you're not*, his mother had added), and though I still had it somewhere today, I had never dared read it again, convinced I would only see it through his, and his mother's, admonishing eyes, a perverted book for perverted people.

I decided now to browse for erotic literature sites, the kind only Anonymous could write. I struck gold quickly, and here found that women were represented far more than men. A great many of the stories were bisexual in theme. You could tell they were written by women because there was foreplay involved, a lot of lyrical build-up, and the presence of an almost Mills & Boon-ish romance. Reading them, I started to understand the male obsession of two women together. Several stories in, I found myself increasingly wanting to be one of those women.

I also wanted to take part myself, and so I registered, gave a username and a brief bio, and was then free to post. But what to write, and for whom? Butterflies floated free and wild in my stomach, and my senses felt on high alert.

My username was L27 and, while I was still pondering what to write, I began to receive private messages: two, three, six, ten. It was gone one a.m. on a Monday morning, just hours before the beginning of another working week. Did these people never sleep? *Do u wanna chat?* asked someone who went by the name of CUMBUSTER. HornyDevil instant-messaged me to tell me that he, or she, was a horny devil, 'which is why its my username, geddit?'

And then I received something from a man who called himself The Pseud. The Pseud's message was different from the rest, longer and more confident, well written. I responded to him promptly, and he replied. I sat up straight now and leaned eagerly into my laptop. My very first chatroom experience was under way.

His username was The Pseud, he would tell me later, because he was terribly pretentious. He loved his wines, drove an exclusive German car, 'and I'm multilingual: French, German, basic Spanish. Oh, and I forgot to mention the tongue factor,' he added. The Pseud, still fundamentally male despite his erudition, was never far from lewdness when we chatted online, and over the next few weeks we would chat incessantly.

The Pseud: 'L27'? I'm guessing it's not your given name, but rather a hastily adopted one for the purposes of this room. Am I correct? It suits you. It has a nice flow. It could be a band name. Anyway, I'm digressing. Let me focus. Hello. UK man here. Fancy a chat?
L27: Hi. Thanks for your message. You're right, it could be a band name. I'm no singer, though. But, yes, I am up for a chat. I'm intrigued by *your* name.

He mentioned the tongue factor. I responded with an emoticon, my first. I asked him to tell me more.

The Pseud: Well, like I say, I'm in a hotel room in Vienna, but I fly back to the UK in a couple of days. I'm at a conference here for work. It has been a long day, and a long evening at the bar. I came up to my room about an hour ago – room 704 – but couldn't sleep. I've been watching a bit of porn on the pay-per-view (€16.99!), and now I'm chatting to you. I've had a few drinks. If you don't mind me being quite so upfront about things, I'm pretty horny right now. I rather fancy a wank. You?

There came the shock of illicit thrill, pulsing with current: a total stranger coming on to me so brazenly. If he had told me this in a bar within minutes of meeting me, I'd have smacked him across the face. But then setting is everything. To read that this complete stranger was on the point of masturbating while writing to me lit me up inside.

I tried out a couple of responses, deleted them and started over, before finally mustering the courage to hit Return.

> L27: Funny, our day sounds quite similar.
> The Pseud: What, you've been at a conference too?

I liked him.

> The Pseud: I know it's late, but I'm actually supposed to be working. I have a presentation first thing in the morning. But everybody needs a little break from time to time, right? Perhaps chatting to you will help stimulate my juices – my creative juices.
> L27: Hmm, wanking and working. Whatever would your boss say?
> The Pseud: Want me to ask him?
> L27: What? Now?
> The Pseud: Sure. He's right here with me. In fact, his hand is around my cock.
> L27: . . .???
> The Pseud: Don't worry, it's nothing untoward. Well, not much. I'm my own boss.
> L27: I'm relieved. May I ask what you do?
> The Pseud: You may.
> L27: Well?
> The Pseud: You haven't asked yet. You've merely asked whether you are *permitted* to. You are.

A pedant! My match made in heaven!

L27: What is it you do, Mr Pseud?

The Pseud: I'm a doctor of the mind.

L27: No, really?

The Pseud: Really.

L27: Really???

The Pseud: We could go on like this all night, if we're not careful . . .

L27: Sorry, but for some reason I didn't imagine a doctor to do . . .

The Pseud: What? Something like this?

L27: Well, yes.

The Pseud: You expected only – what? – out-of-work plumbers, IT geeks? What a snob!

L27: Guilty.

The Pseud: So what do you do?

L27: Plumber.

The Pseud: Oh dear.

L27: I've turned you off? Who's the snob now?

The Pseud: Guilty.

He pressed me for an answer, and I replied as non-specifically as I could. 'Something within the media', was what I typed. But that was all he needed. 'Let me guess,' he wrote back. 'You're a — for — ?' My fingers recoiled from the keyboard and I looked about the room as if I were being watched. How on earth could he know? What had I given away, so carelessly and so quickly? I thought these things were supposed to remain safely anonymous? I pulled the duvet up around my neck, drummed my fingers on the laptop's mouse pad, and pondered my reply. But no words came. I typed nothing.

The Pseud: You're new to all this. I can tell. This your first time?

L27: And you're an old hand?

111

The Pseud: Not so much of the *old*, please.

L27: Ha! An older man, then.

The Pseud: You're no spring chicken yourself, lady.

L27: How on earth would you know that?

The Pseud: It is my job to know such things. I'm right, aren't I?

L27: You are right that I am no spring chicken, yes. But how old are you? This is, by the way, a direct question.

The Pseud: Are we to be strictly honest here?

L27: We are.

The Pseud: So how old are you?

L27: I asked first.

The Pseud: So you did. But I was brought up by my parents – between the wars – to be courteous to women. So . . . Women first.

L27: Between the wars? Good God, Grandad!

The Pseud: Ouch.

L27: I'm 27.

The Pseud: Hence L27?

L27: Wow! You're good!

The Pseud: Too young for me, I'm afraid. Nice chatting with you . . .

L27: No! Come back! Okay . . . I'm 32.

The Pseud: We're getting there . . .

L27: You really are good at this, aren't you?

The Pseud: Among the very best.

L27: 37.

L27: 37+2.

The Pseud: 39?

L27: A gifted mathematician.

The Pseud: I've got a calculator thingy on my PalmPilot.

L27: PalmPilot??? How very 1999. That must make you the wrong side of 40.

The Pseud: Perhaps it does, but then doesn't life always begin at 40? At 39, my dear, it is *you* that is the wrong side of 40 . . .

I'm not sure what I had been expecting to find online while my husband slept off our lunch-party excess next door, but I know that I couldn't ever have imagined hitting it off with somebody so profoundly and so quickly. I'd never had a conversation with a stranger before that had so instantaneously felt quite so *right*. Was it possible to fancy someone you had never met? If so, I fancied The Pseud already. He was an older man – I guessed forty-six, forty-seven – and would, I decided, be handsome, well dressed, impeccably turned out. I'd never really liked beards, but I imagined he had a trim one, the colour of salt and pepper. Hair swept back, reading glasses, debonair in a suit. He would appreciate the finer things in life, the best food, the best wine. He was well read, and was probably listening to opera as we conversed, the swelling drama of Puccini, say, providing the soundtrack to his hotel porn and his intimate chat with me.

L27: Touche. (Sorry, I don't know how to make the accent on the e.)
The Pseud: Touché.
L27: I'm impressed.
The Pseud: Wait until you have reached 47. You'll have learned all sorts by then.
L27: Which is why I'm on here, I suppose. To find myself a teacher.
The Pseud: I can be terribly strict.
L27: And I can be terribly naughty.

A pause of several seconds opened up like a chasm, and I feared I had gone too far too quickly, ignorant as to the etiquette of these things. Perhaps he liked to be the dominant one, his women submissive? I tried immediately to lighten the tone.

L27: Let me guess. You've started wanking again, and you require both hands?

The Pseud: What makes you think I'd ever stopped?

L27: Nobody can type that quickly, and accurately, with just the one hand, surely?

The Pseud: I'm using all available extremities.

L27: So you're something of an expert at webchats, are you?

The Pseud: An expert, no. An enthusiast, certainly.

L27: Are you married?

The Pseud: You don't hang around, do you? Straight in with the personal stuff.

L27: Too probing?

The Pseud: In these forums, yes. I'd normally have gone through several women in the time we've been talking, often simultaneously. We tend to avoid strictly personal stuff in favour of good old-fashioned and very direct smut here – you know: the occasional spelling mistake; fudged sentiment; orgasm; goodnight. With you, an hour in, I'm still on the foreplay.

L27: Foreplay's good.

The Pseud: So my patients tell me. My wife too, once upon a time.

L27: Married and disillusioned, then?

The Pseud: You too, by the sounds of it.

L27: How do you know I'm married?

The Pseud: By the ring on your finger.

L27: It's not as shiny as it used to be.

The Pseud: Whose ring is, at our age?

L27: Smut!

The Pseud: Every good doctor's weakness, I'm afraid.

L27: Thank goodness I don't see one!

The Pseud: Don't speak too soon. You might see *me* soon enough.

L27: That's a bit presumptuous, no?

The Pseud: Not presumptuous, merely hopeful.

L27: Does your wife know you do this?

The Pseud: Does your husband?

L27: No, though I like to think he wouldn't particularly mind. It's all fairly innocent, this. Right?

The Pseud: But that is rather beside the point, no? By doing this without his knowledge, his permission, it accentuates the sensation of being, as you put it before, naughty. And naughty is presumably the point?

L27: Is this a session? Am I paying for this?

The Pseud: Only if you want to.

L27: I think you are right, what you said before. We are getting pretty personal pretty quickly.

The Pseud: It's because we click. It happens. Very occasionally, but it does happen. But then that is why people come in to chatrooms in the first place, in the hope that they click with somebody else out there.

L27: Yes, but it can't be good to click with just any old Tom, Dick or Harry . . .

The Pseud: But I'm not any old Tom, Dick or Harry. The name's Andrew.

A punch to the solar plexus. I reeled, my fingers shrinking from the keyboard again. I looked at my hands. They were trembling. I leaned towards the bedroom wall and heard, to my enormous relief, my own Andrew still fast asleep, snoring obliviously. *Andrew?* What were the chances? He was beginning to unsettle me.

And yet.

The Pseud: You still there?

L27: Just.

The Pseud: Let me guess. 'Andrew' has particular currency for you. The name of your husband, perhaps?

L27: My father.

The Pseud: Let me assure you, I am not your father.

L27: Just as well. Though I'm sure he'd never get connection where he is.

The Pseud: I sometimes have the same trouble. Wi-Fi's not all it's cracked up to be, is it?

I looked at the little time display on my laptop and saw, with horror, that it was just after four. Almost morning. I was due in at work in little more than five hours. I didn't want to leave the chatroom just yet. I wanted to carry on talking to him all morning, and all the next day. I had no idea what to do. Did one play hard to get on these things? If I logged off now, would it keep him keen, or would I never hear from him again – usernames that pass, like ships, in the night?

Perhaps inevitably, he was one step ahead of me again.

The Pseud: Listen, I think I'd better turn in for the night. It's so late it's almost early. I've got my presentation soon, and you have your own day ahead of you.

L27: It's been nice talking to you.

The Pseud: It has.

A pause. Minutes became hours.

The Pseud: We should do it again.

L27: Did you 'finish'?

The Pseud: I think, where you are concerned, tantric might just pay dividends. So, no. I'm conserving.

L27: I'm honoured.

The Pseud: Will you come back to this site soon?

L27: I will if you will.

The Pseud: Until then, then.

And with that, his flashing cursor was stilled. He'd gone, and I was left more awake than I could ever remember being, my heartbeat an insistent pulse in my temple, my fingertips, the back of my knees. I closed my laptop and arranged myself beneath the duvet until comfortable.

I finished inside of thirty seconds.

Six

The Pseud: Do you have a picture I could see?

L27: No!

The Pseud: Ah, I see.

L27: See what?

The Pseud: You were not born pretty, and you didn't grow up pretty. There's more to life than looks, you know. Beauty is only skin deep.

L27: You think I'm ugly? How dare you!

The Pseud: So you *are* pretty?

L27: Might be . . . And you?

The Pseud: Not pretty, no. Never that. More rugged and lived-in, I suppose. I'm told it suits me.

L27: By who?

The Pseud: Whom.

L27: *Whom*.

The Pseud: My wife, in her more attentive moments, the occasional client and, once, on an aeroplane somewhere over the Atlantic, by the woman in the aisle seat next to me. We were in business class, and I concede that she may have been influenced by all the champagne she'd been drinking.

L27: Had she been drinking a lot?

The Pseud: Oh yes. But then I'd been doing the pouring.

L27: So you are quite the flirt, then?

The Pseud: Would I be here talking to you if I wasn't?

L27: Did anything happen between the drunken woman and the rugged gentleman?

The Pseud: Did we join the Mile High Club, you mean?

L27: If you like.

The Pseud: No. Breakfast was on its way, and we were both ravenous.

L27: Shame.

The Pseud: Are you a member yourself?

L27: No! I'm terrified of flying.

The Pseud: Really? What is your earliest childhood memory?

L27: You're not at work, not now.

The Pseud: Actually, I am. It is 3.30 on a Friday afternoon. Where else would I be?

This was a good point. It *was* a weekday afternoon, one of the days my job no longer needed me, and I was home alone, killing time, hanging on his every typed word. It had been a week since we first spoke and we had hooked up another couple of times since, but stolen moments only: once the following day when he was waiting to board his plane back home from Vienna, and again over lunch on Wednesday. He said then that he wanted to talk to me longer and asked when I would next be free. I told him Friday afternoon. When he agreed (actually, what he said was 'We'll see'), I presumed he'd be free as well. I didn't imagine him actually at work. Now I pictured him in his office, a dark, wood-panelled room filled with books on psychology, calming paintings on the wall, and him sitting at a tilt in a leather chair, his latest patient reclining in front of him, her back to him, as she gave vent to her myriad troubles.

L27: You're not talking to me while you should be listening to a patient, are you? Surely that's unethical! Immoral!

119

The Pseud: I'm not, no. I still have half an hour until my next appointment.

L27: Who is she?

The Pseud: She?

L27: Your next patient.

The Pseud: You are aware of patient/doctor confidentiality, I presume?

L27: You're right. I'm sorry.

The Pseud: You're right, too. It is a *she*. She is your age, and in, shall we say, similar circumstances. That is all I am prepared to say.

L27: There are many of us about, I suppose. Perhaps I should get together with her afterwards for a coffee and a chat . . .

The Pseud: Perhaps *we* should get together for a coffee and a chat?

L27: Anyway, where were we? Oh yes, I remember. Your failure to join the Mile High Club with that woman. Missed opportunity, do you think?

The Pseud: Not quite. We got acquainted properly once back on terra firma.

L27: Really?

The Pseud: She was in transit, and had seven hours until her next flight. We headed for one of the airport hotels.

L27: Oh!

The Pseud: You're shocked?

L27: Did the earth move?

The Pseud: Thanks mostly to all the 747s taking off, yes.

L27: So you had an affair?

The Pseud: More of a one-night stand, but during the day.

L27: Not your first?

The Pseud: I'm afraid to say no, it wasn't.

L27: So you do this kind of thing a lot?

The Pseud: Occasionally. I do love my wife but there are – complications. And I have needs. Don't you?

L27: I do.

The Pseud: Which is why you are here talking to me now. You didn't answer my question earlier.

L27: Remind me.

The Pseud: Perhaps we could meet for coffee and a chat?

L27: I'm not sure.

The Pseud: Fair enough.

L27: I don't really know anything about you. I don't know what you look like. You say you are a doctor and that you live in the UK, but for all I know, you could be a redneck trucker from Alabama.

The Pseud: Would you be disappointed if I was?

L27: Actually, I've always had a thing for redneck truckers from Alabama . . .

I still hadn't got used to the sudden disruptions in our conversational flow. If The Pseud didn't ping back a response immediately, I invariably began to panic. I'd scared him off, turned him off; he'd met someone else on one of his other simultaneous chats, someone who intrigued him more. How desperate would it sound to write, *You still there? Please come back, please . . .?*

The Pseud: Sorry, my four o'clock has arrived early. Another time?

L27: Another time.

I wanted to ask him *when* exactly – I needed a time and a date, something to look forward to – but held firm and instead switched off and went out for a walk. I needed to clear my head. But I couldn't concentrate and found myself rushing back home and logging on again just in case. His four o'clock had left abruptly, finished early. It could happen, and I craved it to,

121

needed it to, desperate to open my laptop to his 'Hello?' awaiting a response. Time, when I was speaking to The Pseud, flew by. When I wasn't, it stagnated, it inched by like a worm, in punishingly slow increments. I would stare at the screen, biting my fingernails for the first time since I was a teenager, my heart fluttering inside me like a trapped bird. I could, I supposed, have gone on to another chatroom and chatted to another person, other *people*, but I wanted only him.

Each night, the jangling sound of the keys in the front door would pull me abruptly back into the real world, the world in which Andrew was my husband and I his loving wife. His arrival would always take me by surprise: where on earth had the day gone? I'd scramble up from the sofa, into the kitchen, and quickly begin dinner, rattling pans and opening and closing the fridge as if this were what he unspokenly demanded of me: a busy, industrious wife awaiting his return.

He swooped in tonight, bringing with him an unexpectedly cool breeze from outside. He tossed his briefcase on to the small sofa that sat by the garden door, dropped the *Racing Post* on to the table and gave me a perfunctory kiss on the cheek. 'Nightmare day,' he said, loosening his tie and burping beer fumes into his fist. 'Shall we go out tonight? I could do with a drink.'

I swung around, ready to protest. 'But I'm making dinner.'

We both looked towards the hob, upon which were sat two saucepans, both empty, the gas unlit.

'I was just,' I began, then didn't bother. 'Okay, fine, let's go out.'

I dashed upstairs to freshen up, and saw in the mirror the eyes of a woman full of longing, desperation even. As she applied lipstick, I saw her hands were trembling.

Andrew approached the bottom of the stairs and shouted up. '*Coming?*'

I padded down and slipped my feet into my shoes, Andrew

already at the door. I poked my head into the living room and saw my laptop sitting there, closed, its light still glowing. The Pseud, for all I knew, was waiting for my response at that very moment.

'Lucy? Jesus! Come on, let's go.'

'Coming. I'm just . . . My bag, I think . . .'

'Lucy! It's *here*!' I looked back down the hall and saw him, framed in the doorway, impatient, my handbag dangling from his hand.

We went to the new Thai place that had just opened up nearby, a converted bank that managed to look at once huge but also intimate, with personal booths and low lighting. Our waitress was also our waiter, an exotic transsexual who read out that night's list of specials with an exaggerated lisp. I was distracted throughout dinner, and said no to dessert simply so that we could speed things up and return home. But Andrew, oblivious to my inner torture, was already ordering a second bottle of wine and two spoons for the ice cream. It was, after all, a Friday night. He wanted properly to unwind for the weekend, and he wanted his wife with him.

'Shall we drive to Brighton tomorrow?'

I was biting my fingernails as he spoke, ripping the skin from my cuticles until tiny bubbles of blood appeared. 'What?'

'Brighton. Tomorrow. Like we used to?'

I looked up at him and saw that, though he was talking to me, his eyes were trained on his BlackBerry. Instant email. I'd never bothered with it before, because I had never needed it. I needed it now.

'Okay, fine. Whatever.' I pointed to his BlackBerry. 'I think I'm going to buy myself one of those, or perhaps an iPhone.'

He smiled. 'Really? I thought you never wanted one, never liked the idea of the office in your pocket?'

'I've changed my mind.'

'Okay, sure. Why not? Let me buy it for you. A present.' He

leaned clumsily over the table to kiss me just as our waiter/ waitress was bringing our ice cream. 'I don't buy you enough presents these days, do I?' he said.

We arrived home a full hour later, Andrew dashing up to the toilet, complaining of a full bladder. I headed for the living room, the sofa, the laptop. I whipped it open and saw that three messages had been sent over the course of fifteen minutes, but a full three quarters of an hour ago now.

> The Pseud: Hello?
> The Pseud: Sorry for leaving so abruptly before. I'm home now, my wife is in bed, my daughter out at wherever it is my daughter chooses to spend her Friday nights these days. I miss you.
> The Pseud: Hello?

And now, just as I was reading his final *hello*, there came another message. That exquisite, understated chime. Fate, kismet. A kind of telepathy.

> The Pseud: Okay, you're out. And so you should be. It is Friday night, after all. Hope you're having fun. I think I'm going to turn in now. Speak soon.

My fingers scrambled, drunk on red wine and high anxiety.

> L27: nno dont im b ackk! imback!!!!

Andrew was descending the stairs, and I could tell by his whistling that all the pressures of the office had now dissolved, frittered away until their resumption on Sunday night. He was buoyant, and drunkish, and relaxed. I knew he would be hoping for sex, something we hadn't had in weeks now, possibly months.

I slammed the laptop shut, a little too roughly. It clattered to the floor.

'Oops,' said Andrew, stooping to retrieve it.

He collapsed alongside me, my laptop still in his grip. 'Shall we watch a late film?'

'I thought you wanted to go to Brighton tomorrow?'

'I do.'

'Then maybe we should have an early night?'

He turned to face me, unravelling an arm around my shoulder, his face melting like butter. 'An early night?' He smiled.

'Andrew, I'm tired. An early night. To *sleep*.'

My laptop sat squarely in his lap, both hands resting on it. All he needed to do was open it and read the screen with its incriminating evidence. Then what? Humility, hatred, separation, divorce.

I stood up in front of him and made a ridiculous show of yawning and stretching. Was this really me? 'Sorry, but I'm exhausted.'

'But why? You weren't working today . . .'

'Well perhaps I'm depressed, then.' I held out my hand for the laptop.

And now he did open it.

'Mind if I just check something? Mine is upstairs, and I can't be bothered to get—'

I pounced, snatching it from his grip. He withdrew his hands sharply, as if scolded, and looked up at me with a confused expression, a kind of quizzical half smile.

'Okay, calm down. I'll come up with you.'

Upstairs, we brushed our teeth alongside one another, Andrew trying to catch my eye in the mirror, me stealthily looking anywhere but at his. I caught him shrugging, as if in defeat, then spitting, rinsing, kissing my cheek and making a retreat. 'Night, then,' he said.

I rushed to my room, opened the laptop, and read.

The Pseud: Oh! And there I was thinking you were avoiding me.
The Pseud: Hello?
The Pseud: Are you playing hard to get, or something?
The Pseud: Okay, I give up. Another time.
L27: im h3re]
L27: I mean, I'm here. Have you gone? Knock knock?

Nothing. Silence. Either he was playing me at what he thought was *my* game, or else he really had gone for the night. I waited in horrible desperation, but no further messages came. I wanted to call out, to cry his name out loud. But had I called his name – *Andrew!* – then Andrew would have come running. And that would have proved awkward.

In that moment I irrationally resented my husband intensely. Why had he ordered a second bottle of wine? And why had I drunk so much of it? I'd wanted to come home earlier so that I could – so that I could cheat on him with another man. But no, he, my husband, that idiot, had hampered my chances. He was asleep now, dead to the world and dreaming of his stupid horses, and I was awake, adrift in the agony of an itch that I could not scratch alone.

Before switching off the light and trying to find sleep, I left him one last message.

L27: Okay, I guess you've gone. Sorry. I went out to dinner, and only just now came back. I'm sorry to have missed you. It would have been nice to chat. But when you do get to read this, understand this: I've not finished with you yet.

Brighton the following day was overcrowded, and hot, the Lanes impossible to navigate without a great deal of patience. I had very little patience. Andrew wanted to have lunch at a restaurant he'd seen featured on television the previous week, but couldn't remember where it was, or even its name, so we followed the tiny roads and paths in a series of ever-decreasing circles until I snapped and we ended up at Pizza Express. He attributed my irritation levels (correctly, as it happened) to PMT, and in an attempt to improve my mood took me afterwards to the nearest Carphone Warehouse and bought me my promised iPhone, all shiny and white and alive with illicit possibilities.

We didn't get home that night until gone midnight, and after seeing Andrew to bed and checking the laptop, desperately, to find out whether The Pseud had responded to my previous night's messages – he hadn't – I stayed up until I got the iPhone working. I felt something close to infatuation with it, a palm-sized universe cupped in my hand. I could not have been less interested in all its quirky apps, or its music-storage capacity, its GPS; all that concerned me was its instant access to the web, which allowed me instant access to the site, and, hopefully, The Pseud himself. From now on he could sit dormant in my pocket and buzz me whenever he wanted, and wherever I happened to be.

Progress.

Life with my husband was to grow increasingly complicated over the next few months, pulling each of us in different directions. This is rarely good news for a marriage, but one of the upshots of leading essentially separate lives was that I was free to do as I pleased without inspection.

Andrew's company had recently been taken over by a larger one, which would bring both good and, potentially, bad news. The incoming conglomerate, headed, he told me sourly one night, by large Americans in ill-fitting suits, would buy him out of his existing shares, which would mean an instant windfall of tens of thousands of pounds. But the new regime soon began to bandy about words like *restructure* and *redefining*, which invariably meant that he was now in the position of fighting for a job he had for so long taken for granted. The extra effort required, and the necessary public displays of enthusiasm, rendered him grouchy and distracted in my company, and he would return from the office each night depleted, thin-lipped with a fury he didn't wish to discuss, collapsing instead on the couch in front of the television with a bottle of wine he would drink steadily into sleep. He would awake the next morning pallid and grey, and was often out of the house before I was even awake. Some days he was out of the house before I had even properly fallen asleep, my increasing inability to say goodnight to The Pseud at a decent hour sending my body clock into confusion, and keeping both Andrew and me on entirely separate time zones.

At the weekends he sought only oblivion, at either the races or the football, where he and some of his more longstanding colleagues could let off steam. On these nights he would return home even later, his key in the lock and his stumbling footsteps in the hall dragging my attention away from my laptop, and requiring me to perform for the next quarter-hour a little pantomime: snapping shut the Dell, slipping it under my pillow, and affecting sleep until he'd poked his head round my bedroom door, loudly whispering, 'Are you awake, love?', then withdrawing to his room to fall quickly into unconsciousness, thereby allowing me to pick up where I'd left off. Never once on these nights would he first brush his teeth – a small detail, otherwise lost amongst so many, that nevertheless bothered me more than any other.

We could go days without seeing one another. I felt like a single woman again. To occupy my time away from the webchats, I enrolled at a nearby gym, where I swam, sauna'd, and cycled furiously in the PowerZone room, allowing my unspent sexual energy a viable outlet.

And I certainly needed one, my sexual energy having returned of late and now nearing, it felt, a most disconcerting peak. After at least a year in which I had frankly forgotten all about it, sex no longer defining me the way it once had now that I had discovered a world of bathroom tiles and kitchen fittings, I became belatedly aware again that I was still in fact a woman. Sitting on a bus vibrating at traffic lights reminded me of being fourteen. I could find eroticism in everything: a TV advert filmed in romantic soft focus; the way a man carried himself on the street; the neat fitting of particular pairs of knickers against my, what's it called, my *mons*. Most nights, whether or not I had chatted with The Pseud, I could not sleep unless I had come. And coming once only made me want to come again. I was craven, insatiable, and perpetually a little sore.

At first I worried that I had some kind of condition, but, after reading up on it, it seemed that I may in fact have been experiencing a kind of last-gasp biological thrust. I was almost forty and childless, essentially an anomalous state. Being abruptly hijacked by an overwhelming desire for sex was apparently my body's way of reminding me of its own overwhelming desire for fertilization. I remained adamant in focusing my energies on the former, the desire for sex, and, when I went into the supermarket for some conditioner one afternoon, found myself buying a box of condoms too, just in case.

My sex life with Andrew had stuttered to a halt several months earlier, and the fact that neither one of us had made any real overtures to restart it led me to believe that we could quite easily never have sex again. The last time had been shortly after we'd moved into the house, my pneumonia in remission, the two of us sharing a desire to christen the place. It was a Saturday night, with nothing on the television, and nothing better to do. The sudden desperation in his pleadings aroused something instinctive in me, as did the way in which he removed my clothes: roughly. In that moment, I remembered what sex had once been to us. But then he came too soon and I not at all. We were back watching television within minutes, both of us silently aware that, just perhaps, a door had closed on our union.

Those nights I wasn't chatting to The Pseud, I found myself poring instead over a relationship website filled with people whose own stories were increasingly these days my own.

> LizardKing: Hey guys. I came across this website after a long-distance affair I was having with a MW left me confused and hurt. Reading a lot of the stories here made me realize how common my own tale is, and so in the spirit of the site, I wanted to share. Here goes. About a year ago, I met a woman playing an online video game through a chatroom. We initially became email buddies, and then went from playing the game to chatting more personally via hotmail. It was clear to both of us that there was something unique between us: we were both married, both in our early-30s, both going through marital problems. We clicked in a way I had never done with anyone before.

He went on to explain that, as they became closer, they came to realize that they shared similar experiences and goals, and that they had identical perspectives on life, something neither had with their spouses. He wrote that he never thought of her as anything but a friend at first, but that 'sometimes you feel you've met someone special, and that it would be wrong not to allow the friendship to develop.'

> LizardKing: I get to travel pretty frequently for work, and so one day I suggested I make a little diversion, and go visit her (she lived maybe a three-hour drive away). At first she thought it wasn't a good idea. Her husband was emotionally and verbally

abusive, he had already cheated on her many times, and he clearly had psychological problems. She felt that she wouldn't be able to hide the fact that she'd met me. But a week later, she changed her mind. She didn't want to meet me near her home, and so we compromised and met halfway. I gotta say, neither of us knew what would happen upon our first meeting, how we would feel, what would happen. But the very instant we saw each other, we fell for each other, in every way.

His message went on across one long unbroken paragraph that filled my screen. They checked into a hotel room, and the night they shared, he wrote, was 'amazing, spectacular, the first time I ever felt truly and passionately in love'. But in the days afterwards, she failed to email or text him. Frantic, LizardKing pursued her, bombarding her with messages, and even driving to her town in the hope of spotting her on the streets ('like a stalker!'). She eventually sent him a final message saying that she now regretted that night they had spent together. It had been a mistake. She wanted to give her marriage another go. She then deleted all her social network sites, and all ways of contact. LizardKing was devastated.

> LizardKing: She always used to say that our EA was too strong. Well, the PA was even stronger. So much so that she eventually went NC. I know a lot of you guys have gone through similar stuff, so I wanted to ask: what can I expect now? Is there any way back for us? I never intended for either of us to get hurt, but now we both are. I just want to know she is okay. What should I do?

The responses veered wildly, offering support, condolence, criticism, empathy. One wanted to know what he expected, a happy ending? LizardKing responded with refreshing, if tragic, honesty ('YES!'). He never got it. Instead, he became a regular

131

visitor to the site. 'A problem aired = a problem shared, right?' he wrote hopefully.

Another post, from somebody calling themselves MisterT, read:

MisterT: Okay, so basically xMW broke the NC out of the blue, no warning, and contacted me to say that she'd been missing me like hell this past year, and was dying to see me again.

Am I tempted? Of course I am! But look, it's difficult. She hurt me, bad, and afterwards I had to go back to my wife and try to get my life back on track. It was hard, but I did it. But now it's like all those lessons are forgotten. The woman has badly stirred my feelings! Part of me wants to see her again, and another part wants to run away, afraid of being hurt again. She told me that her marriage is no better today than it was last year, and that she is staying around for the child only. But she has not mentioned any intention of a divorce, so I'm figuring: what's the point?

Thing is, she seems to be offering herself to me on a plate. Who wouldn't be tempted to have that kind of fun? Especially when, at the risk of TMI, I'm not having very much fun at home! But I know the consequences of fun (and I didn't back then!). F***! I was doing so well, but now the old feelings have returned, and I'm confused.

Help!!!!

I read on, fascinated and appalled at the confessions, the exclamation marks, the cryptic shorthand. NC, I eventually worked out, was *no contact*, EA *emotional affair*, and PA *physical affair*. In almost all the cases here, everyone had started out convinced of their own innocence, their pursuit of harmless online fun, but every time each EA eventually became a ruinous PA. Many were repeat offenders: somebody calling herself Miss Sin had posted over 1,600 messages, setting out in detail not just her own multiple affairs ('some of us never learn!!') but also, as past master, offering advice and solace to others.

And many *were* seeking advice. There were people here who wanted to know whether cheating was normal, people struggling to understand whether infidelity really was wrong or simply a natural human instinct. There were those wanting to know precisely why good people do bad things, and asking whether love in and of itself can ever be enough. There were people who wanted to share memories of their own affairs, and others who took the moral overview, having stumbled upon their morals the hard way.

One man, who had already clearly suffered for his actions, pleaded with everyone on the site *not* to have an affair with a married person. In the US, he wrote, 56 per cent of married men and 54 per cent of married women have extra-marital affairs. In the US alone, almost 50 per cent of marriages fail. 'Speaking from experience, having an affair with a married person is insane, crazy, the most dumb thing you could ever do.'

He concluded, beseechingly, by saying that his affair had cost him his job, his life. 'I don't see my kids now, and not a day goes by when I don't regret my actions. So do yourself a favour, all you people on this site: DON'T! JUST WALK AWAY! RESIST!'

This particular post had garnered the most responses, over eight hundred, the vast majority of them sympathetic to his plight and thanking him for such sage advice. But appreciating its message did not mean, as he had so clearly hoped, heeding it. If they did, this particular website would have ceased to function. As it was, it always fielded heavy traffic.

I would return helplessly to this website over the next few months. I needed a channel for my twinges of conscience, for all my confusion. I wanted to see how others had lived, to learn from their lessons, and to realize that it was best, ultimately, to appreciate what I had at home.

It always left me feeling better in myself after a few hours of reading the posts here. And then, I suppose like everyone else on the site, I went off and behaved recklessly anyway. How else was I to learn but by my own mistakes?

In the first few weeks of my relationship with The Pseud, our conversations took place either during the day, when Andrew was at work and he between patients, or else at night, when Andrew was fast asleep in his room, The Pseud in his study at home. But then our communications became more frequent. We came to share everything, at once inconsequential yet intimate: our thoughts on the weather, on a particular TV programme, on what we were having for dinner. He would message me first thing in the morning ('Good morning!'), and then again during lunch ('Bon appétit!'). Once or twice he even messaged me during a session (or so he said). 'I'm leaning back on my chair and listening to my patient witter on, and all I can do is think of you.'

I should have discouraged him, but I couldn't. I knew, also, that he kept his BlackBerry on at night – he'd upgraded from his PalmPilot on my mocking encouragement – and I couldn't help myself but instant-message him when I knew his wife was lying there alongside him. I pictured him turning his back to her to read my words, and pictured too what physical effect they might have on him. It was wrong, clearly, and I felt terrible about my behaviour, really – I barely even recognized myself – but rarely had wrong felt so right, so palpable an aphrodisiac. The old me, the one who would have considered such actions as reprehensible, was gone, vanished. Fed up, frustrated, and old before my time, I had no sex life any more, but I wanted one. And now I had found my male equivalent.

We swapped messages when he was with his family at the weekend, and when I was out at dinner with Andrew. We were self-centred and cruel but, oh, the sheer thrill of it all intoxicated me.

When The Pseud told me one night that he was going on holiday with his family, my stomach plunged. He hadn't had sex with his wife, I knew, for almost a year. A holiday would perhaps bring them back closer together and help them also bond with their daughter. Happy families, with no room for me.

In his final email to me before the flight, he promised to take me with him and contact me as regularly as he could. Fine, I thought to myself. Enjoy your holiday. I resolved – a grown-up resolve – to allow him his space, and not to contact him until he did me, first.

I caved almost immediately.

L27: Enjoying your holiday, then?

It was a little after midday UK time on a Wednesday afternoon, mid-August. He and his family had flown out to Lanzarote the day before. I'd spent the morning cleaning the house. The fridge was full, the garden tended to, its shrubs and flowers in neat little colourful rows alive with the buzz of bees. I sent the message impetuously, my garden gloves tucked under one arm, while standing barefoot on the grass. I regretted it immediately, and certainly didn't expect him to respond any time soon. But he did. My phone vibrated less than a minute later, and I squealed, out loud, with helpless relief. I dropped the garden gloves and ran inside, requiring privacy.

The Pseud: Yes and no.
L27: Neither one nor the other?
The Pseud: Just you wait until you have a family yourself. Then we'll see . . .

L27: I'd rather not.

The Pseud: Wish you were here.

L27: Wouldn't that get a little crowded? I thought you were having *important* family time?

The Pseud: My family barely knows I'm here. My daughter has no use for me any more. She's already met a boy from Newcastle that she cannot imagine ever being separated from.

L27: She'll get over it, I'm sure.

The Pseud: I hope so.

L27: And your wife?

The Pseud: My wife is reading War and Peace.

L27: Ha ha.

The Pseud: I'm not joking. Her book group is a rather self-consciously literary one. It's a big book. We've not exchanged a word since we got here.

L27: I am doing my best not to ask you whether you slept with her last night.

The Pseud: Why, would that bother you? We're just having a bit of fun, you and me, no?

L27: I know, I know. But you'll remember, I'm not used to this. You are.

The Pseud: And I never attempted to hide that from you.

L27: How many other women are you juggling alongside me right now?

Funny how your body temperature can sometimes drop like a stone. Suddenly, I was shivering.

The Pseud: As a matter of fact, none. Just you.

L27: I'm honoured.

The Pseud: You should be.

L27: So, if I may be blunt, how is your sex life with your wife in Lanzarote?

136

The Pseud: Have you read War and Peace? It's enormous, and clearly exhausting. She sleeps the moment her head hits the pillow.

L27: Poor you.

The Pseud: I'm made of stern stuff. I'll survive.

I wish I were, I almost typed out. But I didn't. I pulled back at the last moment. But he had me completely.

I do not believe, with the benefit of hindsight, that I was falling in love with The Pseud. But I felt as powerfully drawn to him as I have to anyone, while at the same time believing I knew exactly what I was getting into. He had confessed, after all, that he had done this sort of thing before – an upfront confession that I admired in a world otherwise full of lies and exaggeration and bald fantasies. He had told me about his midlife crisis, and the clichéd path his life subsequently took with his sudden motorbike obsession and infatuation with mostly younger women.

On one particularly long night that we shared – me in bed, he, I liked to think, hunched over his desk in his study – he explained in paragraphs that spooled out like flung ribbons that when a man reaches the wrong side of forty, he begins fully to appreciate the certainty of mortality. From here on in, he wrote, life is all about the slow disintegration of everything you once held dear. Make the most of it while you can.

'I thought you once told me that life began at forty!' I wrote, trying to lighten the tone.

The tone, however, remained. 'I did, and it does. But only because you suddenly realize, often for the first time, that you no longer have quite so much of it – of life – left. Which means that everything you ever wanted to do before but never got around to, you now feel compelled to do, often straight away – because, well, because you never know, do you?'

In the last three years alone, he revealed, he'd seen two of his oldest friends go, dead before fifty. Pulmonary embolism and cancer. He told me about his life, that he had been married for a quarter of a century ('we married early, too early'), and that things hadn't been good between them for at least a decade.

'Things aren't terrible, nothing like that, but we've drifted. It happens. Initially, having children brings you together. We tried for years to get pregnant, and then after Chloe we tried for several more years for another one, but it wasn't to be. So we focused all our love and attention on our daughter. The apple of our eye. But then she grew up, as children are wont to do, and she shucked off our overbearing attention in painful increments, until it got to the point where she didn't want very much to do with us at all. That's when it gets hard. You look up at your spouse one night over dinner to realize that she is a stranger to you, and one you can't summon up the strength to get to know again. The only thing you have left in common is upstairs in her room, getting ready to go out and leave you to yourselves. And so you sit side by side in your empty house, in silence, in front of the television, staring into an abyss of your own making.'

I thought of myself and Andrew, and how we sometimes did something similar already.

I suggested to The Pseud that this was something he must see every day as a psychiatrist, and that surely he had a remedy for such things?

'I do. But both parties need to want to make that effort. Sadly, I don't think either of us really does.'

And so why didn't they simply divorce?

'Too much effort, I think. Too much fear of being alone.'

I asked whether his wife knew about his affairs, his online life?

'No.'

And did he think she had affairs herself?

'No.'

Perimenopausal, he continued, his wife had lost all interest in sex, and had developed other interests in its place: book clubs, charitable organizations, the local church. He himself, meanwhile, as if to counterbalance this glaring omission within her, had redeveloped a very vigorous interest in sex.

'Going broadband helped.'

Previously, he had had not so much affairs as flings, and strictly fleeting ones: with a secretary the week before she left to go travelling; a colleague he met at a conference in Frankfurt; and another one in Tucson. It was after he had flings with two patients, within the space of a couple of months, that he realized his infidelities, if they were to continue, now required the safety of distance and anonymity. BT laid new cables in his neighbourhood and, as a result, home life had become bearable. Over the past couple of years he had had four fairly longstanding relationships with women he had met in chatrooms. But, he added, he had never met any of them in the flesh.

'Meeting your online lover can be beset with problems,' he wrote, promptly slamming the door shut on that particular possibility in our own relationship, and making me wonder why he had ever suggested we meet for coffee in the first place. To gauge my level of interest, perhaps? I asked him how he knew they could be beset with problems if he had never met one, and he responded with the only emoticon I would ever receive from him: ☺. But I pressed him, insisting he be not quite so vague.

'Perhaps you will find out one day,' he wrote, 'but not from me.'

'So you have never hooked up with anyone you've met online?'

'I didn't say that, did I?'

He explained that there were several other websites he visited, ones that focused far less on the kind of talk we indulged in and more on direct action. He mentioned a few by name and told me that they each had very active communities, people meeting for no-attachment sex, then posting reviews on one another for future prospective partners. I was shocked, and couldn't hide my shock. He'd had several sexual encounters this way, he told me, some of them awkward, all of them exciting, and, he added in a way that made me uncomfortable, 'useful'.

'Useful how?'

'Oh, in all sorts of ways.'

'And how would you rate it?'

'Positively.'

He told me of a club he frequented on occasion. 'For swingers.'

'You swing???'

'Calm your punctuation, my dear. From time to time, yes, I swing. Me Tarzan.'

As if to allay any doubts I might have had over how genuine he was, he went into specific detail about the place, its name, its sauna shop front, the fact that you have to know someone who knows someone in order to get in, the price of a good bottle of wine at its bar, the kind of towels they provide, and the ratio of men to women. More men than women, he admitted, and not always as young as he would like, but physical perfection was not the point in these places. A sense of adventure, he concluded, was.

Helplessly intrigued, I asked him to tell me more.

'Take your husband one night,' he suggested.

I thought for a while for an appropriate response. 'Ha!' was all I could manage.

About a week after he returned, gratifyingly dispirited, from a full week in the company of his wife and daughter on holiday, he asked again to see a picture of me. We were already intimate with one another, he argued. A picture couldn't hurt, and would not pull the veil of anonymity away too much. Even if we were never physically to meet, we could nevertheless take our online affair to a comparable next level. No?

As a kind of incentive, perhaps, he sent me one of him. The

little paperclip attachment on his email pulsed before my eyes like a virus, and my mouse hovered for several anxious minutes before I summoned up the courage to click. There was a moment's pause that seemed to stretch on for ever while the image downloaded, and in that time I imagined he would be revealed naked to me, perhaps even engorged. When the photograph finally pixelated on my screen, I was both relieved and disappointed. He was fully clothed, and rather handsome – the kind of man who looked his age and didn't mind it. I could see why women would find him attractive; I did. He was lean and lined, and, as I had somehow expected, had a salt-and-pepper beard. In some sense, he looked precisely what he said he was: a middle-aged psychiatrist. The tortoiseshell glasses suggested intelligence, the slight smile a lucid, and open, mind.

I had never liked posing for photographs, and consequently had very few to choose from now. I could hardly send him a crudely cropped wedding photograph, so I waited until Andrew had gone to bed to take a fresh one. The half bottle of wine sloshing through my veins brought me the necessary courage as I changed out of my day clothes and put on a white vest, through which the black lace of my bra was clearly visible. I held my iPhone at arm's length, pinched my nipples until they were visible beneath the white cotton, and clicked. As I uploaded it, I helped myself to another glass of wine, prevaricated, worried, took a deep breath, then sent it.

Three minutes passed before I received a response.

'Oh my. Where have you been all my life?'

I wanted to take these words and frame them.

The Pseud: Where do you live, out of interest?

L27: I thought we'd agreed no personal information?

The Pseud: I told you all about my cock last night. Does that not constitute personal information?

This was true. We'd spent several hours the previous night having 'sex'. If, previously, we had been careful with one another, modest almost, then ever since he had come back from his holiday our sex sessions had changed. They were brute now and crude, the typed equivalent of rough sex, if such a thing were possible (and it was), and unimaginably exciting. A single word from him was worth to me a thousand pictures. He had told me what he wanted to do with me, and I explained what I would like to do with him, and on him, each short succinct sentence prompting a rapid response. It was verbal ping-pong, a constant back and forth, both of us keeping up the frantic momentum. Reading over the transcripts later, as I did several times, it seemed cheap and sordid, embarrassing even, and full of typos and sentences like *I'm c-c-c-coming*. But in the heat of it all, it had been amazing. I had lost myself entirely, and wanted to again.

And so I told him where I lived.

The Pseud: I know which city you live in already. More specifically please.
L27: You first.

He told me. The two words that comprised his neighbourhood were also mine. I felt instantly nauseous. Violently, I pushed the laptop away from me. Not for the first time, nor for the last, I wondered whether The Pseud wasn't in fact infiltrating my life in some more sinister way. He was always two steps ahead, knowing somehow where I worked, just happening to share my husband's name, and now living in the same postcode – for all I knew, the same *street*. I glanced up at the window, and towards the houses across the road. Was one of them his? I might well have seen him many times already: at the bus stop, the French deli, the Italian café. I quickly clicked on his photograph again and studied it more carefully. I did not recognize him, but that did not mean that Andrew and I had not already had a café brunch next to him and his wife one weekend morning, or that we hadn't stood next to each other in the queue at the supermarket.

It may have heightened the thrill that, on the worldwide web, you could find yourself talking to someone who inhabited the same city. But this was too close for comfort. The Pseud, I now knew, was my neighbour. Or was he? I racked my brain, wondering whether I had inadvertently given him any indication of where I lived. Did he know? *Could* he? Was he playing mind games with me here? I began to feel very uncomfortable.

The Pseud: You still there?

L27: Sorry. Toilet break.

The Pseud: I love it when you talk dirty to me.

L27: I live . . . not too far away from you. Can we leave it at that?

The Pseud: Ha! So we're neighbours? I could be at your house, theoretically speaking, in five minutes, 10, yes?

L27: But I thought you didn't want us to meet?

The Pseud: I know. I was just saying.

L27: Besides, my husband is home.

The Pseud: Okay, then. You could, theoretically speaking, come to mine instead.

L27: Your wife?

The Pseud: Dead to the world. She's been sleeping poorly for the past week now, so she's knocked herself out. Zoloft, prescribed by the medic in the family. And brandy, self-prescribed. Works a treat. I shan't be seeing her again until I return from work tomorrow night.

L27: Your daughter?

The Pseud: In her room, Skyping the Geordie boyfriend from Lanzarote. I won't be seeing *her* till the weekend at the very earliest . . .

L27: So essentially, you're all alone in the world?

143

The Pseud: And lonely.

L27: What are you wearing?

The Pseud: Talking dirty again. I love it.

The following morning, walking down my high street took on a whole new slant. I felt like a private investigator, stepping furtively between the cracks of the pavement, eyes hiding behind my fringe, wondering whether my online photograph was recognizably *me* in the cold, hard light of day. I watched people milling in bus queues, stepping out of shops, walking with purpose or else strolling with none. I looked incessantly for any man with a beard over a certain age, and saw so very many, as if suddenly the whole world was full of bearded men in their midforties crowding the streets of my home. I imagined mine to be in a burgundy corduroy jacket, unbuttoned to the morning breeze to reveal a Jermyn Street shirt. No tie. Comfortable trousers, sensible shoes. He would be walking towards me at any moment, would look up, recoil in recognition, but then open his arms to me. A happy ending, closing credits.

Or, no, perhaps he was driving? Here came a Saab. The Pseud, I felt, would be the kind of person to drive a Saab. I bent down as it passed, a cruel woman at the wheel extinguishing my dreams. I walked into the deli, then out again, then stepped into several cafés, looking around as casually as I could, brow knitted like a fisherman's knot and terrified of catching sight of him but at the same time desperate to. Was he looking for me too? He seemed to know me better than I knew myself. I didn't put it past him.

I walked on, and oh dear God, was this him now? Up ahead, I spied yet another bearded man, this one in a suit. He was still a way off, and my view was obstructed by other pedestrians, but he looked approximately the right age and, at this distance, ball-park handsome. My legs turned to jelly as I realized, with a sinking sense of uplift, a contradiction in terms that right now defined my confused state: that it *was* him. I was sure. I was *almost* sure. For an instant, I felt a compulsion to – what? – to turn, to run, to dash across the road and into the oncoming traffic, anything to avoid this all too real confrontation with the man who, just last night, had brought me to intense orgasm without even touching me. My legs were getting looser at the knees, and yet I continued onwards, blinking into my fringe, chin tucked into my chest. The distance between us diminished. I could almost hear his footsteps on the paving stones falling into sync with mine. I could also, now, hear his voice. Was it calling me? No, no. He was talking into his telephone, one of those hands-free ones, with a cord trailing from his ear into the folds of his suit, a breast pocket. It was a strong and confident voice. Well-educated, instructional. He was talking, possibly, to his secretary. The secretary he had had an affair with, newly returned from her travels?

He was ten feet away now, less, smaller than I had at first thought, and perhaps not quite as handsome. Less rugged, more lived-in. I was able to get quite such a good look at him because he was still lost in conversation, staring only at the pavement in front of him. His mouth was open and I saw capped teeth, almost too white. Blue eyes, with crow's feet sprouting from both, suggestive of someone who smiled a lot. His beard needed trimming, his hair too. Had I reached out, I'd have touched him.

The moment our paths crossed, he raised his eyes to mine, and the crow's feet deepened. He smiled. I caught my breath, but he continued on, walking by as if I were anyone, just another woman on the street, he just another man. And that, of course, is precisely what he was. It wasn't him. Perhaps I knew it never had been.

The wobble in the knees gave way now, and I needed to sit down. I found a café and ordered myself a double espresso.

When I brought the tiny cup to my lips, it rattled against my chattering teeth.

What was happening to me?

I would like to be able to say now that I managed to keep my dignity in all this, but I can't because I didn't. The sex I had with him was intense and vivid and real. The more we had, the more I wanted.

'I think I want to meet you,' he wrote to me the following night in a post-coital haze, both of us ready for bed and sleep, but neither of us wanting to be the first to log off.

'Is that a good idea?'

'Yes. So let's.'

'When were you thinking of?'

'This weekend. Come up with an excuse for your husband and meet me for lunch. I know of a place. I also know of a hotel nearby . . .'

It was the ellipsis, I think, that made me lose my head, and what I typed next went against everything I had previously believed in myself, that these chats were nothing more than a bit of harmless fun, and would never, ultimately, come between myself and my husband.

'Okay,' I wrote, unsure if I actually meant it or not.

'I'll let you have the details tomorrow. I want you more than I think I have ever wanted anybody, L27.'

I wrote that I felt much the same, and I think I meant it too, caught up in the moment. I can only say now that, at the time, it all seemed entirely appropriate.

Seven

I didn't hear from The Pseud again. Well, to clarify, I did, just the once, and much later, but in effect he simply vanished from my life.

The following day, an email to him bounced back, undeliverable, the address unrecognized. A mistake, surely. I tried again, and again, and then, puzzled and a little panicked, I returned to the erotic website where we had first met, only to find that his profile was no longer up. Because we had never spoken on the phone, I had no number for him, and because I didn't even have his full name, there were few other means at my disposal to track him down successfully.

I began to worry. Perhaps something bad had happened. Perhaps he had had an accident? But no. No. My rational mind hadn't *completely* deserted me. I was aware of course that even if such a thing had happened, his email address would likely have survived intact. I did still have trouble rationalizing it, though. Just a day earlier he was telling me how much he wanted me, how much he thought of me, and now it was as if he had never existed in the first place, had been little more than a figment of my imagination.

I felt as if somebody had died, and fell inescapably into a period of what I can only describe as mourning. Over the next few days I checked my phone incessantly, and re-sent a version of the same querying email ('Where are you???') again and again until my thumbs hurt. Perhaps he had a virus? Computers were always prone to viruses. For all I knew, he was actually as desperate to get in touch with me as I with him, and we were both of us stuck at the end of our keyboards shouting into unnavigable silence.

The hurt intensified. At night, unable to sleep, I cried into my pillow over what I surely knew by now was irrefutable fact: that he had got bored of me, just as he had with my many predecessors. He had reeled me in, had got what he wanted – a typed declaration of my adoration, the bolstering of his ego – and so now it was Game Over, and time to move on to the next one. He'd done this kind of thing before; he had told me so himself. I was a fool ever to think I represented anything more to him than that.

I tried to hate him. Self-pity came easier, an enveloping mope I could not shake off. Even Andrew noticed something was amiss.

'What's wrong?' he'd say.

I could only tell him to leave me alone, that I needed space. When he then gave me space, I resented him for not realizing I needed comfort. I called in sick, and spent what felt like days on my sofa, staring out of the window, hoping in vain for a message to reach me out of the blue: 'L27, I'm so sorry. I hope you'll understand, but . . .'

But nothing. It was over.

I wrote the conclusion to our relationship down on a piece of paper, in the hope it would help. His wife, I scribbled, had found out about us. She had sifted through his emails, learned of my existence and threatened him with divorce. He had promptly capitulated, begged for forgiveness and promised to have nothing more to do with me. But secretly, at night, he pined for me still. All that passion couldn't have been fake. Could it? It couldn't so effortlessly just ebb away. We were both, in our own ways, suffering, both the victims of our circumstances, and stuck in predictable, traditional marriages.

I wrote that I forgave him, but by the time the ink dried – and I'm speaking metaphorically here: the pen was a biro; who writes in ink any more? – I had changed my mind. The way he had treated me was simply not good *n*etiquette. How could he so unceremoniously dump me, without a proffered reason, without an apology even? I was due, if nothing else, an apology.

Another tack, then: I decided to track him down and get an explanation.

It had been a busy day, the habitual nightmare of the daily commute, and I couldn't wait to reach my front door. The battery on my iPhone, like the batteries on all iPhones using 3G, was hovering near empty despite its previous night's charging. I was in a sour mood, another two colleagues having been made redundant, my boss's repeated exhortations that at least *my* job was safe beginning to have an increasingly hollow ring. I got home tired and hungry, but with little strength to do anything about either. Andrew was home already, earlier than usual. I found him on the sofa, doubled over, lacing up his shoes.

'Football tonight,' he said, without looking up.

About once a month Andrew would take clients to a game, where the Premiership would provide colourful backdrop to an evening's enthusiastic drinking and surreptitious pleading that the client did not take their account elsewhere, thereby pushing his job closer towards jeopardy. He would return home belligerently drunk, and I knew that I would wake the morning after to find the toilet in a state that would offend me as a woman.

'Good for you,' I said to him half-heartedly, then stalked up the stairs.

I reached my room, slammed the door and collapsed on to my

149

duvet, firing up my laptop. I heard Andrew bound up the stairs, and quickly pushed the computer to one side. He opened my door and poked his head nervously around it.

'You sure you're okay?'

I looked over at him. He was still wearing his work suit, tie askew, shirt untucked, with evidence of a mayonnaise-based lunch on his lapel. He had put on, I realized now, even more weight recently. He looked jowly, as if lining himself for winter. My heart sank.

'You're going out like that, are you?' I asked him.

He looked down at himself. 'Yes, why?'

I sighed. 'Just go, Andrew.'

'PMT?'

'Get lost.'

He withdrew. 'Don't wait up.'

'Do I ever?' I whispered back.

With him gone, I retrieved the laptop and Googled once again The Pseud's first name, which I presumed was authentic, alongside 'psychiatrist' and the neighbourhood in which he lived and worked. There were more Andrew psychiatrists than you would think. Which on earth was he? Pointlessly, I re-Googled his stupid pseudonym for the umpteenth time, but this time something happened, my breath catching in my throat. I'd found him.

A photograph, no less, The Pseud grinning impishly on a swingers' site. I wiped the tears from my eyes as I read his profile: ADVENTUROUS FORTYSOMETHING MALE SEEKS SIMILAR IN FEMALE. Beneath this was the heading LAST POST. His was just six hours previously, in the middle of his working day. 'I'm rather new to all this,' he lied, 'but I'm willing to be led.'

It was a site I'd not seen before, and full of the kind of men who called themselves CUM2SOON and HEAVYCUMMER, alongside women like STUNNA and seXXXyBitch. Each boasted a photograph that was tiny, postage-stamp-sized, but that advertised their wares in the assumption that full disclosure gleaned instant results. Most of them were naked, many overweight. One woman was posing with a can of Irn-Bru between breasts that started at chest level and finished at navel. Another had drawn a smiley face above her shaved pudenda. One of the men had a pair of Mickey Mouse ears tattooed above his penis. The Pseud stood out for the simple fact that he remained dressed, in a silk shirt, the top three buttons of which were undone. He looked good.

What to do? I considered posting a capital-lettered rant about him, to let everybody on the site know the full measure of the man, but almost everything here was articulated in capital letters. I'd be shouting into the wind at best, and at worst ridiculed as a woman on the verge. There really was no recourse here, no fitting opportunity for retribution.

I had to let go and move on.

I don't know why, but I logged on under a different pseudonym, sat back and waited for others to come find me.

By the time Andrew got home, long gone midnight, singing unquietly to himself, I had signed up to three other websites as SHY THIRTYSOMETHING FEMALE REQUIRES ILLUMINATING, but offered no photograph. Nevertheless, I already had thirty-six messages impatiently awaiting my response when Andrew barged into my room.

'Oh, Lucy . . . ?'

His whisper was hoarse and leering, a holler the neighbours could hear. But he had not caught me unawares. My laptop was already beneath the duvet, and I was busy feigning sleep. I heard him linger at the door, and I counted out his laboured breaths: one Mississippi, two Mississippi, three. Eventually he retreated, and within minutes I could hear him snoring loudly through the walls. I reopened my laptop. Forty-one messages now. I was popular. I propped myself up on my pillow and checked my watch: one o'clock. Early yet.

I should perhaps qualify the boast that I was 'popular'. Every woman on such websites was practically cheerleader-popular. But then the ratio of men to women here was something like ten to one, so even the plainest of Janes could convince themselves of their utter irresistibility within minutes of logging on. One of the many good things about the internet was the levelling of the playing field. The only downside was the quality of men whose appetites we were whetting – few of them, quite frankly, worthy of cheerleading at all. Shame.

I signed up to another erotic story website and received even more invitations for personal chats, with people like Ben, username Paranoidandroid, a young trainee teacher from Bristol who sent me sweet and coy messages by day and rather more lustful ones at night, and a cocky sous-chef. The chef sent hundreds of messages, so many coming in so short a time that I rather wondered whether he was what he claimed to be at all. But I cross-referenced his username with his Twitter account and found lots of photographs of each new meal he had knocked up. He was twenty-five years old, a boy. If he didn't record every-thing he did online somewhere, then it didn't really exist at all. He was also quite beautiful, all cheekbones and pout.

'How can you be a chef if you spend all evening texting me?' I asked him one day.

'I multitask innit,' came the response.

'How do I know you're not simply photographing the work of others?'

'Come over to the restrant one night. Service winds down round 11. I'll rustle u up a post midnite feast in the kitchen, an that way u can see 4 urself.'

I fell into regular correspondence with, of all things, a helicopter pilot, who was much amused when I confessed how flying terrified me. He offered to take me up in his helicopter on a low-flying flight over London, which would cure me of my phobia instantly, or so he claimed. 'If you can survive the turbulence in a copter, you can survive the turbulence anywhere!'

I chatted regularly with a wine importer from somewhere 'down south' whose first message to me was that he liked his women of a certain vintage, with a solid body and a flowering bouquet. He recommended a lot of wine to me, and promised to get me deals on the best new-season discoveries (Andrew would have loved him). And late at night, during breaks between his classes, I talked with a philosophy lecturer from a university in America, who liked to send me his poetry. The lecturer treated our conversations as an opportunity for full and frank honesty, with no colouring-in, no embellishments. I found him fascinating. He was in his fifties, he wrote, and not particularly attractive (he later sent me a photograph confirming this). He was nursing both a red-wine gut *and* a divorce settlement that still smarted. He lived alone, but wanted now to explore his fantasies, 'if I can ever summon up the necessary courage'. While he attempted to locate it, he sent me PDFs of his course lectures on eighteenth-century philosophy, moral theory and practice, which he encouraged me to read and to feel free to comment upon.

He seemed particularly taken with Plato's *Symposium*, which, as he lecture-ishly explained, was a philosophical text dated 385 BC and which concerned itself with the purposes and nature of Love. Love – always with a capital L – was examined in a sequence of speeches by men attending a symposium, and each guest was, at some point during the party, to give a speech in praise of Love. Aristophanes gave a speech about the origin of soulmates: how originally humans had four limbs and one head with two faces. Zeus, fearing their power, had split them all in

153

half, condemning us to an eternal search for that other half to complete us. Socrates was also in attendance, and aligned Love with philosophy and even wisdom.

The lecturer himself wasn't so sure. 'Two decades of marriage, during which I attained love, if not always Love, hasn't left me with anything approaching wisdom,' he wrote. 'In fact, quite the opposite. Women confuse me. My wife confuses me; you, if I'm honest L27, confuse me. What's a nice girl like you doing talking to an old fart like me? Has Love not taught you any better? But of course it hasn't! At the risk of damning his otherwise fine reputation, Socrates was talking out of his ass.'

After a couple of weeks of good-natured chats and only the most fleeting diversion into those fantasies (he liked the idea, though he had not yet tried it for himself, of smacking and of being smacked, and he thought he might like it if I was, in his inverted commas, 'naughty'), he invited me to visit him. It would all remain entirely proper and decent, 'above board, as you Brits say'. He would put me up in a hotel near the campus, wine and dine me and take me to local theatrical productions, and then return me to my room afterwards. 'No pressure,' he wrote, 'but I like to think we'd enjoy one another's company.'

But his mood, I hope unprompted by me, turned sour soon after. He fell silent for a couple of weeks, then suddenly emailed in the middle of what was his night. From the typos in his message, I could only conclude that he was drunk, and in a bad way. He sent me what I initially mistook for one of his poems, a brittle, drunken rage, whose last line was '. . . The difference being, I thought I had a chance with the ladies.' It was actually one of Charles Bukowski's, 'Two Kinds of Hell'.

I wrote back asking if he was okay, if perhaps he wanted to talk on the phone. But he didn't respond, not immediately, nor later. My invitation to visit him, I could only presume, was revoked.

I missed my chats with him, but the truth of it was there were many others to fall back on. Life became full again. I still worked loyally, if robotically, each Tuesday and Thursday, and I found that my days of forced indolence passed quite easily, shopping, cooking, cleaning, tending to the garden. Occasionally I would meet up with former colleagues, venting our way towards eventual catharsis over successive bottles of wine. And I remained married. I knew this because I would see my husband sometimes in the morning, heading out the door in a perpetual rush while I was still descending the staircase to breakfast. We would occasionally dine together in the evening, if one of us wasn't working late, or else entertaining clients. Andrew commented that I seemed happier, and that he was glad about it.

We seemed to have passed a critical point, and I'm not really sure how. But his very presence was no longer bothering me quite so much. I had accepted him as he was, the way, clearly, he had me. We had little in the way of real contact with one another, but we'd fallen into comforting parallel lines, heading in the same direction but distinctly apart, more friends now than lovers, an agreeable fondness replacing lust. He said that we should think about going on holiday soon, that it would be good for us, and I agreed without hesitation, but also without much of an urge to do anything immediate about it.

I was rather taken aback, then, when he came home one evening with two tickets for a short cruise around Scandinavia. We were now well into autumn, but the weather was clement and the forecast good. I thanked him dutifully, relieved more than anything else that the holiday did not require air travel, and later felt myself actually *wanting* to go on holiday with my husband. That at least was my first thought. My second was: I hope I get a good signal on the ship.

*

155

Six weeks after I'd last heard from him, The Pseud got in touch.

'Hey you, remember me?'

It was a weekday evening, just twenty-four hours before we set sail on our cruise. I had an hour before hooking up with the helicopter pilot and was passing the time watching something on TV while chatting intermittently with Ben, my teacher, and the chef, while Andrew, the other man in my life, slept soundly upstairs. I was arranged comfortably on my sofa, with a packet of low-fat crisps and a camomile tea, last Sunday's newspaper colour supplements fanned out all around me. The chef was busy preparing late suppers and every quarter-hour or so I'd receive an update to tell me either that *this linguines wickd* or *just dropd the hake!!* Ben, aka Paranoidandroid, was telling me how he was going to split up with his girlfriend any day now, and asking for both advice and courage, as if I knew anything about either. But I wrote back with Agony Aunt confidence.

The Pseud's message landed into my personal account with an innocent chime, arriving from an email address I didn't recognize. I clicked on the window, and his words speared through me like a lance. There was something taunting, I decided, about *Hey you, remember me?* Too casual, too carefree.

I knew, nevertheless, that I was helpless to resist the question.

L27: I don't believe I do, no.

The Pseud: Ah. I didn't think so. For what it's worth, though, I would like to apologize. Certain things ... shall we say, *happened*. But that's all behind us now. Behind me. I feel in a better position to control my decisions now, and I am hopeful that I can move forward. With you. Urgh, I'm nervous here. Can you tell?

L27: Sorry, are you talking to me?

The Pseud: You're going to make it difficult, then?

L27: No, I'm going to make it easy.

156

I didn't need him any more. I was over him. I had other men to talk to now, and my confidence had doubled, no, *re*-doubled, in his absence. I deleted his emails and deleted my responses to them. Gone. No man was ever going to have such an online hold on me quite so easily again.

How easy it is to write those emboldened words now. How naïvely I believed them at the time.

They call it God's waiting room, or else a retirement home on the sea. The few friends we told about our imminent cruise were quick with jokes that we were old before our time, and *a cruise*?! Whatever were we thinking? They had a point. The cruise ship *was* a retirement home on the sea. We were the youngest on board by decades, but though we felt like errant children at first, we soon slotted right in – a fact that only jarred later. Nothing wrong with befriending the elderly, but this was hardly the ideal getaway for a married couple hoping to put the spark back into their already middle-aged relationship.

We would be sailing in early October, but the forecast was good, settled, warm even. Only fools have faith in forecasts, and by the time we breached Scandinavian waters the rain had begun to lash with such relentlessness that all outdoor activities on board were cancelled. No pool party, then, and no open-air bowls tournament, but instead whist and bingo and Scrabble in the glitter-balled ballroom. And once we'd left Copenhagen, bound for Oslo, the sea was pitching and yawing with a lurching violence, the storm now gale force 9. Almost everybody on board simply retreated into themselves, trying to find a little personal space in which to be ill in peace.

There had been some confusion over our booking, Andrew having reserved us a suite before being told, upon boarding, that all the suites were full. Sorry. In its place, we were given a twin, a tiny cubicle of a room comprising two cot-sized beds separated by a small cabinet. The only light came from a tiny porthole, but because we were below deck, and because the waves were so high, the only thing we could see was water, and our mournful reflections in it.

At first we tried to laugh it off, but two days of persistent vomiting can remove the humour from any situation. There was a much more stoical mood on board, a collective stiff upper lip from people who had lived through wars and still boasted Blitz spirit. In fact, many of the elderly passengers came to the assistance of the staff, who proved far worse at dealing with seasickness than anyone else.

The waters mercifully began to settle as we neared Kristiansand, but it was noticeably colder here, too, and when we docked we as one made a beeline to the nearest department store to stock up on winter clothes. Oslo was even colder, freezing, early October masquerading as late January on its brittle, gale-chilled cobblestone streets. But we cheered as we docked, as some of us had decided to make our way back overland, by train.

The train took a weaving, and distinctly leisurely, route down through northern Europe towards Belgium and France. By this stage we had bonded with our elderly friends, and together we commandeered several carriages. The elderly rarely travel un-prepared, and the breadth of board games available was impressive. I don't think I had ever seen Andrew quite so happy and in his element.

At night I would retire early, leaving Andrew with the men, where, in the absence of wives, they would start to drink their whisky neat and play for money. In the cocoon of our couchette, meanwhile, I indulged in online sex with Ben, who, now that he had parted from his girlfriend and was back living with his parents, had the sexual frustrations of a fifteen-year-old. Ben was twenty-three years old and training to become a teacher of English literature. He sent me poetry, always with an apology, but I liked his poems, even if I didn't always understand them. They were empty and spare, and featured a lot of remote pastures in winter climes. He admitted to occasionally suffering from depression, hence his username, Paranoidandroid. Though he had friends, from university mostly, he wrote that he preferred his own company right now, 'which is difficult given my current living arrangements'.

Since his return home, his mother had made him her pet project again, anxious that he was taking the break-up from his girlfriend too seriously. The attention she lavished upon him, he told me, was suffocating, and he desperately sought an escape route. His parents were night owls and would stay up until the early hours watching old black-and-white films, always leaving space on the sofa for him – a kindness which only made him all the more melancholic. He hid mostly in his converted basement space, subsisting on toast and red wine, and had felt on the brink of giving up altogether, he claimed, until he met me. I, he insisted, had changed everything, had given him a reason simply to *be*. No pressure, then.

> Lucy: A good-looking boy like you? You should be out on the town every night with a string of girlfriends, rather than in your room and talking to me.
> Paranoidandroid: Who says I'm good-looking?
> Lucy: Just a hunch.
> Paranoidandroid: I must have flattered myself. Besides, you are far more interesting than any girl I could ever meet around here.
> Lucy: It's you flattering *me* now.
> Paranoidandroid: You make it easy.

We decided to extend our holiday, Andrew and I, bearing east into Holland and Amsterdam while everyone else carried on towards Calais and home. It was a tearful goodbye, and we exchanged addresses with our new friends. 'Promise to write,' said Marjorie, thrusting a book of stamps into my hands. 'I know you young people don't any more, but do it for me.' I promised I would. Andrew was bereft at leaving them. I feared he might cry.

Amsterdam was raining when we got there, but that was all right; we were used to the rain by now. It had become the abiding feature of our holiday, and it somehow helped bring us closer together, having perhaps developed a little Blitz spirit ourselves. It was nighttime as we arrived, and we were starving. We found a seafood restaurant and ordered lobster, Andrew insisting upon champagne to wash it down.

'What's the celebration?'

He was still unaccountably emotional, the holiday having somehow affected him in different ways than it had me.

'Us,' he said. 'We are.'

He reached over, took my hands and pressed them together in his. I looked about the restaurant to see if anybody was watching. He told me that he loved me, and that he felt more comfortable in my company than with anyone he had ever met in his life, including Alice, his ex-wife. The reflection of the lobster in the flickering candle between us shone in his glasses and I couldn't quite see his eyes, but I could hear in his voice that they were moist. He was talking quickly now, about work and stress, an unpleasant mix in his father but, he hoped, not in him. 'You love me, right?' he said. 'You're glad you're married to me?'

It was not the sort of question, and certainly not in the setting, I could answer honestly. No, it was the kind of plea that wanted only, for now, validation. But that was easy. I wanted to give Andrew my validation, because my truthful answer was yes. I did love him, and I was glad to be married to him.

I looked at him, smiled, and nodded.

'But . . . ?' he said. His voice rose helplessly in fear.

But nothing, I said. I shifted in my seat and could now see his eyes. They *were* brimming. Suddenly I heard myself talking. 'Just that, well – sometimes, sometimes I wish things were more . . . *exciting*. Not just between us, but in life,' I said. 'You know?'

He nodded, in agreement or defeat, I couldn't quite tell.

'But excitement is only ever temporary,' he offered. 'What we have . . . what we have is for life.'

Really? I wanted to ask.

'But,' he added quickly, 'there's always . . . Well, you know . . . other ways. To find excitement, I mean. Ways that don't have to . . .' He pointed a finger between the two of us, '. . . harm us. You know?'

Andrew, I knew, was a man of few words. This was difficult for him.

'What I mean is, I've got you, I've got my horses—'

'And me?' I asked, genuinely intrigued.

'I know,' he said, as if in agreement. 'Well, perhaps you could find something else . . .' He reclaimed my hand and applied more squeeze. 'I think you need something, Luce. Because ever since the house was finished . . .' He swallowed. 'You should go out there and have a little, whatever. Fun.'

The waiter appeared at my elbow, filled our glasses and finished the bottle. 'Another?' he asked. 'Yes,' said Andrew. We waited until he had retreated.

'You're suggesting I have an affair?'

'No! No, nothing like that.'

I had a moment's conviction here, a conviction I felt in the very pit of my stomach, that Andrew was about to admit to being the other *Andrew* as well, the psychiatrist. But no, impossible. Surely. The conviction that he somehow knew about my online dalliances – dalliances I had gone to great pains to conceal – lasted considerably longer than a moment.

'No, what I meant was that . . . Look, this isn't easy for me.'

The champagne arrived, already uncorked, and the waiter poured. Andrew drank. 'There are certain kinds of clubs here. For couples. Husbands and wives. I've looked into them. They sound like fun. I thought it could be a way for us to pick things up again. Because, let's face it, we haven't done – well, anything, for a long time now.'

I felt my cheeks burn.

'I mean, if you don't want to, of course, that's fine.' His eyes shone with excitement and terror. 'But it could be – fun?'

'Dessert?' The waiter was back. We ordered, and he left.

My mouth running away with me again, I found myself telling him about the swingers' clubs The Pseud had spoken of. I claimed that Jane had told me about it, that she'd gone with one of her boyfriends and had found it, I said, my fingers making rabbit ears in the air, 'enlightening'. Andrew nodded, intrigued, but then our chocolate fondue arrived, a spoon each, and we kind of lost the conversational thread. Before I knew it, we had lapsed into silence, a silence that allowed my husband to drink the majority of our second bottle and then call, a little impatiently it seemed to me, for the bill.

Afterwards, we took a taxi to a hotel we'd stayed at a few years previously and checked in. Given what we'd discussed over dinner, I'd have expected Andrew to mount sexual overtures the moment we dropped our bags on the floor and surveyed the bed, which was vast. But my husband looked suddenly exhausted – the cumulative effects, presumably, of a disastrous holiday, a long day's train travel, a confession of the heart and two bottles of champagne. He yawned animatedly, undressed quickly, put on his pyjamas and kissed me full on the mouth. By the time I came out of the bathroom, naked, he was asleep.

The conversation may not have aroused him, but it did me. I lay beside him, texted Ben, and told him that I wanted to barge into his little basement space, take off all my clothes and have him watch as I pleasured myself for his benefit. He'd been asleep when I texted, but was awake now and was soon responding in kind. It had the desired effect.

My relationship with Ben soon took on a whole new emphasis. Having split up with his girlfriend after three years, a run-of-the-mill rollercoaster affair that typifies all first loves, he said that he had had it with women of his age and wanted maturity instead. He asked how old I was, and though I was about to turn forty, which he had already said was his ideal age for a woman, I told him thirty-seven.

While I was on the train from Copenhagen down through Luxembourg and on towards Holland, he too asked to see a picture of me. After The Pseud, I had a strict policy of never sending a picture to anyone, and was tempted to send to Ben a cut-and-pasted model. But Andrew was snoring in the seat in front of me, his head vibrating on the train's window, a long string of saliva stretching from his slack mouth down towards his shoulder, and I just thought, 'To hell with my policy.' I wanted Ben to see me in all my thirty-seven-year-old glory. I raised my iPhone until it was level with Andrew's face but pointing towards me, and clicked. Andrew stirred, but the string of saliva remained unbroken. His snoring was becoming a public disturbance. I kicked his foot, and he fell silent. I checked my self-portrait, which was grainy and slightly out of focus due to the movement of the train, and my hair was mostly over my face, but I was smiling, and I didn't look too bad. I sent it before I could think better of it.

'YUM!' was his immediate response, and I purred in delight. He sent one back. I peered into my phone's screen at the face of a boy who, mathematically at least, was probably young enough to be my son. He was beautiful and bed-haired, with sharp cheekbones and a shy smile radiating out of his limpid gaze. He was dressed in the kind of oversized jumper that my semi-Goth former self used to sport twenty years ago, back when, oh my, back when Ben was just born. I did not share this detail with him.

He accompanied the photo with just one word: SORRY ☹.

Ben had little in the way of bravado, and did not use these online chats to beef up his personality or pretend to be someone he wasn't. Perhaps he did with others, but certainly not with me. With me, he was awkward and sensitive and naïve and gauche, his messages crowded with helpless apologies and dot dot dots and sad faces. Though early on he had told me his name was Ben (not, actually, his real name, as I was much later to discover), his username remained Paranoidandroid. It suited him.

Paranoidandroid: So where are you?

Lucy: On a train in Denmark.

Paranoidandroid: Alone?

Lucy: With my husband.

Paranoidandroid: And you're talking to me???

Lucy: He's fast asleep. Would you rather talk another time?

Paranoidandroid: No, no, it's just that – well, is he bigger than me?

Lucy: Heavier, maybe . . .

Paranoidandroid: What I mean is, could he crush me if he ever found out about . . . Well, this. Us.

Lucy: Us?

Paranoidandroid: (Blushes)

Lucy: I like it when you blush.

Paranoidandroid: If I'm honest, I like it when you make me.

Denmark was long and flat and featureless; few tunnels, and yet I still managed to lose signal regularly. The break in contact was agonizing, yet blissfully so. It added further to the excitement, reaching out across the miles to make contact with the one thing in my life right now that made my heart beat a little bit faster.

Paranoidandroid: Either your husband has woken up, or you've lost interest in me.

Paranoidandroid: Hello, hello?

Paranoidandroid: You know, sometimes I wish I could retreat into this room forever, lock myself away, and live only virtually . . .

Lucy: Wouldn't that get awfully claustrophobic?

Paranoidandroid: You're back!

Lucy: Lost signal.

Paranoidandroid: Is it wrong to be sick of people, of the human race, at the age of 23?

Lucy: Just wait until you reach 40.

Paranoidandroid: I thought you were 37 . . . ?

Oops.

Lucy: I am, but I feel 40.

Paranoidandroid: Life begins at 40. I read that somewhere.

Lucy: Somebody told me much the same quite recently, as it happens.

Paranoidandroid: Who?

Lucy: An arsehole. You wouldn't know him.

Paranoidandroid: I know lots of arseholes. ☹

Paranoidandroid: I wish I was with you right now.

Lucy: If you were, I'd wrap you up in my arms.

Paranoidandroid: I wish I could meet you.

Lucy: I thought you wanted to lock yourself away in your room and never come out?

Paranoidandroid: For you I'd make an exception.

I lost signal again.

> Paranoidandroid: Sorry, did I go too far?
>
> Lucy: No, that's fine.
>
> Paranoidandroid: It isn't. You're married. And I'm young enough to be . . .
>
> Lucy: My plaything?
>
> Paranoidandroid: You get me terribly excited when you say things like that.
>
> Lucy: Plaything plaything plaything. How excited, exactly?
>
> Paranoidandroid: so excited thatI c an't ty--pe stra ight any more
>
> Lucy: Hot flushes?
>
> Paranoidandroid: A lot of blood flow, and all to one place.
>
> Lucy: Where . . . ?
>
> Paranoidandroid: Remind me where you are again?
>
> Lucy: Somewhere outside Copenhagen, I think.
>
> Paranoidandroid: I was going to make a joke about my blood flowing even further south than that. But I don't think it scans. Anyway, it's making me lightheaded.
>
> Lucy: Lie down.
>
> Paranoidandroid: Only if you lie on top of me.
>
> Lucy: I'd rather straddle.
>
> Paranoidandroid: !
>
> Lucy: Forgive me. Got carried away myself.
>
> Paranoidandroid: Is your husband still sleeping?
>
> Lucy: Like a baby.
>
> Paranoidandroid: I've just come. Your turn. Take yourself to the toilet, and prepare yourself for some text sex.

I returned to my seat ten brisk minutes later, my arrival waking Andrew up. Removing his glasses, he rubbed at his eyes, his fingernails excavating the sleep that had built up in each corner.

Consciousness was gradually returning to his features, like a corpse re-animating.

'You okay?' he asked. 'You look as if you've been running.'

Later that night, I received another message.

> Paranoidandroid: I've just spent the past couple of hours on the phone with my ex. *She* called *me*. She wants to give us another go. I know you are the last person I should be asking this, but you are also the *only* person. What should I do?

If only Ben knew just how hot, and also quite how cold, he made me.

I awoke on our first morning in Amsterdam to a chaste kiss on the cheek, Andrew towering above me wearing only a towel, still wet from the shower.

'Guess what time it is?' he said.

I looked at the clock radio by the bed: 2.15 p.m.

He laughed. 'We obviously needed our sleep!'

I lay back, slightly bewildered at having slept half the day away.

'I've been awake for over an hour now, but I didn't like to bother you. You looked exhausted. Anyway, come. Come and look out of the window. They've given us a garden room.'

I reached for the hotel dressing gown and went to join him. Together we gazed down at the Japanese garden with its delicate bonsais and trickling water features. Andrew now repositioned himself behind me, placed his arms around my stomach and cleaved into me.

'Glad we're here?' he asked.

I was. Because the moment required it, I allowed him to turn me around. He swooped in for a kiss that came with an added and, these days, unexpected, ingredient: tongue. It sat there limply in my mouth, and I resisted the temptation to bite down. I pushed my hips towards him, but felt none of the anticipated swelling. Abruptly, he withdrew.

'Shall we go?' he asked.

'Where?'

He had it all planned out, he said. The rain had stopped and the sun was shining. We were going to hire a couple of bikes and cycle around the city, stopping off for lunch, and later for coffee and cake. Then we would come back to the hotel to freshen up, then get ready for dinner. He'd already reserved a table somewhere nice.

'And after that,' he said, his eyebrows arching high upon his forehead, 'a surprise . . .'

Saddle-sore from several hours on an upright bike, and full of Asian fusion food and groggy red wine, all I wanted now was a hot bath, a soft duvet and sleep. It was eleven o'clock at night, but my husband was fidgety and excitable. My *surprise*, it seemed, was imminent. We got into a taxi driven by a large Middle Eastern man with an enormous neck who took us into the heart of the city at speed. His eyes kept finding mine in the rear-view mirror, and I couldn't determine whether his smile was friendly or something else. It was a Saturday night, with a slight chill in the air, but warmer than it had been at any time since we'd left home.

We were heading towards the city's rougher districts, the Red Light mile, the train station, the dodgy hotels. This did not, I decided, bode well. We got out a quarter of an hour later on a humpbacked bridge, whose adjoining roads were all being dug up. Massive JCBs, now idle for the night, blocked most of the way. Every other road was packed with weekend tourists chewing on kebabs, drinking beer and smoking spliffs. Up ahead, a couple of Geordies were fighting with fists, broken beer bottles beneath their feet. Andrew clutched at my hand and we began to weave along the pavement, turning quickly on to a narrow stretch of road that ran parallel with the canal. It was quieter here.

'Where are we going?' I asked impatiently. 'Because, to be honest, I'm exhausted. I'd just as happily go to bed.'

'Don't be ridiculous,' he boomed. 'It's your fortieth birthday. Well, almost.' My fortieth was a couple of weeks away. I didn't want to think about it. 'We've got to do something special, right?' He looked up. 'Okay, we're here.'

I saw a nondescript door. Next to it was a sex shop. The door was open, a curtain of string beads hanging across it. Andrew held them aside and instructed me to walk up a staircase so steep I could have done so on all fours without bending down. At the top it opened out into what looked like somebody's private front room, with a dining table, a sofa and, in the corner, a television screening porn. But there was also a counter, and behind it a man with a goatee, smoking a very thin, self-rolled cigarette.

'I came here once with the lads years ago,' Andrew told me as he encouraged me on to the sofa. With two extended fingers he called the man over and ordered us black coffee and a hash cake each. I was really not in the mood to get high tonight, but so puppyish was the look on Andrew's face that I felt it best not to disappoint. We were on holiday, after all. And who knows, perhaps I would enjoy myself. If nothing else, it would render me supplicant enough to have sex with him back at the hotel, which was presumably the whole point of the evening. Three German men arrived and sat on barstools opposite. They nodded to us genially, then spoke amongst themselves, fighting over the menu.

Half an hour later, we were tumbling back down the stairs and out into the crisp night, desperate for fresh air. The streets were even busier, and to my eyes all the neon signs were bleeding into the canal water to create a kind of hallucinogenic palette of gaudy colour all around me. I leant heavily on Andrew as we walked, or perhaps Andrew leant heavily on me, the pair of us an inverse V, or an A without the rung. Andrew was giggling. I was feeling sick.

'Don't look at me. *Don't look at me.* Just look forward,' he instructed. 'Keep your eyes ahead of you, and you'll be fine.'

It felt like New Year's Eve. So many people, so much human traffic, and so late, Andrew chattering all the while, an unbreakable monologue streaming from his mouth and making no sense to me at all, horses and work and BMWs and global warming strung together like an endlessly extending string of beads. 'Fishcakes!' he concluded at one point. For an hour, or maybe four, it was difficult to tell, we were on a merry-go-round in the middle of the city, the pavement whizzing beneath our feet, the same sites and sights and people passing before us time and again. I would later learn that this was not the case at all, that Andrew was actually leading me on to somewhere else, but kept getting lost. I felt fantastic, and then I felt sick again. I was definitely going to be sick.

'A-ha,' he exclaimed suddenly. 'Still here.'

We were now stood outside a shop front with nothing in its window except for thick black curtains. Somebody pushed past me, a man, and disappeared inside. Andrew reached forward and held the door open.

'Where are we?'

'Remember you were telling me about that swingers' club?'

For a moment I had no idea what he was talking about, but then it came to me: The Pseud's recommendation that I had foolishly repeated. Oh no.

'Well this,' he announced, 'is its Amsterdam equivalent.'

Funny how quickly you can sober up the very moment you feel yourself properly out of your depth. As I walked through the door, a certain smell assailed my nostrils, sharp and chemical and déjà-vu-ish. 'Amyl nitrite,' Andrew informed me knowledgeably. We were in a small, cubicle-sized room, where another man, also goateed and puffing away, handed us a towel each and pointed towards another door upon receipt from Andrew of two large-denomination notes.

We walked through into a bigger room. The walls were black, the ceiling too. Lighting was minimal, coming from a series of wall lamps that sent their scant wattage upwards. There was no furniture, but several scatter cushions across the floor. Trance music played insistently from the speakers, each bass note fuzzy and distorted. The sharp chemical smell was stronger here, mingling now with other, uncomfortably intimate ones. My eyes gradually grew accustomed to the gloom, and I saw, in a far corner, an elderly black woman with a mop and a bucket, cleaning a patch of floor before disappearing into another room. At first I thought I must have been imagining her, but I saw Andrew watching her too.

We were not alone. There were fifteen, perhaps even twenty people, men and women both, the majority older than us, and each in a state of undress. Several of the men appeared to be wearing leather shorts, the women short leather skirts, all black. Almost everybody was topless, and a few bottomless. Seeing so many bared breasts sag so sadly reminded me of the gym. I was less prepared for the penises, small and thin, mostly, and curled into plump nests of pubic hair. I then saw an erection – and just like that, my breath left me, the remaining effects of the hash cake vanished. It was coming towards me, attached to a man of about fifty. He was taut and sinewy, unexpectedly tanned for October. He was naked but for socks and shoes, black with laces, shoes for the office, and he boasted a smile as wide as his erection was long. He was alone, but walking amongst the people serenely, trailing extended fingers over the bare shoulders of all he passed. Many ignored him, intent on their own activities. Several, I saw now, were locked in embraces, men kissing men, women kissing women, women kissing men.

A woman approached us, in her forties but well preserved, her small pert breasts rising to make the clear point to us that both her dark nipples were pierced. She said hello, in English, giving us both a kiss on the cheek. 'First time?' she asked, already drifting off. 'Enjoy.' Andrew, still holding on to my hand, squeezed tightly. I felt suddenly, and ridiculously, overdressed, and yet I wished I had on a further overcoat that I could hide inside. I recalled out of nowhere a statistic, from TV or a magazine, that said more people have a threesome between the ages of forty-five and fifty-four than in any other age group.

I was ahead of my time.

The man with the erection was now in front of us. 'Jusht arrived?' Helplessly, I glanced from his eyes to down below. Up close, it was huge. It curved banana-like to the right. I imagined that accommodating it would require careful manoeuvres. I looked back at his face, which beamed with an owner's pride.

'You'd like to touch?'

I was about to answer when I realized that the question was not directed at me, his lizard gaze having slunk over to Andrew. I glanced at my husband, his face bright pink. He managed no response for a moment, and the moment spooled out like tape. Eventually, he regained enough composure to shake his head. The man now took one sideways step in his socks and shoes, his smile growing further. The tip of his cock, I saw, was glistening in anticipation. He asked me the same question, and my response was purely British: terrified of causing offence.

'Not just now, thanks. Maybe later?'

Over in one corner, a couple appeared to be readying

themselves for full sex. Other people began to crowd around, excited and encouraged. There were many erections now. Andrew, still stricken by my side, asked half-heartedly if I wanted to get undressed. He pointed to another corner of the room, where, in the shadows, lay a wall of lockers. I shook my head. He asked if I'd like to go and watch instead. I wanted to turn and flee, but nodded. Another couple, also recently arrived and not yet undressed, joined us.

'Inge,' said the woman; 'Dirk,' said the man.

The main couple were in their early forties, I guessed, and there was something so perfunctory about what they were doing with one another that it was impossible to tell whether they were a married couple or awkward strangers. He was bent over her, and they began rutting like dogs. There was cellulite, on both of them, and noises too. Grunts of exertion, an unfortunate fanny fart. The crowd pushed progressively closer and shuffled around a bit, the better to give each of us an unimpeded view. The man's scrotum hung low and was entirely hairless. It waggled like a glove puppet as he thrust in earnest. He turned to smile at his audience, and I saw him red in the face, the veins protruding in his neck. The woman beneath him issued a succession of *oh*s that confirmed to me at least she was mostly faking her enjoyment for the crowd. She generously chose to fake her orgasm to coincide neatly with his all too real one. He withdrew quickly, a heavy condom dangling from the end of his immediately flaccid penis.

One of the men approached. 'Nice,' he said.

The crowd had got what it wanted: an ice-breaker. People now began to pair off, stroking and fingering one another in the slow dance of pre-sex overture. Inge and Dirk went over to the lockers, and I watched as the man with the giant erection approached them. Beside me, I felt Andrew begin to stroke my breast through my coat. I turned to look at him to find that it wasn't Andrew at all, but rather somebody else, an older man, wretchedly naked, and grinning. Where was my husband?

Andrew, I saw now, was being led away by a large woman. She had on a garter belt, which looked strangely humdrum against all her bared skin. Andrew's back was to me, so I couldn't see his face, but even from this distance I could tell that his shoulders were tense, his neck locked solid in anticipatory dread. He'd need shiatsu to loosen it.

We were silent in the taxi on the way back to the hotel. There were no words. I focused on the car's clock, glowing green on the dashboard. It was just after two, which meant that we'd managed less than an hour injecting a bit of spice into our relationship. We'd had our little adventure, and now it was time to wipe that particular slate clean and just hope that everything could return to the way it was *before*.

The driver asked whether we minded if he smoked. Andrew cadged one from him, his first cigarette, to my knowledge, in at least a couple of years. The driver opened his window a crack and a properly chilly breeze blew in. I closed my eyes to it and let it pour over my face. Ten minutes later, we were back at the hotel. There would be no climactic sex between us now, neither of us in the mood to instigate any such thing. All I wanted was the oblivion of sleep. As we stepped out of the cab, something caught Andrew's eye.

'*Oh*, look!'

Two doors down from our hotel was a discreet, but clearly upmarket, casino. It hadn't been there the last time we'd stayed here. A queue several people long waited patiently outside it, each new guest admitted only after being frisked first by a couple of burly security guards.

'Come on,' Andrew said. 'Let's go and have some *real* excitement.'

I told him I wasn't in the mood, that I wanted to go back to our room, to bed, and to sleep.

'Okay, won't be long,' he said, and trotted along to join the queue.

I thought that it would be difficult to sleep, that I would be wracked with turmoil and regret, and shame, but I was out the moment my head hit the pillow. I had a dream that I was swimming the Atlantic, the first person ever to do so. People lined the route on strategically placed buoys, applauding my efforts as I dived off a rock on Land's End, and cheering me all along the way. But the world kept turning, incrementally yet cruelly, away from me, and so essentially I was treading water, America remaining as distant as ever, irrespective of my increasingly desperate strokes. It took me several weeks to realize that I was going nowhere. I was tired. The boats and helicopters filming my progress had got bored and returned to dry land, leaving me stranded. My arms grew heavy. Sharks began to circle.

There was a knock at the door. Not so much knuckles as an open palm. I opened my eyes and peered at the alarm clock on the bedside table: 4:10. Andrew? I stumbled out of bed. The knock came again. I crossed the room and opened the door. Andrew.

'Darling!'

He was beyond drunk, waves of alcoholic vapours pouring off him. I reeled backwards, then retreated towards the bed. He slammed the door behind him and lurched after me, giggling like a child.

'I won!'

I asked him not to shout.

'Four hundred euros!'

He showed me several bright blue, crisp notes.

'And how much did you lose before you won?'

175

He looked confused, and shook his head so violently that to stem it he had to grab it between both hands. 'Not the point, not the point.' He shrugged. 'Couple hundred, maybe, but, Luce, you should have been there. Great great crowd.'

I climbed back into bed, and he followed, falling heavily on to the mattress, an arm across my shoulder. I told him to get off the bed, that he wasn't sleeping with me in that state. I banished him to the small sofa on the other side of the room. He roared with laughter.

'Why does it feel like we've been married for fifty years?' he asked.

'Perhaps because you act like such an old man.' I wanted, suddenly, to hurt him.

'Oh fuck off.'

I must have slept then, because when I came to, to the sound of retching in the bathroom and some self-pitying whimpering, the clock read 5:07. Andrew emerged from the bathroom trouserless, vomit spattered down his shirt.

'Help me,' he pleaded.

I led him to the sofa, on to which he now collapsed gratefully, head between his knees, then I took a breath, held it, and entered the bathroom. His trajectory had missed the bowl entirely. There was vomit all over the bathroom floor, the sink, the bidet and the shower curtain. It was dark red, the colour of Rioja, and the stench was overwhelming. I stormed back into the bedroom to berate him, to hit him with fists, but he was now face down on the sofa, fast asleep.

I vowed to myself that I would not cry. I returned to the bathroom, got down on my hands and knees, and began mopping up the mess with all the towels I could find, which I then rinsed thoroughly in the bath before hanging them up over the rail, hopefully clean, to dry.

When I at last got back to the bedroom, Andrew was now

sprawled right across the bed, arms flung out on either side of him as if awaiting crucifixion. I curled up on the sofa and longed for a sleep that now would not come.

Dawn arrived early in Amsterdam, this most beautiful of cities, and I watched the sun bring colour to the rooftops as the streets beneath me slowly stirred. Amsterdam, I knew, would now always remind me of this night, tainted beyond redemption. I got dressed and went downstairs, where I was the only one on this Sunday morning having breakfast at such an early hour. The staff made a sweet fuss of me, pouring me orange juice and offering me my choice of newspaper. The coffee was good and strong, the croissants light as air.

Eight

I went to see a psychotherapist. I found her – where else? – online. She advertised herself as a specialist in relationship problems, and now that I had the clarity of a forty-year-old, officially middle-aged, I realized that that was what I had, relationship problems, and that I likely needed a psychotherapist far more than I did a much younger, and purely virtual, lover.

I had known all along the kind of man I was marrying, of course, but never having been married before, never having even sustained a long-term affair before, I didn't quite appreciate the toll it would come to take. I still loved Andrew, but was unsure if I could claim to be *in* love with him. Was the difference pertinent? I derived comfort from him, from his presence and protection, and also relief that marriage spared me the misery of the human meat market, out night after night hungry for scraps. But then I also *missed* the excitement of the market, the adrenalin rush of being on the prowl, and the ever-ready prospect of passion. Which is precisely why I tried to find it through my laptop instead, and hence the sensitive teacher, the cocksure chef, the helicopter pilot, the lonely university professor.

I needed help.

A couple of weeks after Amsterdam, my birthday passed with a whimper and Andrew was busy weathering his own private storm: a humbling demotion at work, a pay restructure, and an overbearing new boss, the combination of which led to him drinking more, gambling more, and staying out more. I tried repeatedly to talk to him about his drinking, but he would always brush it off, saying that the only problem with it was the one in my head. 'I drink to unwind, Lucy, to have fun. The whole world does. Where's the harm?' He told me to get some perspective. On the nights he stayed in, he would fall asleep in front of the television well before his 10.45 cut-off point, and if I didn't wake him and encourage him upstairs to bed, he would still be there the morning after, looking aged, and grumbling about a crick in his neck.

One weekend I suggested he forget about the football and come to the gym with me instead. It'll do you good, I told him. We could have a workout together, and a refreshing swim. Swim? He laughed, and my face must have told him how disappointed I was, because moments later we were in the car and on our way, a packed sports bag heavy on my lap.

He was wearing a pair of faded white shorts with the legend MEXICO 86 on the left leg, and indecently short. His socks were pulled high up his hairless shins, and his trainers were both box-fresh and helplessly old – a pair of Nikes he'd bought half a decade earlier and never worn. He survived ten full minutes on the exercise bicycle, his legs trembling with exertion, before dismounting unsteadily, shaking his head, and telling me he'd meet me in the café by reception when I was finished. I took my own leisurely time after that, resigned in my solitude, but when I went out to meet him, he wasn't there. I eventually found him in a pub down the road, sipping a second pint while re-reading that morning's *Racing Post*. After a spot of lunch we went to the cinema, our first matinee performance since the first year of our relationship. He was asleep before the opening credits had ended.

Another weekend, I dragged him to a gallery, but he complained of lower-back pain and of being hungry, of an incessant need to pee. As we made our way towards another calorific pub lunch, I looked around at the other couples, hand-in-hand or walking in an embrace, taking in the exhibition with companionable fascination, and I felt a stab of longing. I told Andrew I needed the toilet, and once locked away in the cubicle took out my phone, wondering again why Ben had gone silent this past week. I'd tried to cut back on my online relationships of late, in order to focus more attention on my marriage. But this, I realized, was futile. The helicopter pilot was being persistent, and the chef was making one of his empty promises ('Come for lunch! On me!'), but I wanted only to hear from Ben, just Ben. I began carefully to phrase a message to him, when suddenly I heard a voice. Andrew's.

'Lucy! You all right in there, Luce?'

I put my phone away, flushed, and went out to quieten, and appease, my husband. Plenty of Sunday afternoon remained. I wondered quite how I would get through it.

That's when I thought of seeking out a therapist. A therapist would help, would give me clarity, a way out of *all this*.

She lived a brisk twenty-minute walk from my house, in a large but scruffy townhouse which she shared with a dentist, situated directly in front of a busy bus stop. I took the six crumbling steps up towards the big black door, obstructed by three schoolchildren who sat smoking on them, and rang the bell. *Für Elise* went floating off up the unseen hallway, bringing Barbara, the psychotherapist, bounding down it with heavy footsteps that reminded me of my husband's.

Opening the door to me, she looked flustered and pink-cheeked. Her hair was short and black, a grown-out buzz cut, and she was wearing a large, deliberately shapeless black dress that went all the way down to her feet. She looked clean through me as if I were invisible.

'Do you mind?' she said sharply to the smoking school-children, and then waited, glaring, with hands on hips, until they shrugged, stood up and ambled towards the bus shelter.

Only now did she take me in, with a bright enquiring face, piercing blue eyes, a round nose and full lips. Her cheeks betrayed the cracked veins of middle age, and the ravages of dry skin.

'Marcia?' she asked hopefully.

'Lucy.'

The bus arrived, and distracted her again, until: 'Lucy! Of course. Please, do come in.'

She invited me inside and directed me with waving arms into her office. It was large and cavernous, with two sofas pushed up against opposing walls, and beneath the vast front windows a desk upon which textbooks were piled. More were piled on the floor. On the mantelpiece was an old ticking clock, and above this a large mirror that warped my reflection so unpleasantly I quickly looked away.

'Please, do sit.'

I opted for the sofa in the sun. As I sat down, dust erupted from its cushion and swam tantalizingly in front of my eyes, momentarily hypnotizing me. Barbara offered me no coffee or tea, which was just as well, as I wanted neither but would have accepted both, just to have something to hold on to.

'Mind if I smoke?' she said, sitting behind her desk and light-ing up before I had a chance to answer. Sunlight from the windows was pouring down on to her and she appeared lit from within, glowing like a religious icon.

'Now.' She brought both hands together. 'Let's begin.'

She asked me some questions about myself, and I found that the moment I started talking I couldn't stop, my nerves promptly evaporating into thin air, into all the dust. I had never done therapy before, but could immediately see how easily it could become addictive. It is rare in ordinary life ever to have the opportunity to be able to talk about ourselves and have some-body actually *listen*, without feeling selfish about it. I'm sure at times even my closest friends had never really listened to me, but then I suppose at other times I had never really listened to them, either, my mind already too full of me. If you really wanted someone to give you their undivided attention, maybe you had to pay them.

She watched me, without expression, as I told her about Andrew, our marriage, the house renovation, my pneumonia, my nagging listlessness of late, my fast-disappearing career, and the fact that I was starting to think about having an affair. I omitted to tell her that I was already doing so online; the admission simply wouldn't come.

When she finally spoke, her voice revealed a slight accent, clipped and sharp but pleasing to the ear. It took a while to place it. German.

'You've not mentioned children,' she said.

'Children?'

'Yes. I presume you have none?'

'Correct.'

'And how old are you?'

I told her. Her eyes widened.

'So you cannot have children?'

I explained.

'But children, I am thinking, would change everything. For you, and certainly for your husband.'

'But we don't want children.'

'*We?* Your husband agrees with this?'

I nodded.

'I don't understand. Why not?'

I checked my watch.

'We have time,' she assured. 'Do not worry about that.'

At the end of my hour, she suggested I return three times a week. There was plenty to work with here. She saw me to the door with a fixed smile on her face and said that she was look-ing forward to seeing me again. Perhaps it was the maternal lilt in her voice, or her unwavering certainty, but I believed her.

Do women have a midlife crisis? Because I think I was in the middle of one.

My sex drive was still climbing. I became incapable of walk-ing past a clothes shop without going in, loving the intimacy of the changing room, of new fabric around my hips and thighs, the sensation of silk bra on skin as I leant forward slightly to settle each breast into its cup before fastening it around the back. I bought clothes that clung, that kept my sense of arousal in perpetuity.

Though my husband failed to notice any of this, it was commented upon at work. Female colleagues asked if I was in love or about to celebrate a special occasion, while my boss would look at me askance and more than once wondered aloud whether I was on my way to a job interview with the com-petition. 'Your two days a week are still secure here, you do realize this, don't you?' he'd worry.

I began to enjoy the twice-weekly commute. On the bus into work, I could make eye contact with a man, somebody invariably younger than me, and would allow my gaze to linger suggestively where once I would have blinked shyly away. This reminded me of the power I could just about still wield over certain men; I had forgotten what that felt like.

And it was true that they were almost always younger. A decade previously, and my tastes were exclusively for older men, preferring character and experience over youth. But now that I was regressing, I found myself drawn more to young men in their twenties, still naïve and pretty and unsoiled, boys I hoped would see in me all the character and experience I now possessed. I would hold their stares until they began to blush with a kind of *who me?* incredulity. When they got off the bus, these boys, they would always steal a final hopeful glance at the window as the bus pulled away, and I would always reward them with a farewell look, a coquettish grin to suggest what might have been.

I don't think I consciously wanted any of these boys actually to approach me – and, perhaps frustratingly, they didn't – but I loved the adrenalin of these fleeting encounters. It set the mood for the day, which I maintained with sessions on my iPhone, my virtual lovers as insatiable as me.

'You're going to the toilet an awful lot,' noted Stephanie, a colleague. 'You're not bulimic, are you?'

Though my chef was a lot of frivolous fun, our messages full of flirtatious meaninglessness, it was Ben I still sought out most, despite – or, for all I knew, *because of* – the mixed signals I was getting from him. He'd emailed me on the night of my fortieth, unaware of the anniversary, to tell me that he had indeed got back with his girlfriend, ensuring, if nothing else, that I ended the night lonely and feeling sorry for myself. But then, after a week of torturous silence, he contacted me again to tell me that their reunion had not gone well. 'It's over for ever this time.' I immediately messaged him back, telling him (selfishly) that it was for the best, that he would get over her in time, and that he was a young man, he wouldn't be single and lonely for long. 'And you've always got me,' I wrote.

'All I want is you,' he wrote back.

There were many things, I suppose, that drew me to him the most. One was his fertile imagination. Every now and then, prompted by certain events in his own life that would remain a mystery to me, he would send long emails of unbridled passion, suddenly unleashing a previously hidden voice and recasting himself as fearless romantic-fiction pornographer. They would appear in my inbox without prior warning, and never in the middle of a regular exchange between us. No, these were fantasies he had spent time honing in private, for all I know editing and re-editing until he deemed them just right. I'm sure he got off on them; I know I did. Appraised out of context here, they may seem a little tacky and ridden with purple-prosed cliché. And perhaps they were. All I can say is that at the time they excited me in a way references to Plato and Socrates never could.

Hello, it's me. It's late, I'm alone, and sleepless, and the reason for my insomnia is you. It's been a tough week (don't ask), but I'm through it now and I am right now in an aroused state. I suppose once upon a time I would have just finished myself off quickly and then gone to bed, but you, Lucy, have shown me the benefits of foreplay, even written foreplay (especially written foreplay!). I'm going to enjoy writing this. I hope you enjoy reading it.

I'm imagining us meeting, and me having spent the night at your place. Where is your husband? Who cares! It's my fantasy. Perhaps he doesn't even exist . . . Anyway, I'm imagining waking up and seeing you lying naked beside me, an hourglass in repose on the mattress. My hand traces the curve of your shoulder, the dip of your waist, and the swell of your hips. My hand then falls, as you always knew it would, on to your midriff. My finger circles your belly button, it traces up and then down, and then down further still. You are wet and ready, and hot, so hot, and my finger, and then my fingers, slide into you. You tense, and then you relax into it. You moan, and very slowly you turn to face me. I slide on top of you as your face reaches up to mine, your tongue in my mouth, hungry, your wide open eyes on mine, saying every-thing words never could. I enter you, and we are still, so still. At first we don't move at all, just remain locked together, but then slowly we find our rhythm . . .

And that's just one of my fantasies. I have more. I fantasize, for example, about coming to visit you at your home. It's a late Sunday afternoon, summertime. You are preparing your husband's dinner. He has popped out for last-minute provisions, and more wine. I watched him go from across the road, but he didn't notice me. I knock. You are pleased to see me, but flustered. You are hot. I follow you into the kitchen where there is much still to do. You tell me I can watch, and I do so, seated at the kitchen table. You move from the cooker to the fridge, to cupboards and drawers. Your bottom is tight in a pair of black leggings and as you go about your duties, I reach forward with both hands outstretched and rest them upon your buttocks. You gasp, and, unable to resist you any more, I pounce!

I am now pressed up against you, my whole body, and you can feel how excited I am to be here, so close. You are still trying to concentrate on the cooking as my hands are moving up your waist and on to your full breasts. You can take it no more. You stop what you are doing, you turn to face me. I lift you up and on to the kitchen table, and I remove your leggings. You are wearing no knickers. I push myself against you, teasing you for a while before I finally enter you, and we fuck quickly and urgently, you screaming in the wild abandon of orgasm.

The sound of the front door reaches us. Your husband is suddenly in the kitchen, and you are back at the counter, composed, your back to him, your bright red cheeks concealed from view. You look up out of the window in front of you, into the garden, where you see me scale the wall and disappear into the next garden . . . where, just possibly, who knows, I have another date with another frustrated housewife!

186

I'm joking! Lucy, the only frustrated housewife I want is you! ☺

Okay, so these are only words on a screen right now, but I want more than you can know for them to be reality. Can we make it happen?

There were many such emails, increasing in length and detail, over the next few months. Perhaps it was my state of mind, my prevailing weakness, but it is difficult to convey fully the power these messages had on me back then. To know that someone could have such fantasies about *me* took my breath away. I felt at once grateful, unworthy and powerful, but mostly desperate to do as he pleaded and make them, or at least a more realistic version thereof, come to life.

We were exchanging messages all the time now, day and night. I became so focused on him that I stopped maintaining my other chats in order to direct all my energy on to him. We exchanged thousands and thousands of words, which began to follow a particular, though unremarked-upon, rhythm. The sex between us was thrilling, and I would sink back down into my bed afterwards no longer feeling foolish and alone but instead sated and alive. I came to see it as a proper, full-blown relationship, and fully three-dimensional.

Winter set in, and Christmas loomed, a time of encroaching depression and enforced sociability for everyone. He said he wanted to hear my voice. I had been waiting for him to suggest this for months now, but knew from his initial timidity that the suggestion would have to come from him and him alone, not me. To date, we had shared only that one single photograph each, both of us convinced that these baby steps made us quite unlike anybody else online, a fiction we chose to maintain.

Paranoidandroid: I'd love to hear your voice. I think I'm ready for it.

Lucy: I cackle like a witch, I'm afraid.

Paranoidandroid: no matter. I've always pictured you as warty and green.

Lucy: You say the loveliest things.

Paranoidandroid: and I'd love to say them directly into your ear. Your number, please.

Lucy: Seriously?

Paranoidandroid: I think we've been Victorian enough in our relationship already, no? Time to move into the 21st century, I think.

Lucy: I don't think what we did last night was particularly Victorian, do you? I came over all a-fluster.

Paranoidandroid: Madam, help unharness my breeches, would you?

Lucy: Of course, kind sir, let me loosen them . . . *My*, your thighs! How firm . . .

Paranoidandroid: Your number please.

Paranoidandroid: Pretty please.

Paranoidandroid: Don't make me beg, because I won't.

Paranoidandroid: Please oh please oh please oh please oh please oh please . . .

I sent him my number. A moment later, set to silent (Andrew asleep in the next room), it lit up and revealed a number that I would, moments after our call ended, save under the name HIM. I brought the phone to my ear and, in a whisper, answered. He whispered back. His voice, at last. My heart lifted, surged, flew.

Was I falling in love?

Andrew came home one night a couple of weeks later, ashen-faced. I was in the living room doing bad things on my laptop, but closed it immediately and willed the blush from my cheeks.

'What's wrong?' I asked him.

Words failed him. But his eyes were imploring. He came and sat alongside me, and gripped my hands in his. His eyes were rimmed red, and on his breath was evidence of a post-work drink, maybe two. In a single moment, it came to me. He was ill. Cancer. All that drinking, junk food, a never-ending workload, a mountain of stress. And so here, now, was the inevitable outcome. In my mind I came to the oddly lucid conclusion that my place was by his side, that I would nurse him for as long as he needed me. In sickness and in health. Ben would have to wait.

'What's wrong?' I asked, desperate to know. 'Andrew, talk to me.'

'You love me, don't you? I love you. You know that, right?' He shifted his weight on his buttocks and leaned even closer to me. I could smell beer, whisky. 'I mean, I know we argue, of course we do, but all married couples argue. Doesn't mean we're not still good together. Because we are, underneath it all. Right?'

'Andrew, tell me. What's brought all this on?'

He told me. It wasn't cancer. He said that he'd had an unexpected visitor at lunchtime, Dan, his oldest friend. Dan lived in Scotland these days, but had flown down that morning, all his worldly possessions stuffed in a single bag, homeless at forty-five.

'You wouldn't have recognized him, Luce.'

I last saw Dan with his wife Carol when they came to stay with us shortly after the house renovation. I was never fully comfortable around Dan, who seemed to work hard at being aggressively male at every opportunity, and who brought out in Andrew similar characteristics. Whenever they were together they tried to outdo one another with lewd jokes, and would have the kind of drinking competitions they had back when they were seventeen. The more Carol and I pleaded with them to rein it in, the louder they laughed. '*Women!*' Dan would say to Andrew, to which Andrew would unfailingly reply, '*Women!*' And the laughter would erupt again.

'Carol left him. She kicked him out. Threw all his clothes on the lawn from the bedroom window, for all the neighbours to see. Shamed him in front of his friends, Luce.' All this Andrew related as if it were somehow unimaginable, Carol guilty of the most heinous of crimes.

'So why did she do that?'

His eyes shifted. 'She told him the marriage was over, just like that. No second chances.'

'But why?'

Dan, Andrew eventually told me, had been having an affair. Carol had found out.

'Good for her,' I said.

'But he was willing to *end* it,' my husband, now a stranger to me, implored.

'How long has he been cheating on her?'

Andrew shrugged. 'I don't know. A couple of years?'

'*A couple of years?* But they came to our wedding, together. And we had them over here – what? – just a few months ago. Wait a minute,' I said now. 'And you *knew* about this all along?'

He wouldn't meet my eye. 'Luce, he's my friend, my oldest friend . . .'

It was only afterwards, when I had time to digest things, that I came to realize why Andrew had looked so harrowed. He was fearful that what had so easily happened to Dan, the abrupt dismantling of his comfortable life, could happen to him too, and Andrew didn't want a second divorce. But did this also mean that he too had been carrying on, that he worried I'd now find out? Or did he fear that it would be *me* in Dan's position?

As I said before, there are many questions in marriages that don't always demand immediate answers, and for all sorts of reasons. This was one of them.

After the revelation, he insisted we go out to eat. It was a strange meal, Andrew declaring his love for me over and over, as he insisted that we were solid together, that Dan's experiences were a warning, a shot across the bows for both of us.

He told me that Dan was taking a break from Scotland for the time being. 'Lying low,' was how he put it. After Carol had thrown him out, Dan had initially gone over to his girlfriend's house, a twenty-seven-year-old from Poland whom he'd met after the company she ran with her sister had won the contract to clean his office block. But the girlfriend wasn't quite as ready to put up a forty-five-year-old prospective divorcee as Dan had hoped, and so his life began to dismantle further still. Like us, he and Carol had elected not to have children, which meant that, in theory at least, he was able to pick up and start again wherever he chose. Easier in theory than in practice.

'And he's chosen here?' I asked. Andrew shrugged. 'Where will he stay?'

He laughed, as if to the punchline of a joke. A nervous hand reached for his glasses, which he lifted and resettled on the bridge of his nose. 'Well, that's what I've been meaning to tell you.' He paused, waiting for me to join the dots. I said nothing, forcing him to join them for me. 'I've said he could kip down at ours. In the den. It's only for a while, Luce, until he sorts himself out. A few days, couple of weeks at most. Come on, Luce, he'd do the same for me.'

Strange thing to say. 'Would he need to?'

He looked horrified, eyes wide, jaw slack, like butter wouldn't melt. 'No! Of course not! Jesus, Luce,' he cried, as if I couldn't have been more wrong in my suspicions, as if infidelity were something that happened to other people's marriages, to Dan and Carol's, not ours.

Dan was sat on the sofa watching television when we got back, feet up on the coffee table in front of him. The moment he saw me, he quickly removed his feet and gave an exaggerated dusting to the table. He put down his lager, stood and came over to hug me, a warm smile on his face, friends reunited. 'Lucy, it's been too long.'

'How's Carol?' I asked. He flinched. Curious that my righteous defence of Carol didn't strike me as hypocritical, given that I was behaving much as Dan had (virtually, at least), but somehow it didn't. Were I to have analysed it then, I suppose I would have convinced myself that my situation was different, that Andrew had driven me to it in a way that Carol, a sweet and devoted woman, had not done with Dan.

Out of an innate sense of hospitality, I agreed to Andrew's suggestion of opening a bottle, and over the next hour was force-fully reminded just how uncomfortable I felt around his old friend. He had been drinking for much of the day, it seemed, but unlike Andrew had not taken a breather between lunch and dinner. He still had his thin frame, but a pot belly had developed since I'd seen him last, spilling over his belt buckle. His clothes, which I could only imagine had been the influence of his much younger girlfriend, made him look strange, the jeans too loose and too low, the T-shirt, featuring a giant pair of headphones, too tight across his chest and ponderous tummy.

While Andrew and I were on wine, he was drinking whisky, neat. He dominated the conversation, and rendered it a sorrow-ful one, convinced Monica would not take him back.

'Monica?'

'My girlfriend.'

'And Carol?'

'Carol's over, dead in the water. Excuse the expression, but when a marriage loses its passion, Luce, it loses everything, you know?'

Andrew, I noticed, stared at his feet, as if they contained all the mysteries of the known universe.

'And if she doesn't take you back? Monica?'

The whisky was filling him with a false sense of bravado. I would come to know this because, later, from upstairs in the den, I would hear the plaintive wails of a man ruing his actions and paying for his indiscretions. But now he said, 'Plenty more fish in the sea, eh?'

Dan howling into his pillow upstairs like a wounded seal, I spent much of the night in my secondary role for Ben, the one that required I restore his dented confidence. He had been arguing with his parents, and the misery this engendered was then compounded after a job interview went poorly. 'Why do i bothr?' he wrote. I had a feeling he was drunk, because his messages were careless. He was also uncomfortably candid. He told me that one of the reasons the week with his ex-girlfriend went so spectacularly badly was that he couldn't perform. He wanted to know whether anything like that had happened to me, confronted by a man who couldn't get it up. I explained that this was hardly surprising, under the circumstances. It had been a stressful encounter, and his inability suggested that they should never have attempted the rekindling in the first place. He responded that I hadn't answered his question.

'I just wish I could meet somebody nice,' he wrote, and I couldn't help but feel wounded.

'I'm nice,' I wrote back.

He responded with a smiley face, then added: 'You know what I mean. I would love to meet up with you, I really would. But in so many ways this is so very wrong, no? You're married. I don't want to derail your relationship . . .'

193

I was suddenly sapped of strength. What was I supposed to do here? Beg? Send him a link to Journey Planner, listing the train times between his city and mine? Or remind him, tartly, that he knew I was married when he started sending me all these messages, so why should it suddenly be a problem now? It's not that I didn't understand his fear, his ambivalence, because I suffered that as well, but I needed now for this to become all tangible and real, even if just briefly. And surely he did too?

I'd had no idea such an uncomplicated online affair could ever get so loaded with emotional baggage. But this was becoming frustrating. I was living in a house with two miserable men, and flirting online with a miserable boy. I was forty, and not getting any younger.

'Look, it's late,' I wrote. 'I'm tired. Let's pick up again another time, yes?'

It was the first time I had been testy with him. It wouldn't be the last.

The chef, having gone quiet of late, came suddenly back on the scene, and thank God for that. Out of the blue I received a message from him: LNG TME NO SPK!!!, four short words he nevertheless felt it necessary to make even shorter. He claimed that he had missed me, that he always had more fun online with me than with anyone else. Did I fancy making up for lost time? He had just been promoted, he said. I could come for dinner one night, not in the kitchen but the restaurant proper, a Saturday night after eleven ideally, when the boss was home and he'd be able to shower me with attention. 'It'll be cosy,' he promised.

I didn't really want to meet the chef at all, but in the vacuum left by Ben, I figured that I could use the distraction, see it as a test run, even. I reminded the chef that all his previous invitations had turned out rather hollow.

'NOT THIS ONE!!!' he insisted.

Conditions in the house, meantime, had descended to that typical of all flatshares. Two weeks since he had arrived, Dan was still an immovable houseguest, and when they were in one another's company he and Andrew reverted quickly to adolescence: a messy takeaway dinner in front of the TV, then a few drinks down the pub before returning, merry and raucous, to the front room, and a few more cans. Jobless, Dan had not offered to pay any rent, or cover his food and drink costs, but he had splurged, as a present purportedly for all of us, on a Wii 'as a sign of appreciation'. Andrew loved it, and together they played tennis and golf and boxing on it until late, my husband wide awake well after midnight for Dan in a way he never could be for me.

During the day, Dan was supposed to be out job-hunting, but I saw no evidence of this myself. He did go out on the days that I was home, but usually to the pub around the corner where they now knew him by name, while on Tuesdays and Thursdays, my work days, he appeared to lounge about the house all day in his underpants and a ratty vest. That's how I found him first thing in the morning, often waking after a few hours on the sofa after an interminable middle-of-the-night football tournament on the Wii, and that's how I found him when I came home in the evening, the temperature turned up too high, a lazy grin on his face as he greeted me, and the quick placing of one of my cushions across his lap. 'For the sake of decorum,' was his routine joke. 'Wouldn't want Andrew to get the wrong idea, eh?'

But Dan's annoying presence did have benefits. He hogged Andrew all weekend, and the upcoming weekend featured an important race meet at Newmarket – or was it Ascot? – that they both wanted to attend.

'I thought perhaps we might stay over,' Andrew said nervously a few days before. 'Might lift Dan's spirit. We could make a weekend of it; there's loads of hotels nearby. You could,' he added, with laughable reluctance, 'come with us. If you like?'

I told him fine, go, whatever, and promptly messaged the chef telling him that this Saturday night would be perfect.

He responded instantly. 'GR8!!!'

They left early, first thing on Saturday morning. I was still asleep and didn't even hear them go. They left a joint Post-it note on the fridge: *I'll call you from Ascot, Andrew.* DON'T MISS US TOO MUCH!! DAN. I made myself a coffee, then shuffled into the living room to feed Rummy, only to find that Andrew had already tended to the hamster.

After breakfast I chanced calling a couple of friends to see if they were free, at short notice, for brunch, or lunch, or coffee, a stroll. But one was spending the day getting ready for a date, the other with her new boyfriend. 'It's his day with the kids, so I'll get to meet them for the first time. I'm nervous! Wish me luck!'

And so instead I passed the day alone, wandering up and down the high street, the pall of my domestic chores – I bought deodorant, paracetamol, some night cream – given an added charge knowing that, later tonight, I was off on a date. My eyes were drawn to all the young men that passed me by, so many of them so very fetching in their coats and scarves, their cheeks apple red, their eyes roving. I had lunch in my favourite café, poring over the newspapers at leisure, and resisting the attentions of a rather elderly man doing likewise at the opposite table. Too old, grandad. I got home mid-afternoon, called my mother and endured an hour-long conversation about the awful holiday she had just had, a fly-drive package to Florida, and while listening to her blather I missed an incoming call from Andrew, which went straight to voicemail. I then spent another hour in the bath in meticulous preparation: shaving my legs, attending to my bikini line and ensuring that the natural enthusiasms of my eyebrows were tamed and tempered, plucked and shaped.

By six, I had still heard nothing from the chef, but then this, I reasoned, was always the way with the chef: enigmatically silent until moments before, then abrupt direct action. What on earth would he be like in bed? I couldn't help but wonder. But by seven, my stomach rumbling despite three Ryvitas, I grew impatient and contacted him.

'Still okay for tonight?' I messaged.

His response came a slow hour later that I endured only by directing all my emotions to the television, and some minor celebrities on ice. 'DEFO!! WOT DO U FANCY EATN? KNOW ANY GD RESTRUNTS?'

Hadn't he invited me to his? I reminded him of this.

'OF COURSE! OF COURSE!'

The conviction of his capital letters brought me solace, but when no further messages arrived, I texted again. 'So what time do you want me?'

While I awaited his reply, I got dressed. A new pair of knickers, a new bra, a tight but not too tight dress designed in such a way to flatter my bust and to contain the slight continental drift of my midriff. A little bit of make-up, enough to make my brown eyes browner, and then time on my hair, which increasingly liked to do its own thing these days. I sifted through it for traces of grey, and meticulously plucked any I came across. Then I went back downstairs to sit in front of the television, half a dozen balls tumbling into a cylinder and making millionaires of a lucky few.

As I checked my watch for the umpteenth time, I experienced a wave of déjà vu: me, twenty-five years earlier, on the edge of the settee on a Saturday night, poised to go out on a first date, the anticipation of new adventure mingling with a self-destructive dread that the night would somehow not go well, my mother in the next room chiding me for putting so much faith in the opposite sex. 'You'll learn,' she'd taunt.

I checked my phone, in case a message had arrived silently. Nothing. The reception was strong, the battery, so recently charged, full. I toyed with the idea of messaging him again, as over another hour had passed since my last. New butterflies erupted in my stomach, and I realized that I was hungry. I had three more Ryvitas, with low-fat cream cheese. Then I rushed upstairs to check my face, to brush my teeth, to rearrange each breast in its cup; everything just so. I was ready. Back downstairs again, to the television. A film had started. Tom Cruise. Teeth so perfect you'd forgive him his nose. I switched it off. I went to the loo. I checked my phone. I looked out the window, evening becoming emphatically night. I felt cold, suddenly, so turned the temperature up a couple of degrees. If it was cold now, it would get colder still later.

It took me a long time to fall asleep, and when I did I had bad, taunting dreams. I wouldn't remember a single detail about any of them afterwards, but they woke me countless times through the long night. I gave up and got up early to see Sunday as I so rarely had, at dawn, and was the first to arrive at the gym, where I cycled what felt like thousands of miles on the exercise bike, my legs fuelled by frustration and fury. I swam fifty lengths, and fell asleep, exhausted, on the sunlounger, awoken only by a rumble in my stomach that told me it was time, belatedly, for lunch.

I left the sanctity of the gym in late afternoon, after a facial, a massage, a little cry, and another slumber on the lounger, and arrived home to find Andrew and Dan back already, and halfway through a between-meals curry takeaway. They looked happy and spent. Both kissed me, both aiming for the safety of my cheek. Dan offered me a poppadom. They smelled strongly of beer, and were full of stories of the weekend: the bets, the races, the people, the food, the drink. I wondered whether I should have been suspicious over precisely what Dan had helped Andrew get up to last night, but couldn't muster the strength. I listened to their tales, and laughed when they reached a kind of punchline. But then their stories started to loop, the telling of them so much fun that they wanted to start over. I made my excuses shortly afterwards, Dan phoning for a Chinese while Andrew plugged in the Wii. I padded upstairs, bone tired, the sense of dispirited defeat now overwhelming. I slept a dozen hours, and woke up to the beginning of a new week.

At midday, my phone buzzed.

HEY! WOT HPND 2 U THE OTHER NITE???

I was disappointed by this, but not surprised. Those people who choose to spend so much time flirting online often do so because they can't quite carry it through into real life. I realized this now, being something of an expert on the subject. This was all well and good; I could accept and appreciate it, but what I didn't appreciate was the chef now choosing to play mind games with me, attempting to shift the failure of Saturday night on to me and not his last-minute nerves and no-show, or perhaps worse, a better offer. If he had been standing in front of me, I might have clouted him.

I switched my phone off.

A week later, I received another message from him.

HEY! I NEED 2 MAKE MONEY! FAST! ANY IDEAS???

I would not miss the chef.

Nine

Unable to find any kind of succour from Andrew, who clearly had a man-crush on Dan, the brother he never had, I felt more justified now in being as selfish in my own pursuits as he was in his. I'd had enough of online foreplay with cowards, the futile tease of so many meaningless words. I felt ready for – for *something*. Not sex, necessarily, but a date, a real date, with flesh and bone; the kind of human interaction people used to have back in the twentieth century.

It had been years since I had been out on the pull, and I'd forgotten quite how to do it. I wasn't about to approach a stranger on the street, that level of desperation never a good look on a woman of my age. I toyed with the idea of contacting Jane, who, more than any of my old friends, would relate most keenly to my plight, revel in it even, but I didn't want to share my marital problems with her, or with anyone, wanting it instead to remain a secret. And so, against all my better judgement, I went, yet again, back online.

The hundreds of online dating sites I avoided, because these, I decided, were for people primarily seeking love. I didn't want love. Despite its imperfections, I had it. I quickly found instead a succession of harmless-seeming flirtation sites ('for fun . . . and maybe more'), logged on, and began chatting with someone who called himself Tyke. Tyke was twenty-six years old and lived thirty miles away in a flatshare with a woman who was no longer his girlfriend but now just his friend. The transition, he admitted, was proving complicated. 'She's a diamond girl, but she's not for me, not long-term,' he admitted. 'I've never been very good at flirting, which is why I'm on here, I suppose. And you sounded pretty nice, L27. Hello.'

He told me he worked in an office, his job so dreary he refused, then, to go into any more detail about it (though he did later: sales), and confessed that he had once had aspirations to become a jockey. I wondered whether this meant that he was tiny, pocket-sized. Didn't *tyke* mean little child?

Time was no longer a luxury. And so when he asked for my telephone number after a mere half an hour of back-and-forth instant messaging, I offered it up. I felt no butterflies at the prospect of his call, nor when it came, and our conversation, when it happened at eleven o'clock on a freezing Thursday night, started in a quite perfunctory, matter-of-fact manner. *Hello. Hi. Good to talk to you. Likewise. So, shall we begin?* He had an unremarkable but sweet voice, freighted with wideboy estuary, and was clearly enthusiastic. Pretty soon we fell into some uncomplicated, unimaginative but effective, phone sex. I hung up afterwards, curiously empty.

We spoke again the next day, and the day after that, and before ending with a repeat performance of our first call, we shared personal information largely to fill what would otherwise have been an awkward silence. He went into more detail about his situation with his ex-girlfriend flatmate, and I told him about the state of my marriage. He laughed, and said that it reminded him of his parents' marriage. I later sent him a semi-provocative photograph of myself, which prompted a swift response to say that I reminded him of his parents no more.

'Do you fancy meeting up, perhaps?' he asked the following night. I agreed. 'When is your husband next out?' Pick a night,

I told him. 'It might have to be a little late,' he warned. 'My flat-mate gets suspicious if I go out at night. But don't worry, she goes to bed early.'

We arranged to meet for drinks at ten o'clock on a weekday night, at a bar by the train station. I dressed without anxiety, hardly bothering with my smoky-eye routine, and resolving that he would take me as he found me. But I still chose a dress that flattered, and a colour of lipstick a shade louder than one I would normally have worn. I also drenched myself in perfume and wore a pair of heels. In the cab, I realized that in place of any anticipated nerves lay only a cool determination: this was going to happen. He would not stand me up, would not become another Pseud, another chef. And he would like me. At least I hoped he would. I needed the validation.

I planned it that I would arrive earlier than him, to take my place at the bar and have him see me the moment he walked in. The nerves that had been absent in the cab arrived now, and I spent a quarter of an hour re-applying lipstick and fussing with my hair, convinced that all the men in there – and the place was full of men – knew exactly what my game was.

He was late. My phone rang.

'L27?' he said.

'Tyke?'

He sounded awkward. 'I'm lost.'

I thought he was joking, and so I giggled obligingly into the phone. But he was quite serious. He was, he told me, 'somewhere near the station. But there are loads of exits, and escalators, and I don't know where I'm supposed to be going.'

The streets outside the bar were cobblestoned and not kind on my heels. I had abandoned my drink, and with it my feigned sense of cool, and hurried back towards the station, hoping not to sprain an ankle, while he made heavy work trying to tell me precisely which exit he thought he was standing outside.

'I can see a minicab office,' he began. 'And over the road a kebab place, I think. No, fried chicken.'

'Stay where you are. I'll find you.'

And, twenty minutes later, I did. I recognized him from the photograph he had sent days previously. He had a nice, sweet face, a little pinched perhaps, with something unusual going on around the mouth. But his eyes were warm and friendly and, when he saw me approach, full of relief and embarrassment. If nothing else, his getting lost proved an effective ice-breaker and gave us something to talk about as we negotiated the cobble-stones back down towards the bar. He was indeed jockey-sized, perhaps a couple of inches shorter than me barefoot, but a full five inches given the size of my heels. I felt like a mother coming to pick up her son.

'Look, sorry about all this. I got confused,' he said.

In the bar, he encouraged me to find a table while he went to get us drinks, pulling a five-pound note from a small multi-coloured purse with the word MENORCA stitched on to the front.

The moment I realized that Tyke was somebody I was never going to get serious over – and I realized it quickly – I began to relax and enjoy myself. He brought me a large glass of wine and a pint of lager for himself, which he carried over to the table slowly, tongue protruding in concentration.

He sat next to me, and blushed as he spoke.

'I'm smaller than you would have liked, right, ha ha?' he said, his nervous laugh something I had never noticed during phone conversations with him. He grinned to reveal a chipped front tooth.

'You look just fine,' I assured him.

The compliment brought blood to his cheeks, which spread, then settled. Though I knew he was twenty-six, he could have passed, in this light, for seventeen. His skin was smooth like a baby's. He was dressed in Ben Sherman, Levi's, and a Stone Island jacket, and his fingernails, I noticed, were bitten to the quick. He was tightly coiled, and full of a nervous energy that I could well imagine getting excited on the back of a horse. I realized, with a certain wry detachment, that he would probably have so much more to talk about with Andrew than he ever would with me. Perhaps I could introduce them? They could become friends.

We sat at a large table, glancing around the place as if in search of conversational inspiration. Our last chat, the night before, had been an unbridled one, and I had come loudly into the phone. Odd to think that I knew exactly what he sounded like at the point of climax (a disconcerting goose honk that got longer as it progressed, and always prompted a quick apology afterwards), and odd also to think I knew exactly why he had never made it as a jockey. All this intimacy, this private confession. And yet now, here, sat opposite him and staring into his cute-ish, pinched little face, with its chipped tooth and thin lips, I realized, ridiculously, that the man was a stranger to me. And one who was plainly awed by *me*. I relaxed.

I took the upper hand, and we quickly found the comfortable neutral ground of any first date, and made the kind of humdrum small talk that allowed us to get to know one another better even though we both knew that this was information neither of us really needed, nor would later draw upon. What we actually talked about I can no longer recall, but the time passed, and suddenly the bell rang for last orders, bringing him to the belated realization that he had just eleven minutes before his last train.

I hadn't expected to accompany him to the train station, much less hand in hand, but as the night was now reaching its abrupt conclusion, a change came over Tyke, and he began to tell me, almost desperately, that he had always dreamt of meeting an older woman, and that he couldn't believe it was now happening. Which meant, by extension, that I was his dream woman. I took the compliment.

'Let's do this again, yeah? We could keep it uncomplicated and secret, promise. Your husband would never know. When can I see you again? Maybe we could go to a hotel next time? What do you think?'

We were on the platform now, and beeps were indicating that the train doors were about to close. He came in to kiss me with an open mouth, tongue poised. I offered him a cheek.

'Love you, yeah?' he called out, but I was gone already, to the cashpoint, to the taxi stand, to home.

Andrew and Dan were horizontal on the sofa when I got back, and I knew that they had both been smoking, and that Andrew had sprayed air-freshener in the room the moment he had heard my key in the lock. There was a sharp pine smell in the air, redolent of unlicensed cabs. Takeaway cartons littered the table in front of them, alongside several beer cans and, in a makeshift ashtray, the remains of the still smouldering roach.

'Hi darling,' Andrew said, seemingly unconcerned at my late arrival. He nudged Dan, eyelids at half-mast.

'Lucy.'

'Dan.'

I went to the kitchen for a glass of water, and Andrew followed. At the sink he gave me a peck on the cheek, the same cheek I had offered Tyke just half an hour before, and asked me how my day was. The question was rhetorical. He was clutching at his stomach, and began theatrically to groan, hoping to unpick the thread of my wifely concern.

'Vindaloo,' he said.

'Goodnight,' I told him.

I went to bed satisfied with myself, a novel sensation of late, but the satisfaction soon ebbed away and left me with a sense of anticlimax. I'd finally done it: I'd met someone and gone on a date. But I had expected more from it, more excitement, a greater sense of achievement. It had been a little like unwrapping the best-seeming present under the Christmas tree only to find an Argos foot spa when you had been secretly hoping for a Christian Dior handbag.

I went to see the psychotherapist again.

It was a week later, and I made the appointment for the middle of the afternoon on an otherwise empty Wednesday. She offered me a coffee this time, and while she went to make it I nosed around her office. There were photographs of her family: a husband perhaps in his early sixties, and three children, all boys, all teenagers. They were smiling, interlinked in a collective *cheese*, in cities like Venice, Madrid, Milan and Amsterdam. On the wall above her desk, by the window, was a framed certificate. DIPLOMA IN COGNITIVE THERAPY, it read, underneath which was written her name in an inky cursive scrawl. The date on it was just twelve months previously.

I quickly sat down on the sofa as she walked into the room.

'So,' she began, looking at me kindly but somewhat confused. 'If I remember correctly, you got married?'

'I *am* married.'

'You got married *before* having therapy?' Her mouth fell open, and I couldn't tell whether she was being funny or serious. 'Big mistake. Ha! Never mind. You are here now.'

I settled back and sipped at my scorching-hot coffee. She rearranged the smile on her face to mimic compassion and asked me now to tell her, in more detail this time, about what had happened in my life since getting married almost two years ago. I told her everything I thought she needed to know, and concluded by saying that I had gone on a date a week previously, nothing serious, just on a whim more than anything else.

'And where did you meet this man?' She was intrigued.

'A bar.'

'No no no. I am asking *how* did you meet this man? How did you find yourself in a situation of saying *yes* to being asked out on a date?'

I hesitated. 'I was looking on a chatroom – with a friend. It was just a bit of fun. And he, this guy, seemed . . . well, nice. He asked me out, and I thought why not? So I said yes.'

The psychotherapist brought her hands together in a steeple, both index fingers pushing at the skin between her nostrils, which pushed the bulb of her nose up and out until it resembled a snout. She did this several times until she sneezed, which may have been the objective all along. She told me that, deep down, my problem was an obvious one. I felt as if I didn't deserve my house, my husband and my contented life, and that I was now punishing myself accordingly, opening it all up to risk. She told me not to worry, that this was in fact common. 'We all deal with guilt, all of the time.' She told me that my mother sounded as if she needed a doctor herself, my mother being the likely root of all my deep-rooted problems, and that she could recommend one: her husband. He was expensive, she conceded, but he would be worth it. 'I think she might need help.' Did I want to put my mother in touch with him? If so, I could do so now. She stood up and offered me her cordless phone, which was big and green and plastic. I told her no, thank you, I would think about it, but that I would rather focus on *me* right now, if it was all the same to her.

'But your mother,' she said, almost pleading.

'Okay, fine,' I said, my voice rising, 'but right now I need to talk about *me*. With you.' I looked at the clock on the wall. I still had another fifteen minutes. 'Can we do that?'

She leaned back on her chair until it creaked, and stared blankly at me before allowing herself a smile. She clapped her hands once.

'Good! You are getting angry. It is good that you are getting angry with me now.' She leaned forward on to her desk. '*Progress!*'

Though now I couldn't say for sure why, I returned to see the psychotherapist a further eight times. Gradually, and so subtly at first that I never quite realized what she was doing, she came to do more and more of the talking, telling me about her husband, in relation both to my mother and also to herself. 'I am drawing parallels,' she pointed out once, but these parallels would become increasingly oblique to me as the sessions went on. She told me that she had been married a long time, over twenty years, and that they had endured a lot, 'but we are reaching the end of it together, and this I think is what is important.'

'The end?' I repeated. They were dying?

'Figure of speech, my dear.'

When I was permitted to talk, I often didn't want to stop. I cried energetically throughout every session. But the psychotherapist had one overriding goal, which was to reconnect me to my husband, to forgive him his at times selfish behaviour, and instead to see only the good in him while acknowledging the negative that sometimes lurked within me. 'You are a union, remember!' she'd say. She also encouraged me, time and again, to realize that there was a hole in my life, and that I should fill it in the way so many women did.

Elsewhere, Tyke was texting me almost every day and leaving messages on my voicemail. He wanted to meet again, to pick up where we had left off. He was proving persistent. I wanted to forget all about Tyke, to pretend he had never existed in the first place. And the best way to do this was to replace him. I found another website, gave myself another pseudonym – JL – and browsed hungrily. A man called Johnny Jay contacted me.

'Almost the same initials!' was his first message. 'There's got to be something in that?'

'One way to find out,' I responded.

A week later, dressed in another new set of lingerie and one of my wardrobe's most flattering dresses, I met him, as I had Tyke, at the train station. He was blond and handsome and impeccably dressed, thirty-one years old, and he towered over me. The rush-hour was dispersing all around us and we stood motionless in its midst. He hugged me, presented me with flowers and, rather forwardly I thought, leaned towards my cheek and gave a lingering kiss to one corner of my mouth. Though we hadn't exactly discussed it, I was expecting a meal – our date was early, 7 p.m. on a Thursday evening, conveniently clashing with a key football match for Andrew – but instead Johnny Jay took me to the pub on the train station concourse, where we sat at a table that afforded us a bird's-eye view of the milling commuters. It was cold, and I kept my coat on while he went to the bar. He came back with a couple of glasses and a bottle of fizzy wine.

He grinned. 'It was on offer.' From his jacket pockets he withdrew a couple of packets of barbecue-flavoured crisps.

He sat down not opposite me, but alongside, drawing his chair up close, one hand draped around my back and settled upon my hip. I gave him a look that I hoped would rein in his enthusiasm a bit, but was confronted with eyes alive with unstemmable mischievousness.

He told me, unbidden, that he used to be an actor, and that he was currently 'resting' (his quotation marks). Right now, he was modelling for the kind of clothing catalogues that came through people's front doors at Christmas time. Low-level stuff, he admitted, but the pay was good, and it left him with a lot of free time. He had had several walk-on parts in television dramas, a few minor roles in rep, and had been the face of a coffee advert in Austria. Had I ever been to Austria? He told me he didn't like

209

relationships, but freely confessed that he was hooked on the thrill of the chase. 'I like women, *a lot* of women.'

I had, then, what I can only describe as an out-of-body experience. I did not recognize the woman sitting next to him, this other version of me, tarted up and throwing herself at strangers. Had I really fallen for the charms of such a vain-glorious fool so easily during our webchats? Surely not. But then I recalled, with squirming embarrassment, that he had been just as gauche from his very first message, and even more so when we spoke on the phone, *me* calling *him*, and keying in a crucial 141 before doing so. We had had several filthy sessions, he coming across like a lurching Casanova who spoke only in porn cliché that got louder as we both reached our respective climaxes. I may have been tipsy at the time.

I was nowhere near tipsy now, and still could not believe that I was out on a date with someone who called himself Johnny Jay, and who sat with his legs quite so ostentatiously apart. His laughter was a horse's bray, and scattered munched crisps every-where, the hilarity prompted by his own unironic witticisms. It was this, I think, that convinced me I had entered a parallel universe and was now a quite different woman at forty than I had been at, say, thirty-eight.

'You do this a lot too, do you?' he asked.

'Do what?'

'*This*. Meet strange men from the internet for sex.'

'For sex?'

He laughed. 'Why else? For friendship? Ha!'

'Why, do you do it a lot?'

'All the time.'

I was about to ask him why such an obviously good-looking man would choose to meet women online when he could so easily do so in real life, when I realized that he actually very probably did both, and saw little discrepancy in either. When he wasn't out crawling bars for women, he was at home crawling internet sites for them.

'Let me guess. You're a novice?'

I nodded, and he grinned in a way that revealed to me every last tooth in his head. He leaned forward and placed an open palm high up my thigh. His hand was warm.

'I'm a very good teacher. Listen,' he said, and indicated with a jerk of the head for me to come closer. 'There's a little hotel I use just around the corner. Cheap. We could be there in five minutes.' He thrust his face into mine and kissed me. 'Got your credit card? Cash?'

I edged away from him and reached for my wine glass, but it was empty.

'I'm hard for you already. Want to feel?'

He looked like a boy not yet able to control the excitement he felt. Helplessly, I glanced between his legs and could see the outline of his penis flush against the tight denim of his jeans. His eyes grew wide as they took in mine watching him.

'Just let me go and freshen up,' I said.

'We can do that at the hotel. Some of the rooms have bathrooms.'

'No,' I said. 'Here.'

It was after eight o'clock and the bar area was packed. I was grateful for the smoking ban so that I would be able to leave this place and not take an ashtray stench with me. The toilets were by the staircase, which led back down and out on to the swarming concourse. I wondered whether Johnny Jay would be leaning over the bar rail to see if I was making my getaway, but even if he were, what would he have done: make chase? I left by the main exit and walked out into the rain.

There was a three-week gap between my penultimate and my last visit to Barbara. The psychotherapist had left a message on my voicemail telling me that she was unable to see me 'for a while', and would contact me again if and when she was. Another voicemail – left, alarmingly, in the middle of the night, when my phone was off – arrived a couple of weeks later, telling me that it would be business as usual this coming Wednesday if I was interested, and could I please text to confirm. Though I by now doubted that the woman was helping me in any tangible way, I did, and found myself looking forward to the looming appointment, something to peg the rest of my empty week on.

Barbara had changed. I saw this as soon as she opened the door. She looked older, beleaguered, defeated round the edges. There was no offer of coffee, and she led me into the front room in silence. Sitting behind her desk, she was agitated and distracted.

She would normally have asked me how my week was, but this time she announced that she wanted to talk to me about children.

'Again?'

Children, she ploughed on oblivious, are important, 'the *most* important'. Though she had already, in previous weeks, labelled me a control freak terrified of having children for the simple reason that it would upset the self-centred rhythm of my life, she insisted that my having a baby would help me achieve a happiness that was otherwise denied me. 'Children are the solution!' she cried, as if it were an advertising jingle. She began to tell me that just two years previously she had suffered a miscarriage, and that shortly afterwards her mother had died unexpectedly.

'You think about that for a moment,' she said. 'Think about your mother dying without you having made her a grandmother first. How would you feel about that?'

'I'd survive,' I replied truthfully.

'But Lucy, I really do think you should give the matter your full attention. I didn't want them once either, you know, but look at me now. They are my entire life! I know you have your doubts.' There were tears in her eyes. 'I understand your doubts. But jump in. With, as they say, both feet! It will give your life purpose! Focus! These things you need!'

I did not fully understand her hectoring and asked whether this was what psychotherapists were supposed to do: judge, encourage, coax and bully their patients? She laughed sourly.

'You expect me to be like psychotherapists on the television? Lucy, my dear, my darling, this is not television, this is real life. You are a middle-aged lady. Don't flinch. You *are*, more or less. And from what you tell me yourself, you haven't done very much in your life that you are happy with. This is why you are suffering! Because of this! And I am simply trying to show you a way out. This is why I ask you these two things over and over: think about having children; and send your mother to my husband.'

I emailed her that night explaining that I was unsure about the way my treatment was progressing, and that I wanted to take a few weeks to think things through before deciding whether to continue, but hoping, I added, somehow fearful that she might abandon me should I subsequently change my mind, that she would keep the door open.

I received no response.

Ten

When the inevitable happened at work, I suppose I should have been prepared for the news that I all along knew was coming. But I wasn't. I took it badly, and stumbled out into the lunchtime-busy streets afterwards in a fit of propulsive tears and bewilderment.

The economic crisis, I was told, was to blame. It was ongoing, and worsening. So very sorry. 'Those bloody bankers,' my boss lamented. It wasn't just me; it was three of us from our already anorexic team. We'd already each lost three days of the working week; now we would lose the final two. 'There's just no way round it, I'm afraid.' My boss willed upon us all a necessary stoicism. 'Be strong. Bounce back.'

At least, he added, we had the comfort of our redundancy packages. We were then asked to load up our personables and move out. The recent Oxbridge influx watched us go, feigning shock but glinting excitedly at the opportunities it threw up, the young usurping the old, the new New World Order setting down its roots and getting, for the time being, comfortable.

It was early April, but still cold outside, and the cold numbed me to further sensations. With my cardboard box under my arm, and my collar up, I stemmed the tears and walked the eight miles home. Dan, I knew, would likely be there to greet me. I was not looking forward to that.

'You might be depressed,' Andrew told me that evening, anxious at the sight of me fully dressed but already in bed at seven o'clock. 'Shall I make an appointment with the doctor?'

I slept for fourteen hours. I felt heavy, sluggish, but it wasn't necessarily an unpleasant sensation. It was a sensation that encouraged more sleep, and so I slept all afternoon, woke briefly in the early evening, and was then out again for the whole night and morning after. I went downstairs for breakfast and found Post-it notes from Andrew that I couldn't summon up the strength to read. By the time I opened the fridge, I was no longer hungry, and went straight back upstairs to bed. At some point on the third evening, the telephone rang. My mother. Andrew answered and took it upon himself to share my news with her. This was how I came to wake at some point on the fourth morning of my unemployment to find that a present had been sent, via Royal Mail, from my mother: a large cardboard box, its flaps sealed down with Sellotape. I searched for the scissors.

For all her inability to show me her maternal love, masking any emotions she may have felt for me with quips and criticism and scorn, the presents she would intermittently bestow upon me – often out of the blue and nowhere near my birthday – seemed to me to try to make up for this: underwear, spices, plants, ornaments. And now these: cushions. I opened the box to find two of them, both embroidered with flowers and, in their centre, homilies. One simply read LOVE, the other IT'S LOVE THAT MAKES A HOUSE A HOME.

These I brought up to my room with me, and placed them on the bed, where I spent most of the next week.

By Saturday, though, I felt better. Andrew was out somewhere – I'm sure he had told me beforehand, but I retained no memory of it – and I spent the day in the garden, gazing up at the blue, blue sky, breathing in the fresh air, and taking pride in the flowers that were now coming into bloom. By early evening

I was watching television when I heard his keys in the front door. He came into the living room, dressed in his full Ascot finery.

'You're up!' he said.

'I am.' I smiled. 'Good day?'

He came to give me a kiss on the cheek. There was no alcohol on his breath. This was unusual. I sat up, relieved.

'Where's Dan?'

Andrew looked almost excited. 'Surprise! He's found somewhere else, somewhere nearby. He moved in yesterday, took the rest of his stuff before we left today. Thanks for being so patient with him, Lucy. I appreciate it. He does too.'

'What time is it? Why are you home so early?'

'The race is over. I wanted to be with my wife.'

'Makes a change,' I snapped, instantly regretting my tone. 'A *nice* change, is what I meant.'

He went into the kitchen to make me some camomile tea. Over the past week, I had had more camomile tea, and more soup, than anyone could possibly want. My bladder was permanently full.

We spent the next day, a balmy Sunday, together. The pace was gentle, my husband's demeanour kind. He spoke to me slowly and gently, as if I were hard of hearing, or else so sensitive I might break. He seemed nervous around me, and anxious. We went for a light lunch around the corner, and then, because it wasn't too cold, for a walk through the neighbourhood's pretty park, something we had never done before. It was almost romantic, the pair of us sitting side by side on a weathered bench with the inscription *Alfred Carmichael & Ethel Carmichael: Together in Eternity*. I had a vision of Andrew at sixty-five and me at sixty-one, and decided that it didn't seem so bad, not really. He asked if I was cold, and for a moment I feared that if I said yes he would produce from nowhere a warm blanket to drape carefully over my knees.

We popped into the video shop on the way back, which was of course a video shop no more but instead full of Blu-ray discs and Xbox games. We returned home empty-handed and allowed ITV to entertain us into unquestioning submission. We had an early night, Andrew tucking me into my bed and, before he left, planting a dry kiss on my forehead.

'Goodnight,' he said.

'Goodnight,' I replied.

I could have screamed.

I exerted, at first, a lot of effort on my recuperation. I began by arranging my days into chunks in the hope of keeping myself sufficiently busy that I would no longer feel a compulsion to stray. I was adamant to turn a corner; there would be no more Tykes in my life, no more JJs, or anybody else. I was restrained on my laptop, and used my iPhone only to make and receive calls. My monthly bills shrank.

Each morning I would rise to make Andrew's breakfast and see him off to work. I would feed Rummy, retrieve him from his cage and allow him the run of the living room. Three mornings a week I would spend at the gym on the various instruments of torture to be found there, and on other mornings I would go through the house tidying up things I'd already tidied the previous day.

Patricia, next door, was now working from home full-time, another victim of the economic crisis. She spent her days chasing freelance graphic design gigs and refusing to be down-hearted. 'I've got Poppy to feed; I must remain positive.' Over the garden fence one morning she asked if I fancied joining her for coffee and cake, 'the necessary indulgences of those on the home front.' She grinned.

I arrived expecting it to be just me and her, but found her

hallway cluttered with prams. In the kitchen I was introduced to several local mothers, whose infants crawled noisily around the floor. They were women who had once had high-flying careers now temporarily sequestered exclusively in motherhood. Some took this fact better than others, and those who didn't advertised the fact loudly. They were smart and funny (and none of them asked me why I didn't have any children myself, Patricia having presumably forewarned them before my arrival), but they were bonded by a common theme, and it was difficult not to feel outside that. Friendships were harder to create the older you got.

On a typical day, I would more often than not forget lunch, my appetite vanished, my midriff grateful for it, and instead would spend my lunch hour and beyond online, scouring the internet not for men but rather work. I had been told by several former colleagues, now unemployed themselves, that there might be some freelance production work out there somewhere; you just had to seek it out. With a microscope, it seemed. I could never find any.

On a whim, I enrolled in adult education classes, and twice a week studied Introductory Italian at a community college. There were perhaps half a dozen ladies in the class, all in their late forties and early fifties, and who dressed in clothes I could never afford but all too easily admired. Over coffee and rich cakes in the café across the road afterwards, they would tell me that they had been on the adult educational circuit for the past few years now, and that it was 'ever so much fun'. Like the Racing Widows, they had husbands who were consumed by their work and themselves, and children who were old enough no longer to need them full-time. In the past year alone they had studied French, English literature and screenwriting together. I asked them what they hoped to do with all this knowledge, but they looked at me as if the question were nonsensical. They offered no answer.

Sometimes I would travel into town afterwards and wander through a museum or gallery, shamed by the realization that a great many of them I was visiting for the first time. Such places were magnets for the single and the unemployed. There were so many of us now, each of us victims of the financial climate, and all with time on our hands – time spent, if not at museums and galleries, then at matinee performances inside otherwise empty cinemas. On several occasions we would catch each other's eye across an empty floor and we would smile in humbling recognition before moving off, very deliberately, in separate directions.

I'd arrive home each day shortly before six. If Andrew didn't have a works event in the evening, I would cook us dinner. If he did, I would cook for myself and stew in front of the television until he came home. He rarely arrived later than ten, and no longer came home drunk. He had become docile and domesticated, and doted on me like a dog. Never once did he make overtures towards sex, seemingly content for us to pass our evenings in uncomplicated inactivity.

We never really argued either, but in time I'd have done anything to make sparks fly. Trouble was, I could never find anything tangible to clash over. Our relations had become *nice* – a hideous, insidious, ruinous word in certain circumstances. Nevertheless, at the end of the day, *nice* did provide a certain comfort out of which I couldn't quite navigate myself. I had the intent, certainly, but not the necessary follow-through. I was becoming stagnant.

I had my first Introductory Italian exam eight weeks later, and passed with a respectable score. In the café with my fellow students afterwards, I could now *chiedere* for a cappuccino with confidence and *complemento* the waiter on his pleasant *contegno*. But he had no idea what I was saying. Despite what his cheekbones suggested to us, he wasn't Italian at all. He was Slovenian.

I could, I suppose, have gone to Italy and tested my novel fluency there. I used to like Italian men; perhaps I still would. I liked the idea of a weekend alone in Venice or Rome, a shopping trip to Milan. It was a plan, a plan that, like so many others, would no doubt fritter away, and which soon enough I would forget all about.

The motherly coffee mornings, meanwhile, were becoming more difficult to face, and most times I would sit there smiling wanly, feeling increasingly lost in their company. The women naturally talked an awful lot about motherhood, often to the exclusion of anything else. I felt my presence hindered them in some way. The heavy sluggishness of depression was returning. I wanted only to sleep.

My days lost all sense of shape and form, and I began more and more to drift. I stopped going to Patricia's for coffee. I decided not to enrol for Intermediary Italian, Venice and Rome a lingering pipe-dream well out of reach. I allowed my annual gym membership to lapse, and fell helplessly back into old ways and bad habits, losing myself to the online world I thought I'd left behind. I began to hate so much in the house, finding fault where before had been only perfection: in the skirting boards, the doorknobs, the choice of Venetian blinds, the colour of the bathroom tiles. I found plenty to argue over with Andrew now, sniping at him endlessly over dinner and deliberately hiding the remote control. I was petty and ugly. I lost my remaining friends, never now responding to their calls, their texts. Self-pity is rarely pretty; mine was hideous. I could cry for hours, unprompted, sometimes loudly, sometimes silently, the tears endless, generating themselves tirelessly from who knew where inside me.

'Your eyes are very puffy these days,' Andrew said to me one night. It was 10.43, a Wednesday, which left us just two minutes until he made his nightly overtures. In my head I counted from one to sixty, and then again: 10.45, on the button. Responding instantly to his body clock, he stood and yawned and rubbed his eyes. He picked up his phone and his *Racing Post*, then looked down on me, eyebrows arranged empathetically across his brow.

'You should wear make-up,' he encouraged. 'It suits you.'

I listened to his footsteps up the stairs, so untroubled and unsuspecting, Andrew yet again leaving me to my own devices. I couldn't decide whether this was because he trusted me implicitly, or because he had long since stopped caring. It had been a long time, after all, since I felt that Andrew actively cared – an accusation, I knew too well, he could just as accurately level at me.

A wave of remorse passed over me again, so very familiar by now. When I started out doing all this, I thought I was somehow adhering to a slightly higher moral ground – distraction not divorce – but the lines were becoming increasingly blurred. I knew what I was doing was wrong, and that my actions were hardly fostering decent prospects for any long-term happiness Andrew and I may yet have been striving for. But every time I reassessed the situation, and decided that Andrew wasn't so bad after all, and that it was solely myself at fault, something else would happen to change my mind.

A few days previously, he had come home from work late and in a distracted mood. In a wifely desire to be good, I had made him dinner, a recipe from one of the under-employed cookbooks on the shelves, my efforts, I hoped, to act as a peace offering.

He came into the kitchen with a plastic carrier bag heavy with two bottles of Scotch. The meal – a lemon and thyme chicken casserole – was already steaming on the table. He managed to both look at it and ignore it completely.

'Lucy, why don't you pick up the flyers from the doormat?' he asked me. He held four of them in his hand, advertising local pizza and curry houses. They'd arrived, as they did several times a week, at some point in the afternoon. 'It pisses me off that I have to come home to them every day, you know?'

I had no idea what he was talking about. They had never bothered him before.

He loosened his tie and retrieved one of the bottles of Scotch from his carrier bag.

'I mean, for fuck's sake,' he said, sighing. '*Christ*.'

I watched him pour his drink, then as he reached for the freezer door in search of ice.

'There's no ice,' he told me impatiently.

'I'll make some after supper,' I said, indicating the meal in front of him.

He looked at it properly now, and shook his head. 'I'm not in the mood.' He sauntered off into the living room, taking the glass and the bottle, but no ice, with him.

We never picked at the stitches of this particular confrontation afterwards, largely because we never revisited the scene of most of our arguments. They settled quickly, for Andrew at least, dissolving into nothing more than the fabric of our marriage, some rough, some smooth. But they never completely dissolved for me, and so whenever the guilt resurfaced I had only to recall one of these frequent episodes to relocate my resolve. I was doing what I was doing because, ultimately, I wasn't happy.

I wasn't happy.

Eleven

Old habits die hard, they say. But they die all the harder if you've nothing to replace them with. My life that summer had opened up into the emptiest chasm. I was going slightly but undeniably mad, and had started, latterly, to talk to myself. But then somebody had to.

When I reasserted myself on my laptop, then, it had felt as if I were reacquainting with an old friend. Life as I had known it had quickly returned in the typed words on the screen, and I had gone straight to my private messages on the forum where it all began, unchecked now for almost two months. I'd had visions that there would be hundreds of messages waiting for me, all manner of hairy, under-employed men desperate for a little L27/JL/JuicyLucy magic. There were just seven. Nobody bothers an inactive account when there are so many active ones vying for attention. Two were spam. One was from a man called DRRTY D4VE, two from Ben, one from the long-forgotten helicopter pilot. I decided to leave Ben's till last.

'U cum highly reccomended!' wrote DRRTY D4VE. 'Me 2!'

'Fly the friendly skies?' the helicopter pilot wondered elliptically.

A wave of over-familiar ennui washed over me. Did I really have the strength to go through all this again? Had I really no better way of passing my days? I deleted both.

The seventh was from somebody called Sue.

Sue: Hello Juicy. It's Friday night and I have had a couple of glasses of medium white, I'm a bit bored, and so I idly looked at your profile because I liked your name. And what do I see but the most beautiful boobs ever! Thank you, is all I can say . . .

I had forgotten about the boobs. Sue was referring to a night months ago when, frustrated with Ben's endless prevarications, tired of the chef's meaningless witterings, and slightly sad that my university professor from America had stopped contacting me, I'd taken a grainy colour photograph of my tight T-shirted chest, decapitating me at the neck in pursuit of anonymity, and posted it alongside a minimal description of myself as a woman up for it. I had called myself, though now I struggled to remember quite why, Juicy.

The message from Sue had been sent a couple of weeks previously and I toyed with responding now. It was a Friday night, after all; I was back online whether I liked it or not; and I craved the spice of human interest. Maybe a woman would be better. I wrote that I had been away and had just come back to her message. If she was ever around for a chat, I typed . . . and then, because I didn't know how to finish the sentence, I left it as it was. I clicked SEND.

She responded immediately, offering more dispiriting proof that some of us at least were online, and poised, all the time, day or night, reaching out and forever hoping to grasp at something if not quite real, then at least virtual.

Sue: Hey, Juicy! Nice to hear from you! So, yes, another Friday night, and I've got another bottle open. I thought perhaps I'd offended you by contacting you, a woman contacting another

224

woman on a site for straights?? But, hey, it's all just a little fun, right? You are straight, I'm guessing? Me, I'm a bit of both. Perhaps you've read some of my stories on the erotic forum? Mostly fiction, I'm afraid to say!

I quickly browsed one of her stories and was pleasantly surprised. It was good and, if fictitious, nevertheless full of very specific detail. I responded, and said as much.

Sue: Well, I suppose at least some of it is based on reality. ☺ I did see my flatmate masturbating once, although in very different circumstances, and I have to say I almost fainted! It was so unexpectedly exciting! Ever since, I have loved to watch men and women play with themselves, and I love to be watched myself, although only by women. I'm very strict about that! It doesn't happen very often, me being watched, I'm afraid [long sigh], but when it does – wow! I'm single at the moment, and have been for almost a year now. If it wasn't for my fingers, I'd be a desert down there!
Sue: Oops, TMI??

She asked if I had Skype. I did, but then I abruptly remembered Ben's messages, still waiting for me. Ben hadn't emailed me direct for months, and neither had he called or texted. The fact that he was now messaging me on the website neither of us had communicated via since first hooking up didn't bode well. Nevertheless, it suddenly became imperative to see what he had to say for himself.

Juicy: Sorry, can I get back to you later? Something has just come up.
Sue: ☹ Sure!!

His first message was an intriguing one: 'CONFLICTED'. The second, in lower case, managed two words: 'forgive me'.

Perhaps I was emotional, premenstrual, habitually low, but this left me confused, and out of confusion rose anger. How was I supposed to decipher or decode what *forgive me* meant? Was it so hard for people online to say what they really wanted? And what, exactly, was he craving forgiveness for? For bottling out, for messing me about? For disappearing from my life? I wondered, fretfully, whether this wasn't perhaps a cry for help, a suicide note even. Surely not?

I checked the date. It had been sent a week and a half ago. I reached for my phone, keyed in 141, and punched in his number manually. I still knew his digits by heart; I always would. He answered on the first ring, an emotionless 'Hello.' Neither happy nor sad. But alive. I hung up.

I had previously resolved to put Ben out of my mind for ever, and out of my life for good, but my resolve always was weak.

Falling back in contact with him, picking up from where we had left off, proved disarmingly easy, and once again we were in daily contact. I'd had a similar relationship with smoking, although it was easier to quit the cigarettes.

It was another average weekday night, an uneventful dinner at home before the invariable early night to bed, to sleep. Andrew was in the kitchen disposing of the remains of our meal. I could hear the plates scraping and the wine glasses being stacked in the dishwasher. I had asked him repeatedly not to put the new wine glasses into the dishwasher; they smudge. But he never did remember. I could hear him whistle as he worked, and though his whistling never did approach any recognizable tune, he sounded, as Andrew so frequently did, uncomplicatedly content. No mention had been made of the latest argument, nothing too serious, a two out of a possible five on the Richter scale, but it was still brooding inside me. He ran up the four steps that took him from our kitchen through to the living room, where I was sitting on our plump white sofa. He swooped in and gave me a chaste peck on the cheek as if we were, to all intents and purposes, a happy couple unhindered by simmering, lingering resentments.

'What are you doing?' he asked.

I could smell the hoisin sauce on him. Red wine stained his lips. He sat beside me, his full weight causing the cushions to lift me up into the air, the laptop almost falling from my knees.

He had brought with him another bottle of wine and two clean glasses. He poured, and handed one to me. It was shortly before ten o'clock, a Wednesday night that could have been mistaken for any other Wednesday night.

Seeing me return my attention to my laptop, he began to scroll earnestly through Sky+ with all the concentration of a man operating heavy machinery. He asked if there was anything I wanted to watch, and when I failed again to respond, he cued up the Channel 4 racing he had taped earlier in the day, despite the fact that he already knew the outcome of each race.

Gazing into the laptop's glowing screen, I started typing.

Andrew spoke again.

'What are you doing?'

'Shopping.'

'But the fridge is full.'

'Clothes.'

'But your wardrobe's full!'

He laughed, and waited for me to do so too. Then he turned back to the television.

Lucy: Hi!
Paranoidandroid: can you talk?
Lucy: sort of.

Paranoidandroid: I miss you. Have you had a good night?

Lucy: same old same old.

Paranoidandroid: you sound sad.

Lucy: not sad, just frustrated, I guess.

Paranoidandroid: I *do* like a frustrated housewife . . .

Lucy: which means you'll come and whisk me away, r[ight?

Lucy: Sorry, there's no [in 'right'.

Paranoidandroid: are you drunk?

Lucy: tipsy.

Paranoidandroid: i like you tipsy. Drink more. Do it for me.

'Andrew, I think I'll have another glass, please. I like this one.'

Andrew was sat leaning forward when I glanced over at him, both hands curled into fists between which he was clutching an imaginary bridle and winning the 4.10 at Epsom. He broke off to refill my glass, and then his own.

Lucy: I'm doing it now. But I think it's making me too tipsy to be talking to you.

Paranoidandroid: all the better to take advantage of you . . .

Lucy: this is true.

Paranoidandroid: what are you wearing?

Lucy: not very glamorous, I'm afraid. Black skirt, black tights, grey top. If you could see me, you'd probably think I just got back from a funeral.

Paranoidandroid: ah, but women in mourning are very attractive . . .

Lucy: I'm definitely a morning woman. Last thing at night, too

Paranoidandroid: you just left off the full stop! Very unlike you, Miss. Grammar

Lucy: like I said, tipsy. Normal rules do not apply

Lucy: FULL STOP.

Ben usually typed quickly. If a response didn't ping back within seconds, then he was planning to say something bold. I knew him well by now, and I loved these tantalizing silences, the stretching of seconds, the knowledge that I would like whatever it was he was preparing to say. I reached again for my glass of wine.

Paranoidandroid: i dare you to take off your skirt. just stand up and shimmy out of it. Tell your husband you're hot, or something – but don't let him touch you. i don't want him touching you.
Lucy: little chance of that.

I was tempted to do as he bade, but couldn't. I didn't want to flaunt my cyber affair quite so cruelly in front of my husband. And so, tucking my laptop under my arm, I stood up. Andrew, distracted, dragged his eyes from the racing and laid them, briefly, on me. I sought some kind of emotion on his face, as if to give me reason to stay, but in vain.

'Going to bed?' he asked, checking his watch.

'Yes. I'm tired. See you in the morning.'

His eyes lingered on me only briefly, then he turned back to the television.

So much of what happened online was fantasy, I did not need to let Ben know that I was now upstairs, in private. He wanted to play a game here, and in my own way I wanted to play too, albeit in comfort, in my pyjamas, the pyjamas I would never let him see were he and I ever to meet.

Paranoidandroid: have you done it yet? i'm waiting.
Lucy: I have.
Paranoidandroid: what was your husband's reaction?
Lucy: My husband is watching television.
Paranoidandroid. You're wasted on him! I want you to describe

to me your tights. Can you see the outline of your knickers beneath? . . . Are you wearing any knickers?

An hour passed, in the way that hours online always do: in the blink of an eye. I looked up to the clock on the wall and saw suddenly that it was almost eleven. Outside my door came sounds of my husband climbing the stairs, bound for the bathroom first, and then bed. I knew he would not come in to bid me goodnight. But just in case, I closed the laptop and tucked it under the duvet. The five minutes it took him to prepare for bed before actually getting into bed lasted an age, but then all of a sudden he was out, snoring away.

Paranoidandroid: are you still there?
Paranoidandroid: hope so. ☹
Lucy: I'm still here.
Paranoidandroid: it's gone 10.45. has he gone to bed yet?
Lucy: he has. Shall I remove my tights now?
Paranoidandroid: wish I could, personally. With my teeth.
Lucy: Come over, then. He's already fast asleep, and will be till sunup. Can't you hear him snore?
Paranoidandroid: it would take me hours!
Lucy: I'm going nowhere, Ben. *Run!*

Was this too needy of me? The lack of an immediate response suggested I had, once again, shocked him. I quickly typed out another message.

Lucy: give me a few minutes. I'm going upstairs to my room to get more comfortable.
Paranoidandroid: ☺ comfortable's good.
Paranoidandroid: you still there?
Paranoidandroid: or have you abandoned me? Perhaps you've

fallen asleep?

Paranoidandroid: or perhaps you're having sex with your husband?!

Lucy: I'm here now. And, no, no sex with my husband.

Paranoidandroid: does he suspect us, do you think?

Lucy: what is there to suspect?

Paranoidandroid: you know what I mean.

Lucy: would you like him to?

Paranoidandroid: I'm not sure . . .

Lucy: well, he doesn't.

This wasn't strictly true, but Ben needn't know this yet.

Paranoidandroid: praps just as well. i never was much of a fighter.

Lucy: yes, perhaps just as well.

Paranoidandroid: i hope I'm not ruining your marriage.

Lucy: do you?

Paranoidandroid: ☺ well, perhaps not! but i am, after all, the younger man here. It should be you leading me astray . . . But then I instigate a lot of it, don't I?

Lucy: you instigate as much as I permit you to, young man.

Paranoidandroid: you are beginning to turn me on.

Paranoidandroid: and I'm getting tempted to ask you to meet me in person, in the flesh. We could go for dinner, or something

Lucy: just dinner?

Paranoidandroid: you can have dessert as well, if you insist.

Lucy: you've been suggesting this for a long time now, Ben.

Paranoidandroid: I know, I know . . .

I started to cry. One of the benefits of keeping this strictly, or at least mostly, textual, with no webcams, was that I could cry as

231

much as I liked while we conversed, and Ben would remain none the wiser.

> Paranoidandroid: i think I'm worried about the risk . . . The questionable morality of it all . . . I know we shouldn't be doing this. I feel like a terrible person.
> Lucy: I don't think you're a terrible person.
> Paranoidandroid: and then i feel guilty, and i can't sleep, and i torture myself, and

I sighed. We had been here before, many times, and we returned to this territory increasingly as our relationship progressed, Ben so often afraid to engage fully with the real world. It disappointed me, and upset me because I found myself wanting more than just his messages. I wanted to meet him, to be with him. But then I was drawn to his crises of confidence too, and the fact that he never hid them from me. By failing to hide behind a concocted bravado, Ben was the first real man I'd ever met online.

When I first encountered him, the best part of a year before, it was on one of the websites that specialized in erotic stories. This was not a site for people who wanted quick relief over garish bedroom photographs, but for people who craved, I suppose, a slightly higher form of smut. The stories were often witty and well done, and genuinely arousing. They could run on for pages, those writers unable to find publishers for their X-rated Mills & Boon stuff effortlessly finding hundreds, if not thousands, of readers here.

Ben was not only one of the writers, but was also to be found lurking within the message boards, those margins where readers would gather to swap stories not merely about their own experiences in erotica, but also the state of their relationships, their hopes and fears, a surprising number of those posting offering mutual support and encouragement. This always fascinated me: they'd come in for sex, and leave with friendships. Ben's posts, in which he related his relationship problems, and what it was like to be back living with his parents, were sweet and funny and rather soulful, and made him, for me at least, stand out. I clicked on to his personal profile, liked what I read, and then dared send him a private message. His response was immediate, and within a few exchanges he was suggesting that, 'if I didn't find it too forward', perhaps we could swap personal email addresses. I set up a Hotmail account immediately, under a pseudonym (not my first, and by no means my last), and we were soon in a room of our own. Privacy.

Our conversations were not sexual at first, but rather the kind any two people would indulge in when still trying to get to know one another. Each of us was keen not to overstep any invisible boundary; we were ridiculously polite with one another, and wary. We blushed easily. He told me I reminded him of an old teacher of his, his first crush. I responded that he was the son I never had, then promptly took it back. 'Crikey, just how old are you???' he teased. We were connecting on a sweetly simplistic, even romantic level. Which books do you like? Which films? What is your favourite colour? Your dreams, your hopes?

We messaged each other once or twice a week, and then once or twice a day, and then every day, and then every night. The messages became increasingly passionate, and sexual. I began to care for him, and it seemed he cared for me too.

One time, exchanging messages well into the middle of the night, and me at least fairly drunk on red wine (it helped the nerves), he said that he wanted to hear my voice again, that he had fantasized about it endlessly since that time we first spoke. I admitted that I wanted to hear his again too.

Although at one time I had vowed to myself that this was a line I would never cross – no pictures, no webcams, no phone

233

numbers ever given out; diversion not divorce – for Ben I had made an exception. I had agreed then that he could save my number. Moments later my phone had vibrated. With my husband's snores singing in the room next door, I snatched it up and answered it. My voice shook. His own whispered response – just two syllables, *He-llo* – left me unaccountably excited.

'Well hello,' I said again, unsure quite what to say next.

'I don't know what to say next,' he said.

I smiled. 'Well, that's a start.'

'It is. Um. Okay, your turn.'

The awkwardness had soon mellowed out, and we talked like teenagers – a recent reality for him, ancient history for me. Before either of us really knew it, we'd overcome our nerves altogether, and suddenly our mutual desire tumbled forth. My very first attempt at phone sex with Ben. He had made me come in a single minute; I hardly had to touch myself. Never before had I experienced such racing excitement.

But the post-coital aftermath reverted us promptly back to awkwardness, neither knowing how to follow it, both aware again that we were strangers, strangers who had just, in a manner of speaking, had sex. I felt myself pining for a cigarette.

'I'll . . . That was nice,' he stuttered. 'Thank you. I'll say good-night now.'

Our messages for a full week afterwards had gone back to kind and timid – confirmation, surely, that the sex had been a mistake; too fast, too much, too soon. Though both of us, of course, knew that the timing had been perfect, and that once we got over ourselves, we would be doing it again, and again, and again.

Before long, I was not only in lust with the boy, I wanted to protect him. He was vulnerable, in so many ways, and for so many reasons. He was bringing out in me a maternal instinct I didn't even know I had, and the irony was not lost on me. Here

I was in a virtual world looking for a mate, ideally someone younger – someone younger, went my logic, would be less complicated, and less of a threat to my marriage – and instead I'd found a son to mother.

I would like to suggest that I can't remember precisely everything we wrote to one another that night when we were back once again talking about the possibility of meeting up, but that would be a lie. Not only do I remember it with clarity, but I have the entire transcript saved in the Messenger archive. By six o'clock the following morning, the summer sun starting to peek between the curtains making me abruptly aware of the time, we had reached a kind of impasse.

Paranoidandroid: so when is he next going to the races?

Lucy: this weekend.

Paranoidandroid: and he'll be out all day?

Lucy: all night, too. Won't be back until Sunday.

Paranoidandroid: so if we wanted to meet you'd have no interruptions? You wouldn't need to be anywhere else?

Lucy: None whatsoever.

Paranoidandroid: what's stopping us, then?

Lucy: Your admirable sense of propriety?

Paranoidandroid: it's six o'clock in the morning. i've lost all morals.

Lucy: what's stopping us, then?

Paranoidandroid: nothing! let's do it!

A minute later, another message came.

Paranoidandroid: oh, actually, it may be difficult this weekend. i . . . you know . . . oh. ☹

235

By this stage in our relationship, I had come to recognize Ben's cold feet all too well. Each time he suggested us meeting, he would later retract it and then disappear for a period, as he had now. And then we would start over, from the very beginning again. Clearly, we would never actually get to meet unless one of us affected direct action.

And it wouldn't be him.

So it would have to be me. This was no surprise. I must have known all along where that weakness of mine would lead me.

To here, to Bristol. The hot shame brought on by what I was about to do did not prompt in me any second thoughts; I was too far gone for reality checks, for sensible behaviour. By this stage in my descent, whatever was going to happen next already felt written, done, fate.

I took a train out west, telling Andrew I was going to visit an old friend. I had a whole backstory prepared just in case, but he didn't ask. It was high summer, the end of July, and as close to reliably clement as Britain got. I wore a floaty dress that, if the sun hit it direct, seemed transparent. It was for this reason, I concluded, that the Rigby & Peller combination underneath had been a worthy investment. I took a book with me for the journey, but couldn't concentrate, so I sat back in my seat as the train leaned into the curves and brought the city closer to me by the minute. I was eager to get there.

I had been busy, and efficient in my detective work. I had scrolled through the hundreds of conversations we had had, all saved in the Messenger archive, and re-read them. Early on, he had told me that he had recently graduated, and had also told me from which university, and from which course. I looked at his university online and found footage, subsequently posted on YouTube, of his graduation. Two minutes into the surprisingly professional six-minute film – it boasted opening and closing credits – Ben's face came into view. A name appeared in subtitles beneath him, and it wasn't 'Ben'. At first I was shocked and offended by this, that he had masqueraded under a false name for so long now, but then this was hypocritical of me. He knew me by Lucy, and Lucy wasn't my real name, either. It was definitely him; I recognized his face, his voice. He was speaking enthusiastically about graduating and his hopes for the future. He looked so innocent, so optimistic. And so beautiful.

Next, I Googled his real name and found that he had contributed to a website of amateur poetry and short stories. His upbeat but modestly crafted biography read: '*I like my poetry – all the usual suspects – and my literature, and I occasionally write my own stuff. But mostly I'm training to become an English teacher to, God help me, teenagers.* I found a link to his Twitter page and was surprised to find he had quite a following for such a loner: over 600. He tweeted regularly, and mostly between what seemed to be a wide network of graduates and fellow trainee teachers. Most of the posts concerned rare job opportunities and frontline missives from those already employed, the majority of them in inner-city schools and regretting their career choice: *The kids are hell. Wish I'd trained as a plumber instead!* But he also tweeted about general things: an album he'd just bought, a new novelist he'd just discovered, and indulged in the occasional haiku: *Burdened with qualifications/Now burdened upon society/Tea, anyone?*

I revisited his Twitter page half a dozen times a day, an entirely different side of his character unravelling to me over 140 characters. I hung on his every entry. One spoke about an upcoming poetry reading that some old friends of his were putting on, an open mic night for anyone 'with verse inside them'.

'Free wine!' he wrote. 'While it lasts!! It's an open-door policy, so bring your friends, the more the merrier!!'

This was, then, an invitation. I booked my train ticket immediately.

*

The train pulled into the station mid-afternoon, three hours before the reading began. This was fine by me; I needed some time to compose myself. I sat amongst the soft furnishings of an arty independent café and nursed a large caramelized hot drink until it turned cold, watching streams of young people glide past the front window, their pale skin soaking up the hot sun.

I found the venue, a small bar, easily. A six o'clock start meant, in reality, 6.30–7.00. It was empty save for some early arrivals and two bored bar staff. Half a dozen more were gathered outside, all smoking furiously, and frequently casting furtive gazes up the street to see if anybody was approaching. The moment somebody did, they dropped their cigarettes to the ground and bustled inside. I stood at a safe distance, on the opposite side of the road, desperate to catch my first glimpse of him. My body coursed with all the caramelized sugar, and adrenalin.

I did several slow circuits of the block until, eventually, more people began to arrive, one after the other, and pretty soon the small space was filling up. I crossed over to it now and followed as four people went in. There was a young woman standing at the door with a tray and I helped myself to a glass of red wine. Tinie Tempah, I think, cawed from an iPod mounted on a small but powerful set of speakers. I still hadn't seen him, Ben, but there was a crush of people now, and I was in no particular hurry, wanting to relish the moment, to stretch it out and make it last. I stood halfway between the bar and a small makeshift stage in the far corner. On it was a lone microphone stand, its lead trailing off towards a wall.

Several people surrounded me now, all in their twenties, wafting the combining aromas of their recently extinguished cigarettes, perfume and aftershave. I watched a series of complicated handshakes take place, and heard cries of 'Long time no see'. Looking at so many of the young men here, I had to fight the temptation to hike up their jeans for them before they slid from their snake hips altogether and ended up in a denim puddle between their shoes.

Others were standing off a little from the crowd, determinedly by themselves, gazes focused intently on the sheets of paper they held in their hands and upon which, presumably, were scribbled the poems and short stories later to be read in public. It was going to be a long evening.

I turned around, and suddenly there he was. Standing perhaps ten feet away from me, Ben – or *Jake*, his real name – in the flesh, at last. He was holding a glass of champagne in his right hand and talking to a woman. I heard his voice, and watched as he rearranged the flop in his fringe. My veins flooded with something powerful.

More people joined him, three, four, old friends clearly, from university. He was taller than I had imagined him, six feet at least, and he was wearing clothes that marked out his calling in life as a self-conscious creative type: battered Converse trainers, skinny jeans that hung low on bony hips, threadbare T-Rex T-shirt and, over that, a pinstriped suit jacket, probably Oxfam-purchased, and coming artfully apart at the hem. His face was bright and fresh and eager, his hair deliberately wild, his skin so very smooth. *I* was more likely to grow a beard than he was. His eyes were deep brown, and when he smiled his lips parted to reveal neat, orderly teeth.

Would he recognize me? The sole photo he had seen of me to date had been blurred, my hair tumbling over my face enough to make me, in person, unrecognizable. Plus, my hair was different these days, shorter. And, if I was honest about it, newly dyed as well. More grey had been starting to show through.

I needed another glass of wine, and went promptly to get it. The bar was throbbing now with the unfettered glee of a student union. It was difficult not to feel old in such company, but I

239

drank from my glass, my teeth sharp against the rim, and then walked forward, suddenly bold.

From the stage came the howl of feedback. I looked up and saw a young face under a maelstrom of hair, a good-looking young boy in thick, tortoiseshell glasses.

'Is this thing on?' he queried, tapping at it. 'Can everybody hear me?'

A reciprocal roar made him take two steps back. He smiled. He introduced himself, then laughed nervously as he declared the start of this bar's inaugural – and, as it would turn out, final – open mic night for recent graduates of the English Lit degree course. There would be at least a dozen scheduled readings, he explained, and if anybody else wanted to recite something impromptu, then, well, it was an open mic night, so come on up.

'A couple of agents and the odd publisher may be in the crowd,' he said, causing everyone to swivel their necks in hope of spotting them, 'so give it your best shot.'

I expected, perhaps unfairly, to be bored rigid within minutes, but the stories and the poems were beguiling and funny and rather charming. Even the ones that didn't quite work were rendered endearing by the red-cheeked enthusiasm of their delivery.

Ben was the sixth person to go up on stage, pushed up there by two friends. He stood in the lone spotlight, blushing furiously, his fringe falling over his face. He cleared his throat, unsuccessfully. He cleared it again. He looked up, directly into the microphone and then out into the crowd, and if I could have drifted up there – by osmosis, by the sheer propulsion of my love – to offer succour and encouragement, then I would have. My heart was in my throat.

'Um,' he began. 'This is . . . well, it's a sort of poem. It's called "In Every Sunflower".'

He read with quiet purpose for two minutes, two minutes that flew by in seconds, the blink of an eye, and I drank every word he spoke deep down inside me, where they fizzed and bloomed and resonated. I'd like to say that the poem was about me, was *for* me, and that I alone understood its oblique references. But in truth I had no idea what it was about. I liked it, though. And that's all that mattered.

Placing my empty wine glass under my arm, I clapped perhaps a little too loudly, bringing unwanted attention from those around me. As he left the stage, several people came up to me asking if I was an agent, and may they have my card, my email, and would I mind terribly reading their manuscript?

It was all over by nine o'clock, the student-union ambience resuming in earnest. By now on to my third wine, I cast around the place until I spotted him, on the periphery of a circle of friends, laughing at something being said by somebody else.

Now or never, I thought, as I lurched forward.

'I like your poem,' I told him.

He looked at me, looked *down* at me, my head at his shoulder height, and smiled. 'Thank you!' he said. He began slowly to squint. Could he hear the hammer of my heartbeat? 'Have we met?'

'I'm here with—' I pointed, 'with a friend. We were just passing. She's over there. I thought we'd come and see what this was all about. You know?'

The squint frowned. 'Oh, right. Right. Good. So you liked it? My poem?'

'I—'

'Jake? *Jake!* Laurence has arrived.'

Ben turned to face a tall girl with perfect skin. '*Really?*' He sounded excited. 'Where?' She began to lead him by the hand away from me. Over his shoulder, he called to me, 'Laters,' and was swallowed by the crowd.

I was about to move off to somewhere, anywhere, when a man

appeared at my shoulder, a man, like me, older than most of the others here. Judging by his suit, he was a professional. He had a glass of red wine in his hand, clearly not his first. His lips were already stained from the previous glassful. His tongue, too. An agent, surely.

'So, what did you think?'

I shrugged, and smiled. 'I liked them. I thought they were . . . touching.'

'But derivative as well.'

'Um, I don't know, really . . .'

He grinned. 'Apologies. I tend towards the critical.'

'Well, it's true some were better than others. I particularly liked,' I said, but before I could recall the title of Ben's poem, he smiled, nodded impatiently, and clinked his glass with mine. 'Alistair.'

'Bernadette.'

'Irish Catholic?'

'Second generation.'

'Me too.'

'With a name like Alistair?'

'My mother had a thing for the Scots.'

'I see. So, why are you here? Friend or agent?'

'Neither. I'm a lecturer at the university. This lot,' he said, indicating with a careless nod of his head everyone in the vicinity, 'used to be mine last year.'

I asked what he taught, and he answered English Literature.

'Half of them want to be writers, the other half – those who realize they'll never get to *be* writers – to follow in my hallowed footsteps. I keep telling them they are too young, to go out and discover themselves, the world, before they teach. But do they listen?'

'And should they?'

'To me?' He affected a look of outraged horror. 'Of course!'

'Why are they too young to teach? Isn't it all still fresh in their memory, all that information and education, their youthful enthusiasm?'

'The only jobs in teaching they'll be able to get right now are at the kind of inner-city schools nobody wants to teach at. And besides, they are not as good as me, none of them, so it's a pointless dream.'

'That's a bit harsh, isn't it?'

'So, my dear, is life.' He spied my wedding ring. 'But you know that already, right?'

I raised my eyebrows at him, and he clearly liked it that I did. The oldest man in the room, perhaps no more than five years my senior, and it was to him I most naturally gravitated. Ben, I could see, had now moved beyond my orbit. I excused myself to Alistair and went to find a toilet. In the cubicle, I lowered the lid, sat on it and took out my phone.

Lucy: Hello stranger, long time no speak. Missing you. Missing me?

I needed urgently to empty my bladder, did so, and flushed. As I pulled up my knickers, my phone buzzed. I sat back down on the lowered lid.

Ben: Lucy!! How funny! I was just thinking about you! So so so glad you decided to contact me again. I thought I'd lost you for good, that you'd forgotten all about me . . .
Lucy: You're not quite so forgettable, Ben.
Ben: Glad to hear it. How have you been?
Lucy: Fine. What are you up to?

I went out to the sinks, where I splashed water on my face and checked my reflection. My eyes were enormous, full of the most exquisite terror. I patted my cheeks down with a tissue and went back out on to the gallery floor, which was surely by now filled to capacity. I squeezed my way over to the front window, where the majority of people were milling. My phone buzzed again.

Ben: I'm actually out right now. At an open mic night. Poetry, short stories, that kind of thing. Remember those poems I used to send you?
Lucy: I'm proud of you!
Ben: wish you were here. ☺
Lucy: You should have invited me. I'd have come.

I could see him now, through the crowd. Still surrounded by people, but his head bent towards his phone, the glow from which pulsed across his features and did kind things to his cheekbones. Somebody to his left walked away, and I could see now his thumbs on the keypad. I smiled.

Ben: well, you know me, I always bottle it at the last moment. ☹
Lucy: Shame. What's with all the emoticons? Not like you!
Ben: sorry! Sorry! I think I must be drunk. Are you at home?
Lucy: No.
Lucy: I mean, yes.
Ben: make your mind up!!
Lucy: I'm somewhere in between.
Ben: sounds de—

I looked up to see him once again engaged in conversation.

I felt suddenly exposed, playing with my phone directly opposite him. He needed only to look up. I wandered around again, making my way slowly back towards him until I was so close I could smell him. He was talking to Alistair now, the older man clearly drunk because he was full of vocal enthusiasm for

244

Ben's reading. Alistair laughed, and patted him on the cheek before moving off. I hung back.

    Ben: sorry, got distracted. Sounds deep.
    Lucy: That's okay. I'm not sure really where I am.
    Ben: you sound sad. i really do wish you were here, you know.
    i would make you smile.
    Lucy: Prove it.

His circle of friends moved outside, where they could light up. I moved back to the front of the bar and stood mere feet from them, the pane of glass the only thing that separated us. A glass of wine had been discarded on the floor, still half full, and, unthinking, I stooped for it and swigged. More people joined them on the pavement. Ben kept laughing, his cigarette-less hand playing constantly with his fringe. He stood flamingo-like, one foot on top of the other, maintaining an impressive sense of balance for one with so much drink inside him. There he was, three feet from me, and yet still unreachable, off in another universe altogether.

I had expected him to look more browbeaten in the flesh, more nervous, unsure of himself. His messages to me always possessed an undercurrent of wariness, an absolute lack of self-certainty at his place in the world. But now, at this moment, he seemed to have discovered his element. I looked at him and saw a young man full of confidence, someone just starting out in the world and ready to make an impact on it.

I finished what remained in the discarded wine glass, then left, wanting now only to return home. This had been a mistake. As I reached the train station, my phone vibrated.

    Ben: sorry, waylaid again. Well, I would prove it to you if I could.
    If you were here right now, I would – well, I would . . .

Lucy: Go on . . .

Ben: I would take you into my arms and kiss you, and I would press myself up against you so that you knew exactly what effect you had on me, and let you know exactly what my intentions were.

Lucy: I'll be there in 5 mins.

Ben: if only!!

Lucy: You're all talk.

Ben: perhaps I am. ☹

Ben: But then again sometimes I'm all action as well. I am decisive. I am! Seriously. If you were here, tonight, now, you wouldn't recognize me, Lucy. You'd say, Ben, what's got into you!

I ran.

I ran the way people flee the scene of a crime, leaving the railway station far behind and retracing my steps across town and back to the bar. A light rain was falling, and I didn't have my umbrella. I slowed down, not wanting to arrive too hot and flustered, alarmed-looking. But my pace remained swift. I couldn't have slowed down any more if I wanted to. My dress swirled lightly around me, and the rain was intensely pleasurable against my skin. I turned successive corners and then eventually, there, in the distance, still glowing from all the activity inside, was the bar. A few more people were on the pavement now, oblivious to the rain. I could not see Ben. I crossed the road and walked inside.

The waitress was back in her place, offering another tray of wine. I helped myself to two glasses and pushed my way through the throng with impolite elbows towards his wall. Where was Ben? I turned, and quickly caught sight of him, standing at the opposite wall in a group of half a dozen people. As I approached, he looked up and did a double-take. The comprehension came gradually into his face, almost in slow motion, like a cartoon. I was right in front of him now, inches away. This was it.

He swallowed. '*You?*'

I nodded, breathing yogically through my nose.

'We chatted briefly before, right? You said you liked my poem?'

My legs almost gave way, but I buckled my knees, held firm, and choked down my disappointment. *Maybe I should just leave now, escape while there is still time, and pretend none of this has happened*, I thought to myself. Instead, I persevered. 'Yes, yes. I did. I do.' I held up a glass of wine. 'Thirsty?'

His smile was one of confused amusement, simultaneously abashed and intrigued by this odd woman before him.

'Oh, okay. Right. Thank you.'

He relieved me of the glass and, as he did so, I tossed back my damp hair, hoping that it would reveal more of my face to him. Would he recognize me now? He took a long swallow of wine. *This* was it. Surely?

'Jake,' he said, offering a hand. 'Jake Marshall.'

'Not *Ben*?'

'Huh?' The frown that settled across his brow was deep, three distinct tramlines. He shook his head as if to wake up, to clear it of the confusion that had clearly settled. 'No, *Jake*.'

And then, quite suddenly, the room fell clean away from him as comprehension *finally* dawned. His eyes widened, and continued to widen. His jaw went slack. I tried to smile, but my mouth was tight. He stepped to one side, away from the conversation and the crowd, and nodded at me to follow.

'L-*Lucy*?'

'Ben.'

'But what— How . . . ?'

I started talking, in quick rapid spurts, the words tumbling. I was in Bristol, I told him, visiting a friend, and I was walking back to the train station when I passed the bar and, to kill a little time, popped in. Then I saw him, convinced it was really him, and – well, I just couldn't help myself. What were the chances? He didn't mind, did he?

My confidence as I spoke diminished rapidly, like water down the plug, and soon I felt emboldened no more but wanted only his approval, for him to nod agreeably, to make good on his earlier boast that he would kiss me and hold me to him, that everything would be all right, that we would be all right. But he was Ben again now, not Jake, and timid.

'But I . . . I mean – what did you . . . ? And why . . . ?'

His face was fantastically red, and his stuttering helplessness had rendered him impossibly sweet. I wanted to reach my hand up and stroke his face, to tell him *there there*, that everything was all right. I very nearly did. But that would have brought me to the attention of his friends, and I knew him well enough to know that he would not have wanted that.

'It's okay,' I said. 'I'm not here to make a scene. I'll leave. My train,' I added.

He nodded, relieved or bereft, I couldn't tell.

I gave him my wine glass and turned to go, pushed my way back through the crowd and out into the street, then back towards the station. It was raining harder now. I resisted the temptation to turn around to check whether he was following me. I didn't need to; I knew he'd be there, that I would any second now feel his hand reach out and pull me back by my arm, to spin me around and turn my life into a page from romantic fiction. I walked slowly, measuring my steps, getting wet but not caring. I could hear nobody behind me. But then he had been wearing trainers, hadn't he? And trainers were silent.

Pretty soon, it came: a presence over my shoulder. I inclined my head, a nervous smile ready in place to greet him as he drew level. But it wasn't Ben. A middle-aged man blundered past, huffing, earphones plugged in, a pair of trainers on his feet. He made eye contact as he passed, and smiled. But he didn't stop. He too had a train to catch.

I arrived at the station with ten minutes to spare and sat at a window seat gazing out, refusing to believe that my cinematic moment was going to be denied me. I heard from the platform a whistle blow, and the train juddered once before beginning steadily to move out, my back to its destination, my eyes facing a retreating Bristol, and its gallingly empty, *Ben*less platform.

Twelve

No mention of me on his Twitter page afterwards, nor his blog. No text messages, no emails, no explanatory phone calls, no further contact via the erotic website. I knew this because I checked hourly and more. I scrolled through his tweets as if for clues, a morsel of hope, then Googled anything that might have been some kind of hidden message. But he had hidden them well.

Andrew was on a bender. Paris the previous weekend had been profitable. He'd won thousands of pounds across several races, one of his biggest wins to date, and he wanted to celebrate, with Dan mostly. He'd also had a busy client week, business lunches spilling into all-evening sessions. I only ever saw him now either drunk or hungover or on the way out the door in pursuit of both, he as thoroughly self-contained in his world as I was in mine. At weekends, I resumed my trips to the gym to help burn off all my anxious energy.

'You look different,' Andrew said to me one night, red-faced and tired, dressed in a pair of pyjamas I hadn't seen before. We had bumped into one another on the landing outside the bathroom. An attempt at conversation seemed the very least we could do.

'Different how?'

'I don't know. Just . . . different. You eating okay?'

My friend Kerry came round, for the first time in months, uninvited but in need. It was a novelty to have a friend in the house again. She called, and, when I deliberately didn't pick up, left a message. 'We should have a catch-up,' she said, her voice urgent and nervy, frantic almost. 'In fact, I'll come over now, on the off chance, yeah?'

I was listening to the message a second time, just to make sure I'd heard what I'd heard, when she knocked, her fist confirming her nerves, six raps inside of a second.

Kerry was in many ways the last person I wanted to see, but, arriving bruised and battered, she quickly put my own problems into perspective. She had been having a relationship with a Polish man she had met at her local swimming pool. The inevitable had happened, and his wife had found out. She'd come across Kerry's address on her husband's phone and had gone round for a showdown. This explained the black eye and split lip. 'She was a big woman.' It was a shock to see her like this, so literally beaten by love, but I felt empathy, both of us defeated by what we wanted most.

Andrew came home in the middle of what was an intense conversation. As if to prove her gratitude for my being such a good listener, she kept on talking. Andrew was drunk, and stumbled into the living room singing a terrace anthem. The last time he and Kerry had been in the same room she had thrown a glass of wine over him, for reasons I had long since put to the back of my mind. I braced myself now for retribution.

It took him a while to see straight.

'*Christ!* What happened to your face?'

Kerry turned pointedly and shooed him away, as if this were her front room, not his. Andrew shrugged, then dutifully disappeared, taking his song into the kitchen, where he raided the fridge before climbing upstairs. 'Where was I?' she said when he was gone.

We talked, she and I, until two in the morning, repeatedly rehashing her situation until it could bear no further examination. After she left I realized how tired I was, but I knew I wouldn't sleep. I hadn't been sleeping for days, so I went to bed unexpectant. Each night I had relived every moment of my evening in Bristol, convincing myself that it could all have turned out so much better if only I had done *this* instead of *that*, not confronted him quite so brazenly, or else confronted him differently, perhaps told him upfront that I loved him, that I was sorry, that I thought we had something, that we could be good together, and that he needed me, he really did, he just didn't realize it yet, not fully, one of those unknown knowns. My mind wound itself up in ever-decreasing circles, spooling tighter and tighter.

I desperately wanted the oblivion of sleep. What I wanted more, in lieu of a friendly ear, was somebody to talk to, somebody upon whom I could fully unload, because this was too much for me alone. There was no going back to Barbara, so one morning, rising from another sleepless night, I sought out a different psychotherapist, one more directly specific to my needs: a psychotherapist who specialized in online addictions, which I feared was quite possibly what I had here: an addiction.

His name was Dr Benn – two ns, as his receptionist would later point out, requesting I make the necessary amendment to my cheque – and he was able to see me quicker than I'd anticipated, just a day after my enquiring email. He was a short bus ride away, in a small but solid office block that somehow conveyed, to me, authority. A boxy anteroom contained a middle-aged receptionist to answer the phone in a conspiratorial whisper, and she made me a cup of tea while I waited. I had arrived almost half an hour early, and sat watching the clock count its seconds.

Eventually, the door to his office opened and a woman, a large hat concealing much of her face, strode past me towards the door. A moment later the doctor appeared in the door's frame, a tall, thin, gaunt-looking man in his early forties with a long nose, his eyes rendered enigmatic behind a pair of thick glasses that seemed to reflect every available light around him.

'I'm glad I could see you so soon,' he said in reaction to the tears that filled my eyes the moment I took a seat in his office. 'I had a last-minute cancellation just moments before your email arrived. Coincidence or fate, I wonder?' He smiled.

His office had none of the personal touches of Barbara's. It housed one very plain desk and two chairs. Much of one wall was taken up by a vast bookcase cluttered with psychology books – *A Guide to Your Inner Self*, *The Madness of the Ordinary*, *The Inner Well-Being* – alongside other, more general books arranged as if to suggest a rather precise and even pedantic mind: Oliver Sacks next to Oliver James next to Clive James next to Clive Cussler. There were books on crystals, and one on the order of the universe. There were real crystals too, displayed on the mantelpiece, of all shapes and sizes, pinks and blues mainly, and, by the open window, a wind chime which tinkled gently in the breeze.

He took the chair from behind his desk and positioned it alongside mine. He was wearing brown corduroy trousers and, as he crossed one leg over the other, I was reminded of my history teacher at school. Everything about him radiated calm, his voice, like that of his receptionist's, rarely rising above a whisper. He handed me a form to fill in, personal questions requesting contact details, the name of my doctor, any allergies or illnesses I had, and while I wrote he explained that this first session was merely one of assessment, 'to see whether we feel comfortable with one another and whether we feel we could work together in helping you. I'm going to ask you a series of questions, and I will be taking notes on this pad, and I will also be taping the session for later reference.' He indicated a small recording device on his desk. 'Are you fine with this?'

He asked what had brought me to him today in such haste. Unlike with Barbara, I told him everything, explaining my succession of inappropriate relationships with people I'd met online. 'Inappropriate?' he asked, eyes on his pad as he scribbled. I answered that I had been having virtual sex with people online. He handed me a tissue, because I was crying again, this time profusely. I then explained, perhaps in mitigation, that I all but had my husband's approval – to have some fun – though he, Andrew, didn't quite know the extent to which I was pursuing this.

'Explain this to me,' the doctor said.

I told him about Andrew's gambling, his racing, his work, his drinking. I told him about my job situation, the vacuum in my life.

'Children?'

I answered, then told him, with a smile, about Rummy, our hamster.

I told him about the conversation Andrew and I had had a few months ago on holiday, about pursuing our own interests, albeit with vague guidelines and unspoken limits. He had his gambling, I could have my *fun*. I told him about our virtually separate lives, and my endless craving now for new male company, for validation, sex, perhaps even for love. Was that wrong? The doctor didn't answer, but instead waited for me to continue. More quickly now, I told him about Ben, and where my obsession had so recently led me.

He wanted to know about my childhood, my parents, my upbringing. He was interested to learn about my mother's

254

nervous breakdown when I was just a baby, her sporadic violent nature thereafter, and also about the father whom I described as a drinker, feckless, and mostly absent. He interrupted here to ask if he had also been a gambler. I realized that, yes, he had. My father had had a thing for the dogs. He put down his pen and offered up a gentle smile. 'So,' he said, 'you've married a version of your father?'

This prompted from nowhere a torrent, a flood. The psycho-therapist sat quietly while I cried, as if permitting me to do so, and then, when I had stopped, asked what it would take to make me happy. If my life were a book, say, what sort of book would it be? 'A confused one,' I replied. He nodded. 'And how would the book end?'

I thought about this for a while, then shrugged.

Towards the end of my hour, he said he believed I had certain attachment issues, and also abandonment ones. These, he suggested, would likely have come from not bonding with my mother as a baby, and would have been further compounded by a drinking and gambling, and absent, father. He said that I had clearly been holding in a lot for too long now, that there may be some unresolved feelings of grief, and that I was suffering from anxiety and fear of so many things, not all of which were within my control.

He said that I probably had, in some ways, a caring and com-passionate marriage, but that there was room for improvement. He reiterated that I had married someone with similar charac-teristics to those of my late father, and so understandably it would be easier to seek temporary comfort in a stranger than it would in Andrew. He said that my obsession with Ben, if obses-sion was what it was, was probably a catalyst for something else – a desire for change, perhaps. And he said that these were issues he would like to take forward with me should I wish to do so with him. I found myself nodding eagerly, hungrily, almost in desperation: *help*. He said that he would not be telling me what to do at any stage during our sessions, but that he would hope to enable me to work through the issues myself, and would be on hand to support me in whatever I ultimately decided.

Making my way home afterwards, my face, I knew from my reflection in shop windows, was still swollen from all the tears, but I felt lighter than I had in a long time, and more hopeful. It was only after a quarter of an hour – previously an unconscionable amount of time – that I remembered my iPhone, still switched off and languishing at the bottom of my handbag. I reached for it now, and switched it on, helplessly hoping that Ben had been in touch, that he had somehow been aware of my suffering and that it would do me the world of temporary good if he were to reach out and make contact.

But there was nothing.

A small consolation: if this *was* an obsession of mine, then at least I wasn't the only one.

The psychotherapist had told me that, if nothing else, I was in good company. Online adultery, he explained, was increasingly a global obsession, perhaps the defining one of the new century, social networking sites and websites so geared now to facilitating it that they were increasingly being cited in divorce cases. Marriages had been breaking down since time immemorial, but never before directly because of the existence of Facebook and Twitter and Friends Reunited.

We had become a world of nostalgia freaks, hours spent in front of our terminals and phones and iPads, tirelessly tracking down old friends and past loves, not always intent on reigniting old fires, and yet the reignition of fires was nevertheless the all too frequent outcome whenever an innocent email ('Hi! Remember me?') resulted in a date.

The sites I had frequented were representative of thousands of others, and many far more serious in their intent than mine. The psychotherapist told me that I was, relatively speaking, a minnow, seeking only a little company, a bit of fun. I'd not even had physical sex yet. But there were other websites that operated *solely* to link people who wanted affairs but couldn't be bothered to put in the legwork first, sites of which The Pseud was likely all too aware. MEET LIKE-MINDED SINGLES NOW, they read. Or, MARRIED WOMEN LOOKING FOR DISCREET AFFAIRS. They were genuine, and very popular. For £140 for women, but over £600 for men, I could have been *this* close to a lifetime's worth of introductions to men happy to meet me – a woman they didn't yet know existed – not for romantic walks in the park and hopeful glasses of wine over dinner, but solely and simply for uncomplicated sex.

I was amused by this thought. *Uncomplicated* sex. I was a forty-year-old woman and hadn't yet once managed uncomplicated sex. Even the most impulsive sex, in my experience, brought its own baggage. But that was the thrust behind such websites. Everyone else was at it, why not you?

Later, I began increasingly to wonder whether my own dalliances would bring about the demise of my marriage, whether Andrew would find the evidence on my computer, whether he would care, whether he would sue for divorce. I was technologically savvy enough to know precisely how to protect my laptop's history from him, but unless I deleted every text message from my phone, I was hardly covering my tracks.

It was even harder to hide from him my state of mind, and I had feared the morning after my debacle in Bristol that even someone as unanalytical as Andrew would realize something was up. I had been crying for much of the previous night. I couldn't think about him, about Ben, without my bottom lip crumpling again, my resolve splintering once more.

257

Andrew and I encountered one another briefly over Weetabix. I felt his eyes on me, but he said nothing.

My next appointment with the psychotherapist was the following week, and after another emotionally draining hour I felt in great need of caffeine. It was a bright, late-summer's day, and love was palpably in the air, couples passing me arm in arm, flaunting their happiness, their perfectly uncomplicated lives. I chose my favourite café and sat by the window as I always did, where I could watch them pass and feel contentedly sad about myself.

My coffee was brought to me by a waitress with a stud that went through the top of her nose, right between her eyes. Light glinted on both baubles. She smiled brightly and said, in a crunchy Eastern European accent, 'La-tte.'

I thanked her and, as she retreated, saw what I thought was Ben peering in through the café's window, his hands shielding out the sunlight. I shook my head as if to wake up, but, no, he was still there, Ben, now striding through the door towards me, bringing in some of the breeze.

Surely not, I thought. And yet . . .

He was dressed almost identically to the last time I had seen him, but in place of the T-Rex T-shirt, he now wore one that read MC5.

'Hello you,' he said.

I reached for my coffee, mouth open, and continued to stare in disbelief.

He indicated the empty seat. 'May I?'

From somewhere I found my voice. 'Of course, please.'

The waitress appeared again. 'Yes?' He ordered a lemon tea with honey, and then explained, as she went off to make it, 'Bit of a sore throat at the moment.'

'The honey,' I said, 'should help.'

'Here's hoping.'

He removed his jacket to reveal long bare arms, hairless and lightly browned by the sun. His eyes were pink around the rims, his lips slightly chapped. A few whiskers conspired together at his chin but rather lost all will by the time they reached his cheeks.

'Do you have any idea how long I've been looking for you?' he asked.

'Tell me.'

'Two days. I've been doing some investigating, a little private detective work. I re-read through all our conversations and found that you'd mentioned where you live, more or less, and that since losing your job you loved to while away the afternoons in cafés. Do you have any idea how many bloody cafés there are in this street alone?' He laughed. 'I've been looking in every single one of them, morning and afternoon, since yesterday!'

I still couldn't be sure if this was really happening, if he was really here, so I reached out and touched him. I felt flesh; he was real.

'You should have told me you were coming. You have my number, after all.'

'And spoil the surprise?' He grinned, and I could see now that he wasn't quite as confident as he had at first seemed. Nerves were present. '*Are* you surprised?'

'How couldn't I be? I thought I'd put you off for good.'

He blushed deeply. 'Ah, yes – look. I'm sorry about that.' He reached his hand across the table and dared take a hold of mine. 'But talk about surprises! You really caught me off my guard. My friends were there, and . . .'

'. . . And I embarrassed you?'

'No!'

'Me, of all people, at your poetry night, and old enough to be your mother?'

259

He shook his head vehemently, sweetly. 'My mother? God, no. Anyway, my mother is – what? – forty-eight, forty-nine.'

'Ancient.'

'No, it's just that – well, it was a big night, I was nervous, and then . . .' He trailed off, and smiled the most convincing of apologies.

'I thought you'd think of me as a bunny boiler or something,' I said.

'Bunny boiler?'

'*Fatal Attraction.*' It was clear I'd lost him. 'What I mean is, I thought I'd scared you off. For good.'

'You? Never! In fact, I was honoured that you'd made the journey . . .'

'So honoured that I didn't hear from you again.'

He blushed once more. 'No, well, as I said, you did take me by surprise, and I reacted terribly, so terribly that I didn't have the courage to contact you afterwards. I thought you'd hate me for it.'

'I did. I *do.*'

He squeezed my hand, and my flesh dissolved into his.

'I know, I know, and I'm really sorry. I want to make it up to you. That's why I'm here, now.'

The waitress arrived with his tea. I saw him take in her nose stud, and smile. He was a handsome boy. She smiled back, a pretty girl far closer in age than I. He watched her retreat, but I saw no lust in his eyes. The lust only materialized when he refocused them back on to me. This was good.

'I realized that if I didn't take action now, then I would probably lose you for good. And I don't want to lose you, Lucy. I've no idea what we've got, *if* we've got anything, but I know that I want to – well, to at least try to get to know you in real life, in the flesh, not via some email address.'

'You got bored of all my messages?'

'God, yes! Absolutely! Didn't you with mine? All that fore-play, and all of it headed nowhere. I wanted what was next.'

He laughed, and I laughed too. I wanted this moment with him never to end. Even as it was happening, I knew that after-wards this was what I would most hold dear about my time with Ben: a conversation over coffee and lemon tea.

'So . . . ?' I said.

'Oh God, I don't know. I've no idea, really.' He looked cast down, abashed. 'It took all the courage I had to make it this far. I think I need a guiding hand from you now.'

He told me that he had spent so long looking for me yester-day that he couldn't face the journey home. 'I ended up in a dodgy B&B. It was all I could afford. No breakfast, a shared bathroom. I think I stink, I'm afraid.'

He blew on his tea and took a tentative sip. Its vapour clouded about his eyes, and I took the opportunity again to wonder whether this wasn't all a dream. But I could feel his pulse hammer away under my middle finger. I shifted in my seat slightly, and realized I was wet.

'If you stink, you'll presumably be wanting a shower?'

His eyes widened. 'Is your husband home?'

'Not for another three hours.'

'Are you far from here?'

'Just around the corner. Three minutes. I could be . . .' I hesitated. 'I could be washing your hair within five.'

He swallowed, and I watched as his Adam's apple travelled up the length of his supple neck, and then back down again.

I used a shampoo with a heady watermelon fragrance to it. Fat and heavy in my cupped hand, plantlife green and oozing thickly between my fingers. The water was gloriously hot and strong. I looked up into his face and he looked down on to mine, millimetres apart. He bent his head towards me, as if in prayer, and, taking a step back from him, I began to massage the shampoo into his scalp. He was, I knew, staring down on to my naked body, my breasts, my stomach, my pubic hair. I would have trimmed if I'd known he was coming; I'd have repainted my toenails. I hoped he liked what he saw.

I felt his hands on my hips, steadying himself as I continued to work the shampoo into his hair. He took a single step towards me, which brought his erection up against my belly. I looked down; we bumped heads. I almost apologized, and could tell he was similarly inclined, but neither of us wanted to break the spell by being ordinary and humdrum, and so we remained silent. He tilted his head back now, and allowed the water to rinse off the suds. I placed my hands flat against his shoulders and let them travel down across his chest and abdomen, and finally around his cock, which jerked upon my touch, astonishingly hard. I heard him gasp.

A second later, his sperm gushed on to my stomach in fast, urgent spurts. Quickly, so as not to lose the moment, I began to masturbate him. He groaned, his knees buckling, his hands bearing down heavily on me, my feet losing their grip below. When it was over, I brought him to me and embraced him. I laughed.

'Oh God, I'm sorry, I—'

'Shh,' I whispered.

I kissed him, our very first kiss, and then I soaped him down, and encouraged him to do so to me, which he did meticulously, across my breasts, my stomach, my crotch. We stepped out of the shower and into towels. His cock, I noticed, was hard again. At twenty-three years old, premature ejaculation was not the end of sex. I held him by the hand and took him on the most alien walk I'd ever taken in my own house: naked, in the middle of the day, with a man not my husband, also naked, and into my room where, with the curtains still daringly open, we made a year's worth of foreplay at last count for something tangible, something real.

'We've crossed a line now, haven't we?' he said afterwards. I gazed deep into his worried eyes. 'We have,' I told him. 'I think we might just have derailed my marriage.'

I could have stayed there with him, in bed, for the rest of the day, the rest of my *life*, but when I unconcernedly gazed over at the clock I realized with a start that it was now somehow a quarter to six, which meant that Andrew would be home any minute. Ben was downstairs and out the front door before I'd even had a chance to kiss him goodbye, to ask when I would see him again, to thank him for . . . everything. I was left on the doorstep in his wake, instantaneously bereft, and after he had disappeared around the corner I went slowly back into the kitchen to think fully about what I had just allowed to happen.

Andrew was home so shortly afterwards that I knew they must have crossed paths. He breezed into the kitchen, pecked me on the cheek and reached into the fridge for a beer. He asked what was for supper, and seemed disappointed when I confessed I hadn't given it any thought yet.

'No matter,' he said, looking at me once, and then twice, as if seeing something different in my face, something that hadn't been there in the morning. 'Shall we go out instead?'

'Rather not, if you don't mind?'

He shrugged, took his beer and the nearest takeaway menu from the cutlery drawer, and retreated into the living room. I heard him turn on the television and talk animatedly to Rummy as he helped him out of his cage. I looked around the kitchen, whose design had once seemed so important to me, the fulfilment of every modern housewife's dream, but which now looked merely like a kitchen, a place to cook, or not. I peered out of the window, and saw my ghostly reflection peering back. My hair was mussed up. Andrew hadn't noticed. And if he had, he hadn't commented. Same thing. From the living room now I could hear him muting the television as he called for a curry, shouting at me to ask if I wanted one. I couldn't find the voice to say either yes or no, and so he simply ordered two of everything.

In the moment's lull between him ending the call and finding the remote control to turn the sound back up on the television, I heard my own phone, still on the bedside table upstairs, chiming once. A message! I bolted from the kitchen, raced up the stairs, banging my hip on the wall as I ran and crying out a helpless *Ow!*

Andrew shouted after me.

'What's got into you?' he said.

Ben, was what I wanted to reply. Ben.

We met again a week later, a proper assignation this time, at a nondescript greenbelt hotel halfway between our cities, and alongside an anonymous A-road just minutes from the nearest train station. It had been Ben's suggestion, relayed in a furtive whisper during a late-night phone call. Seeing as we were living out his fantasy, he said, he wanted to do it properly. And he wanted to remain, to me, *Ben*. 'Jake isn't worthy of you,' he said.

An affair, he pronounced after the second time we had sex, was necessarily secretive and sordid, so what better place than a nondescript greenbelt hotel in the middle of nowhere? It made it more exciting. As we checked in – and I paid, with cash rather than credit card – we giggled infectiously, the tang of bad behaviour written across our faces. But the young receptionist behind the desk could not have been less interested.

'Do you do room service?' Ben enquired.

'We do, sir. Will you be requiring some?'

'After we've emptied the minibar, yes,' he whispered into my ear.

The receptionist heard him. 'There is no minibar, sir.'

He looked crestfallen, one ingredient of the fantasy already snuffed out. But the moment we reached the room, a dull grey rectangle with a bed in the middle, a single wall lamp overhead and, on the wall opposite, a painting of rolling hills dotted with sheep, he threw me down on to the mattress and fell laughingly on top of me.

All chitchat was superfluous now. Chitchat, in one form or another, was all we had done for a full year before; now was the time for action. Squirming with determination on top of me, he hoisted up my skirt, yanked aside my knickers and entered me. The nylon duvet gave off sparks of static, and I could feel my hair being unflatteringly teased by its electricity. He came quickly, but before he could register any disappointment that I hadn't, he withdrew and began to plant kisses on my neck, between my breasts and my navel, before positioning himself between my legs.

We spent two hours afterwards lying in each other's arms and talking about anything and everything, unburdening secrets, revealing layers. After a certain age, particularly with a regular partner, the post-coital experience usually meant sleep. It was bliss to be reminded of how it used to be. It made me young again, a teenager, that time when talking nonsense felt like the best, the *only*, way to pass an afternoon. His eyes, up close, were multiple hues of brown, chestnut and oak, with flecks of almond. He smelled of chocolate and cigarettes. His tongue ended in a point. I wanted to take it between my teeth, and keep it there.

Almost abruptly, we realized we were hungry.

'Can I do it?' Ben pleaded, already picking up the phone and calling for room service. 'And how much will that be?' he asked of the Hawaiian pizza on offer. His response made me laugh, an elongated *Whaaat?!*, before slamming the phone down in incredulity.

'Daylight robbery,' he said, jumping out of bed and pulling on his clothes. I suggested we go out to dinner, my treat.

'No need! I'll go out and get us a pizza. It'll be fun, eating in here. Just the two of us. Stay there, right there. I want you naked until I come back.'

Alone in the room, I tried not to think too hard about all the cracks I had fallen through in order to find myself suddenly *here*, and doing *this*, with *him*. There was a small television in the corner, so I switched it on. It was cold in the room, and knowing that this was not the kind of hotel that provided bathrobes, I put on Ben's Suicidal Tendencies T-shirt and sat back on the mattress, my knees drawn up to my chest.

I went to the bathroom to clean myself up, a room the size of a broom closet, with rusty brown stains in the sink and toilet pan. The toilet paper was rough. I flushed the chain, and the system's innards gurgled and grumbled, and didn't quickly cease.

It was seven o'clock. I had to be home by midnight at the latest, and knew that at some point in the evening Andrew would likely text me to check that everything was okay, and whether I wanted him to pick me up from Jane's. There was no football tonight, so the offer to pick me up after my night out – Jane, though she didn't know it, was my cover story – was his way of showing he still cared. I set my phone to silent.

Ben came back a quarter of an hour later with two large pizza boxes, each with extra pepperoni. Student food. We ate side by side on the bed, feeding one another triangles of greasy melted cheese and slippery sausage. The moment he finished a slice, his hands were on me again, hungry and insatiable. We managed half a single pizza between us before tossing the boxes aside. He turned me over, trailing his fingers from the nape of my neck down to the small of my back, and tentatively positioned himself behind me.

'You don't mind, do you?'

'Be my guest.'

He giggled nervously, and the headboard began to bang. Somebody in the next room pounded on the wall – I imagined a lonely middle-aged businessman – and shouted at us to keep the noise down. Ben withdrew, terrified. I turned around and coaxed his enthusiasm back.

'Quietly this time,' I instructed.

He took my face in his hands and tickled me with his kisses. 'Sorry.' He pushed his tongue into my mouth, then retracted it. 'What about your husband? If he knew about us? Would he kill me?'

'One way to find out.'

He grinned, and lunged for me again. 'Mrs Dent, you are a very, very bad lady.'

Afterwards, we took a cab to the station, and stood on opposite platforms waiting for our trains. It was just after ten o'clock. I was exhausted, and a little sore. Ben waved at me and blew me a kiss. His train came first. He boarded it, his face pressed up against the window, and I watched as it took him away from me. Mine arrived shortly after, and brought me without delay back to my life. Andrew was asleep when I got home.

A text arrived as I was climbing into bed. 'I had fun!' it read. 'I really really like you. More please!'

I turned off the light, slipped the phone under my pillow and fell effortlessly into sleep.

The next day, after the initial elation had subsided and reality resurfaced, I felt sick. I'd had my fun. I'd finally done it – twice. But now I felt horrible. I had tainted my marriage. I cried violently, starkly aware that this was now very real. I resolved that I wouldn't, I couldn't, I *mustn't* do this again.

But my craving soon returned, palpable, unignorable. And so it continued.

Over the next few weeks I lived only for Ben, conducting a frenzied and furtive affair of the kind I previously thought existed only in beach-read novels. What was happening to me?

One of my most overbearing character traits was that I was an incessant, inveterate researcher, forever wanting to find the source of every detail, to corroborate suspicion, fact, or, in this case, an explanation for my own erratic behaviour. Research was part of my job, of course, but I couldn't help that curiosity spilling over into all other areas of my life. If, for example, I watched something on television that made reference to something I wasn't personally familiar with, I would immediately Google it. If Andrew was with me, then I would share with him my findings whether he wanted me to do so or not. If a book mentioned a fascinating fact on a part of the world I knew little of, I would Google this too. Watching a half-hour episode of *Mastermind* could take twice as long as I continually pressed pause on the remote in order to search the internet first.

In truth, I didn't really need much in the way of thorough corroboration – I would not plough through reams of information, cross-referencing one kernel of knowledge with another, and make notes – but merely to browse, to scratch that persistent itch, and ultimately to raise an eyebrow in appreciation before moving on and quickly forgetting what it was that I had so desperately wanted to learn more of only moments before.

But in this case my thirst for knowledge was hard to sate. My online obsession was making me lose sight of who I was, who I had been. Was I abnormal, ill? Bipolar, even?

Typing a rough approximation of my problem into the search engine, it took me several moments to summon the strength to hit ENTER, fearful of what I might find. The results came up instantaneously. I clicked, skimmed and immediately unclenched. I was, it seemed, in good company.

Okay, right. So I had been experiencing something that was referred to as *online disinhibition*: a loosening – or even complete abandonment – of those social restrictions that would otherwise exist in normal face-to-face interactions. Inhibited in real life, I, and millions like me, became loose cannons online, the anonymity that the internet gave me, gave *us*, permitting me to say and do things I wouldn't dream of doing anywhere else.

Though webcams compromised this to a certain extent, the keyboard didn't. The moment we choose a pseudonym and enter cyberspace, we become *other*, suddenly judged solely by our words rather than our appearance or all the other usual restrictions imposed upon us by our *selves*. This is why we encounter such extremes online – in chatrooms, on Twitter – so much hate, so much invective, so much violence, and brazen nudity from the kind of people who wouldn't even go topless on a beach.

I read on, intrigued, about something called *solipsistic interjection*: that although the conversations and relationships we entered into online *seemed* real, they also existed in a quite distinct parallel universe which was hard to take entirely seriously. Who were these people we were talking to quite so frankly day and night? Were they who they claimed to be? Did they even exist at all? How much of what they came to represent was what *we* ourselves imagined and invented for them in pursuit of what so many of us wanted online – the perpetuation of fantasy?

But what about my overriding, keening sense of morality – that I was doing wrong by Andrew here – which flared up inside my head all too frequently like the most piercing of migraines?

An article I located on the science of love explained this to me, outlined the difficulties we all face in sustaining the kind of romantic love that takes *boyfriend* and *girlfriend* all the way to *husband* and *wife*. If romantic love had evaporated between Andrew and myself, then it had likely been replaced by a deep sense of attachment from which it was difficult for either of us to extricate ourselves, even if occasionally we wanted to. And that deep sense of attachment could still be felt while simultaneously developing a romantic love for somebody else.

This frenzy of feelings I was experiencing over Ben, then, was, scientifically speaking, entirely ordinary and commonplace. As was the teenage fact that he was all I could think, dream and wish about. The state of new love, it seems, is so often defined by its levels of obsession – a state characterized by feelings of exhilaration and often intrusive, obsessive thoughts. So obsessive in fact, that they share many characteristics with the manic phase of manic depression – even minor obsessive-compulsive disorder (OCD).

So I was manically depressed; I had OCD.

Had I actually been diagnosed with either by my doctor, he might have prescribed Valium or Prozac. But because all I had done was fallen for someone I shouldn't have, I was reliant upon only myself to see me through.

No wonder I was in such a mess.

Fact was, I was a proper adulterer now, and totally beholden to my phone. The moment it buzzed, I dropped everything, grabbed my bag and rushed to the door, heading towards wherever that day's assignation happened to be: another hotel, a distant park, an anonymous Starbucks. Ben was emboldened, more of a man in my company, he told me, than he had ever felt before. 'It's like I'm playing a role,' he grinned. 'Method actor.'

After such a long-nurtured online affair, sex became our overriding priority. It occurred in hotels, mostly, though we almost had sex on a commuter train once. This tipped the illicit into the potentially – for all I knew – illegal, and I lamented the days when trains were split into individual, sealed-off carriages, with no CCTV. I relayed this to Ben, and he looked at me distractedly. 'Hmm,' he said. 'I think I saw those on TV once.'

The sex continued to be almost preposterously passionate, the stuff of bodice-rippers. The foreplay lasted hours, Ben seemingly fascinated with every part of my body, as if he had never seen the female form before. I had never previously been aware of being so meticulously scrutinized, and admired. He would kiss my toes, my shins, the cleft at the back of my knees; every inch of me open for his appraisal.

And I appraised him, too. Though I may have been more familiar with the male body than he was with the female, seeing him naked was like discovering it anew. I was used, by this stage in my life, to softened muscles and perpetually relaxed stomachs, to hairless legs, and to all the strenuous effort that sex repre-sented. But Ben could have been chipped out of marble, his body full of definition. Everything was taut, and tight, and firm. My fingertips became excessively sensitive as I ran them over his chest, his abdomen, his loins. I found it difficult not to whimper with gratitude at my good fortune.

He was beautiful.

'My last girlfriend was really quiet,' he told me. 'She didn't like sex very much, I think. But with you, it's different. Lucy, you're amazing.'

And with every session, I grew in confidence, taking increas-ing control in bed, my insatiable lust redolent of my youth but so much more satisfying, because this time I knew precisely what to do with it. We did it standing up and lying down, in the shower and in the bath. Each time after coming, it would take him minutes to be ready for me again, and I myself would come repeatedly, three, four times in a session, until I was bruised and exhausted. And yet still I craved more. It was as if I wanted as much of Ben as Ben had to give, and I wasn't satisfied until I left him feeling thoroughly used. It had been years, *years*, since I had felt so gloriously spent.

One afternoon, in yet another hotel, wearing nothing but a pair of stockings and black high heels, I located his G spot. The look on his face as he came, reflected in the wall mirror in front of us, was equal parts pleasure, relief and reeling shock.

'How? How did you do *that*?'

I did it to him again. To feel him buckle against the flat of my palm, his erection bouncing wildly in front of my face but untouched, transformed me, for him, into some kind of sexual magician. He crumpled to the floor. 'Again,' he demanded.

Our liaisons had little of the real world to them, and just as well, because how else was I able to keep them concealed from Andrew quite so easily? They had a soft-focus quality, suspended in a bubble, and somehow did not, at least at first, impinge on my everyday life. I was living in a dream, and I wanted to perpetuate it.

The bubble did not expand. It couldn't. We did not go out on 'dates'. We never went to a restaurant together, never saw a film, never strolled hand in hand along the river at dusk. Our relationship was largely physical, dictated by a mutual need built up by so many nights of online preparation. And though that rarefied sense of purely platonic romance had diminished, its physical counterpart remained, for me, a thing of wonder, almost magical. *I could go on doing this for ever!*, I convinced myself. It happens all the time. I recalled stories, some real, some no doubt apocryphal, of seemingly happily married couples who maintained secretive affairs over decades, and often with much younger partners. These were relationships that never got tired because they never permitted them to. No arguments over the monthly bills, over plates left unwashed in the sink; no dirty socks. Just intermittent wining and dining, and sex, and love, and romance.

Was I capable of that? Did I *want* to be capable of that, a deception perpetuated endlessly?

I convinced myself that, yes, I did, and, yes, I could, it was worth it, at the same time realizing that of course I couldn't, and that I needed to end this *now*, before either of us, both of us, fell in too deep.

I recalled the experiences of friends like Jane and Kerry, how they would regale me with their own frantic, messy love lives: how perfectly they had started, how inevitably they would soon sour. But they had always, to my mind, picked the wrong men, so what did they expect?

It's easy to be critical from the outside looking in, but just as easy, I was learning, to lose any moral compass when you find yourself in the same situation.

Thirteen

'What are you doing Saturday night?'

This he asked me one day, curled up on a not particularly comfortable hotel bed, post-sex, our breath synchronizing in the otherwise humming silence of a Thursday afternoon.

'Saturday night?' We had never spent a weekend night together before. 'Why?'

Ben was smoking a cigarette. He'd taken to lighting up after every session, thrilled to be doing so in a non-smoking room. 'I've been invited to a party, a kind of get-together/catch-up/pre-Christmas thing for uni mates.'

'And you want *me* to come?'

His moment's hesitation should have forewarned me, but it didn't. '. . . Sure. Why not?'

Me, at a party full of your friends? was what I wanted to say. Instead, shamefully lifted by the idea that he might want to introduce me to his friends at last, I told him okay, yes.

On the Friday, over a Chinese takeaway in front of the television, Andrew had asked what I fancied doing over the next couple of days. He'd been out on consecutive weekends recently, so the question took me by surprise. I told him, instinctively, that Jane was going through a crisis. '*Another* crisis.' I was going to spend the weekend with her, I claimed. We'd be going to a spa, then dinner. There would be tears, I added with a roll of the eyes, the lie coming so easily to me. He shrugged, and said *fine*, but didn't look particularly put out. He helped himself to more pork balls, and we resumed watching TV.

After he went to bed and, so I believed, to sleep, I ran the bath, submerged myself and leisurely shaved my legs, working up to my bikini line. I maintained a bikini line these days, but opted out of the Hollywood option, complaining to Ben that the itch was simply too torturous. 'Brazilian'll do fine,' he responded, as if making an order from a takeaway menu.

It was to this I was currently attending when Andrew knocked and entered, his bathroom as much as mine, of course, and there being no such thing as privacy in a marriage. His face told me he had been asleep.

'Sorry,' he said, 'bursting.'

I watched him pee, taking in my first sight of his penis in months. After flushing and reinserting it into his pyjama bottoms, he turned and started to talk. I left my crotch and refocused on my legs. He was telling me something about Dan, Dan and his new girlfriend, a woman he had met in a wine bar. He regarded me with almost biological interest as he spoke, though he made no outward comment. I brought my knees together, shielding myself from further view, as if to say: *it isn't yours any more.*

There was a lot to say about Dan's new girlfriend, clearly, because he was still talking, sitting down now on the closed toilet lid. The bath was getting cold, and I didn't want to prune. Besides, I was tired. As I made to stand, he reached for a towel and handed it to me. I could feel his eyes all over me as I stepped out and on to the mat. I wrapped the towel around me and went over to the mirror, where I began the slow process of plucking tiny hairs from underneath my brows. Andrew, still on the subject of his friend's new girlfriend, continued to watch, an indistinct reflection behind me.

Suddenly he was up against me, his arms extending around my body.

'You're making a lot of effort for Jane,' he said, not quite accusingly, but not entirely innocently either.

'A woman's work . . .'

He pressed his groin into my bottom.

'Not now, Andrew. Sorry.'

He stepped obediently away. 'When was the last time?' he wondered sadly.

'I don't know.'

'We should, more often, don't you think?' He must have been thinking about Dan, about Dan's new girlfriend, and all the sex they'd be having. I glanced at his reflection again, and he took this as an encouragement of sorts, taking another step back towards me. 'You're glowing, you know?'

'Well, the bath *was* hot.'

'No, I don't just mean now. I mean the last few days, weeks. You're – well, like I say, you're glowing. It suits you.' He was blushing. 'You should – I don't know . . . you should glow more often.'

I turned to thank him and gave him a quick peck on the cheek, the most miserly of compensations. 'Thank you,' I said.

Later, I packed an overnight bag the way I would for a weekend break. I took with me four changes of clothes, three pairs of knickers, three bras. My vibrator, and some sensation-enhancing cream (for him). I packed my black high heels and a pair of flats. Stockings, tights, but also some socks (it was getting cold at night). I packed make-up and perfume, some night face cream. I took a couple of paperbacks, three magazines, a snack in case I got hungry on the train. The bag was heavy; I couldn't really lift it. I took out the paperbacks, and left just one magazine, figuring that I only had the concentration span these days for gossip. I ate the snack, suddenly peckish. I had no idea what I was doing. I packed a box of condoms, ribbed for my pleasure. And then at last I went to bed.

Saturday morning passed like treacle. I busied myself in the garden while Andrew watched repeats of the racing on the Racing UK channel. We had a light lunch together in the kitchen, then I went upstairs to repack, to ready myself and give my face a final once-over. I brushed my teeth, and flossed, ready as I'd ever be.

From the hall, I shouted goodbye to my husband, sprawled in his usual pose in front of the television, quickly opened the front door of our house, and left.

I could hear the party before I could see it, a dull, heavy bass snaking up the otherwise quiet street towards us as we made our slow and possibly hesitant way in hand-holding silence. I couldn't work out if the reservations were mine alone, or whether we shared them, both of us realizing, secretly, that it was too late to turn back, that we would have to see it out now, come what may.

The house was at the end of an elegant cobblestoned street, a tall but scruffy Edwardian semi spread over three floors, with four steps leading up to a door that was already open. Several young people were congregated there, the boys wearing T-shirts, the girls short skirts despite the biting cold, and all of them drinking from cans of lager and passing round a spliff. Ben couldn't have known them because he didn't greet them, and so pushed past and down the carpetless hall, pulling me with him into a large, open-plan living room that led into a kitchen-cum-dining room. It was into the kitchen we headed first, to drop off our bottles of wine and to fill up a couple of plastic cups with the nearest thing to hand. Ben poured out two full measures of schnapps before he even realized what it was. It was thick and sweet, but did everything it could to fortify me. I needed fortifying.

There were maybe a dozen people in the kitchen, each

leaning into the next and aiming their chatter directly into one another's ears over the din of the music, so loud that I feared for the building's foundations.

Ben winced at the taste of the schnapps, but drank it down all the same before reaching for a bottle of lager. He led me by the hand out of the kitchen, along the corridor and up the stairs, our feet picking their way between more bodies sprawled across the steps, the boys splayed out casually, legs apart, the girls with their knees up to their chins, and giggling coquettishly much the way I once did in order to suggest to boys that, yes, I was amenable and approachable, you'd like me, you would, please say that you do. Ben appeared to be on nodding terms with several of the people here, who nodded languidly back, before allowing their laconic gazes to fall on me. I smiled uncertainly, said hello to a couple of the girls, and received precisely no responses from any of them.

Upstairs, the hallway led off into three separate rooms, each large bed-sitting rooms, with the beds folded up into sofas. There were maybe twenty people in here, more in the hallway itself, and we poked our heads into successive rooms before Ben finally settled on the third. I could feel hot sweat pool in his hand. He was nervous.

'Jake!' somebody shouted, and I had to remind myself that their *Jake* was my *Ben*.

A young man with fresh-looking acne scars on his cheeks, his hair salon-fashioned into a maelstrom of disarray, came over to embrace him hip-hop style, shoulder to shoulder, and suddenly I was adrift, Ben's hand no longer in mine but in the grip of his friend's.

'Caius!' he said. 'Long time. How goes it?'

'Cool,' Caius responded.

Ben was consumed into the middle of half a dozen bodies, hugging each of them in turn. Four girls and two boys, all of a similar age, presumably the former university friends. Somebody handed Ben a can of lager, and he dispensed with his now empty bottle, dropping it carelessly at his feet. Somebody asked him what he had been up to, and I found myself eager to hear his response. But I was now a distance from him, three feet at least but also a million miles. I kept a kind of ready welcome smile on my face in case it was needed, and felt suddenly self-conscious about the amount of lipstick I was wearing. All the other girls here were deliberately pale and make-up-less, dressed androgynously yet beautifully feminine none the less. Why, I wondered now, had Ben wanted me to wear my Nicole Farhi dress? I looked like one of the mannequins out of Robert Palmer's 'Addicted To Love' video – a reference to 1986 that would have been lost on him.

Pins and needles in my feet, I shifted my weight and concentrated on the music. It was music I recognized, made by bands of Ben's generation and, though I liked it and wanted to join in the throng in the far corner and dance to it, I felt that this would only draw attention to myself, like a mother jiving during a school parents' evening. I could smell from somewhere a heady whiff of marijuana, and wished that somebody would pass me the joint.

The few minutes Ben left me standing loose was an eternity. But, drawn-out re-introductions over, he held his hand out towards me now and I stepped over the invisible threshold and into what I hoped would be a welcoming circle, but which was pointedly not.

'Everybody,' he said, 'this is Lucy.'

I was appraised by six pairs of eyes, but clinically, as if I were something in a Petri dish. I stretched out a hand ready to shake the first one that came my way. None did. A couple of boys raised their beer cans in greeting, and one girl smiled uncertainly. All towered over me; even the shortest girl there was still a full forehead taller.

'You weren't in our class, were you?' said Caius. He started laughing, and everybody else did too. 'Just joking.'

'No,' I said, trying to laugh as well. 'No, I wasn't.'

I expected Ben to continue with his introduction – Lucy, my *girlfriend* – but he didn't. I was on my own. The silence between us swelled.

'So . . . what do you do, then?' one of the other boys asked.

I decided not to tell them I was currently unemployed.

'Media? Wow. Remember that girl from halls, Jake, who did work experience at the BBC, or was it Channel 4?' Caius said then, and they all laughed loudly and talked rapidly about this girl. And abruptly I was forgotten, back out of the circle without having moved an inch. Somebody brought more drinks, more people joined the group, the conversation continued to flow, and the laughter grew more manic, more exclusive.

I excused myself, claiming I needed the toilet, and disappeared quickly off down the hall and joined the queue for the loo. I leaned heavily against the wall, belatedly aware of how much I had drunk. I watched people come and go on the stairs, alone and in pairs. It was dark here in the hall, and nobody met my eye. I heard the chain flush successively and, once or twice, some painful retching. The door opened, and the two girls ahead of me went in at the same time. Whatever they did in there took a quarter of an hour. When they finally came out, my excuse of needing the toilet was no longer fictitious.

When I came back out again and into the hall I saw an unexpectedly familiar face. His name was on the tip of my tongue. He saw me, and strode confidently up.

'Why, if it isn't Bernadette!' he exclaimed, laughing heartily and embracing me. It seemed rude not to respond in kind, so I did, lost inside this unexpected, but somehow welcome, bear hug. A peer, at last. He was a handsome man in, I guessed, his late forties, with the kind of self-possession about him that allowed him to wear a crushed velvet jacket without looking entirely ridiculous. I felt flattered that he remembered my name, or at least the name I had given him, with deliberate irony, back at the open mic night. But I couldn't recall his.

'Alistair,' he offered readily. 'We met at the open mic night thing the other month.'

'Of course. Hello.'

'And what brings you here?'

I hesitated. 'I'm with . . . someone, a friend of – well, of who-ever's party this is.'

His smile was lascivious, a smile that contained all sorts of suggestion. He had in his hand a large glass of red wine.

'Well, in that case, you are more than welcome,' he said, and bowed slightly.

I shook my head, confused.

'It's *my* party,' he explained.

I found it difficult to conceal my surprise. 'Forgive me, but this doesn't look like the house of a – well, it doesn't look like your house.'

'Not my *main* house, granted,' he was still grinning, 'but it is mine. I rent it out during the year to students. Some of my tenants wanted to throw a party to celebrate something or other, in the way that only students can. I told them that they could, on one proviso.'

'That you were permitted to attend?'

'Precisely.'

I felt unaccountably grateful to be talking to him; somebody on my level who wasn't looking over my shoulder to see who else they should be talking to instead of me. We were still in the hall, close to one another, and impervious to all those that clambered by.

'Don't take this the wrong way,' I began, 'but what would a man like you be wanting to get out of a party like this?'

He removed from his jacket pocket a thin, long spliff and

paused to light it. The flame reflected in his glasses and showed up the intimate detail in his skin, a yellowish, purplish swirl. He inhaled, then passed it to me.

'I could ask you the same question, but then I fancy I know the answer already.'

I hadn't smoked in a long time. My head spun.

He smiled as he said: 'You and Jake . . .'

A hot geyser of blood flushed into my face. How on earth?

'You need hardly be a detective, my dear.'

'If you say so.'

'I noted the lingering looks you were giving him at the bar. You remember, across a crowded room. I'm surprised, frankly, he couldn't feel your gaze at a hundred paces. *I* could.' He leaned into me, chuckling. 'To be honest, I felt somewhat jealous. Of him. Don't you envy the young? All that attention, and so frequently oblivious to it all. He'd kill to have a woman like you look at him so lovingly when he's our age.'

I looked at him and blinked slowly. '*Our* age?'

'Indeed.'

'How old are you, if you don't mind me asking?'

'Forty-seven. You?'

'Younger.'

'Then my sincere apologies! Drink?'

I leaned forward on the balls of my feet, and could see down the hallway into the room at the end, where Ben was still engulfed in conversation with his friends.

I looked back at my forty-seven-year-old compatriot. 'Why not?' I said.

He took me by the hand and led me gingerly back down the stairs.

'There you are!'

Ben looked drunk, and happy, his eyes bloodshot, his lips

curled back into a compressed smile. An hour had passed, maybe more. He looked from me to Alistair, and back again. Both Alistair and I, I knew, were thinking the same thing: which one of us was he talking to? Alistair stood up.

'Jake, my good man.' They shook hands. 'How are you?'

'I'm good, Alistair, I'm good.' While still addressing him, he shifted his heavy-lidded gaze on to me. 'You've not stolen my . . . ?'

'I wasn't aware she was yours!' he beamed.

'So glad to see Women's Lib alive and kicking in Bristol,' I said, still seated on the kitchen's small sofa. 'I'd rather neither of you discussed me as if I were your property . . .'

For a moment Ben looked pained, and I regretted snapping at him. Alistair kept laughing.

'I thought I'd lost you,' Ben said to me.

I was well on my way to properly drunk now, Alistair having mixed a succession of drinks for me in his kitchen with the skill of a seasoned barman, or seducer. 'I'm surprised you noticed.'

'Lucy, don't.'

'At this juncture,' Alistair announced, 'I think it wise for me to say that I believe I hear my telephone ringing in another room. I shall leave you both to it. Bernadette, or Lucy – both suit you, my dear – it has been a pleasure meeting you again.'

I checked the time on my phone: gone midnight. Andrew had left a message: ALL RIGHT AT JANES? Ben sat down next to me, confused.

'*Bernadette?*' he said.

Having never had a proper affair before, I wasn't quite sure of the etiquette. What right did I, a married woman after all, have to complain to him for deserting me at a party filled with his friends? He was merely catching up. I couldn't help but wonder about the conversation I had prompted the moment I had left them to it.

Ben squirmed on the cushion next to me, very likely pondering his own behaviour. We looked at each other, so full of things to say, questions to ask, mutual complications to unravel. We said nothing.

There came to my ears a distant sound, a kind of high-pitched tinnitus, probably imagined but nevertheless constant, and it took me a while to identify it properly. Alarm bells.

An hour and a half later, Ben and I were walking back to the hotel I had booked online the previous night. The streets were empty. His arm was draped over my shoulder, not just out of affection but also to help him remain upright. He had gone back to his friends after making sure Alistair hadn't been up to anything with me, in order to say what turned out to be a protracted goodbye. I, meanwhile, milled about in the kitchen, where a young woman told me she was just coming out of a black depression and did I fancy sharing some vodka and Ribena with her? She told me I looked like a good listener, and so I proved to be, she spending the next sixty minutes unspooling her entire relationship history in exchange for what she believed was my measured assessment and sensible advice.

We got back to the hotel late, where Ben quickly revivified himself – yet another perk of his youth. He pushed me up against the door as it closed, and grabbed a breast with one hand, but I quickly took control, whispering advice into his ear and enticing him gently to the bed. The sex was messy and enthusiastic, Ben reclaiming me for himself with uncustomary vigour, and me happily allowing him to do so. Twice.

He fell asleep shortly after. I lay alongside him and thought about Alistair back at the party. 'I'm a walking cliché,' he had boasted earlier, and encouraged me to guess his story. I thought of the most hackneyed I could: wife and two children, none of whom needed him very much any longer, which was why he was

284

there, at a party full of kids, attempting the classic kind of midlife reinvention. He turned crimson as I spoke, but laughed aloud and said, 'Absolutely right, more or less!'

He told me that a year earlier he had left his wife for one of his recently graduated students. He had confused sex for something more profound, a chance to start over. 'She left me within a month for somebody half my age, the little bitch. Can you believe it?' He was now living in a small flat off campus, most of his salary going to his wife to help pay for the house that they had bought together a quarter of a century previously. 'The only thing that keeps me solvent,' he lamented, 'is this place. The students trash it, but then their parents pay for it. One day, I really ought to sell up, run away with the money and start again properly.' He was suddenly solemn. 'Come with me?' he said.

'Why ever for?'

'Because we're both looking for something here we can't find. And I hope you don't mind me saying this, Bernadette, but you shan't find it with Jake. With me, however, you just might. I have lived, and I have learned some valuable lessons along the way. Who knows? I might just now be the man I was supposed to be all along.' He grinned, and I found myself piqued, and touched, and saddened. And yet still intrigued enough to hear what he had to say next. 'And you might just be the woman I prove it to.'

It was shortly after this that I had received the text from Andrew wanting to know if all was well, my husband with his good heart in spite of all I had done, and was continuing to do, to him.

Beside me, Ben was sleeping silently. I didn't sleep. I couldn't. The drink was keeping me awake, and plenty more besides. What was I doing? I looked over at my young lover, a sleeping beauty who belonged with them, his friends, a girl his own age, not with me. I closed my eyes as if better to envisage a tangible future with Ben, and of course I couldn't. I could see only

Andrew, for better or for worse, the man I had married, the man to whom I was married still. I cried silently, for him, for Ben, for the situation I had landed myself in, the situation I now needed to extricate myself from, to go back.

I got up at four o'clock and spent five minutes tiptoeing quietly through the room before realizing that Ben was not going to wake any time soon. I dressed, then switched on the television and watched the early-morning news. Shortly before dawn I packed my bag and left, leaving a note and some money, in case he was short. *Had to go. Something came up. Speak later x*.

It was cold, the first proper hint that winter was looming. The early-morning streets were freezing, but it refreshed me, the air tickling my nostrils like eucalyptus, the breeze bringing tears. My shoes were loud on the cobblestones, and I wondered how many people I was disturbing as I walked with purpose past their windows. There was nobody else about. I cast around for a taxi, but none came, no traffic whatsoever. It took half an hour to reach the station, and another half an hour before my train arrived. I bought a coffee, a croissant and a newspaper. I sat at my usual window seat, six up from the toilets – the train as complicit in my affair as anything else – and arranged myself accordingly, spread carelessly over both seats to discourage anyone from coming to sit next to me. But the carriage remained empty. I found my headphones and cued up some music on my iPhone. One of Ben's favourites came on, and I hummed quietly along.

Presently the ticket inspector arrived, humming a tune of his own. I unplugged my ears. 'Good morning, Miss,' he said, adding a biro'd squiggle to my ticket before handing it back.

Miss? It had been a long time since anybody had called me Miss.

Fourteen

Strictly within the confines of his featureless office, week after week, my therapist Dr Benn made me revisit my childhood – the source, he claimed, of so many of my problems, and the cause of my multiple frustrations. He suggested, amongst many other things, that I should learn how to grieve – over my late father, the late aunt who was for so long my surrogate mother; to grieve, to let go, to move on. I'd compartmentalized issues in the past, he said, had put them in boxes to deal with later. Now was the time to open them up at last. He counselled me to accept my mother's failings, to accept Andrew's failings, but more than that, to accept my own failings. He suggested that I sought this fantasy world of Ben in much the same way I sought fantasy as a child, closing the door to my mother's mood swings in order to lose myself in Enid Blyton instead.

He recommended I proactively start looking for a job again, which would help rebuild my self-confidence from the ground up – self-confidence forming the building blocks of all that is best in human endeavour. He commended me for what I was convinced was a selfish streak, because he thought I had too rarely put my own interests first. 'Selfish gets a bad press,' he said, 'but if you don't think about yourself from time to time, who will? You have needs; there are intimacy issues; you cannot ignore your sexuality.'

After weeks of doing all the talking, it was good at last to hear him talk back, and as he did so I nodded and blinked and made countless mental notes, ingesting everything he said in the hope that he would help solve the puzzle of my life and make it right again.

Speaking about my affair with Ben, he said, 'Look at it like a bridge, a bridge you take from one place to another, one state to the next.' This bridge, he continued, could take me from marriage into another relationship, or it could lead to a single life once more. Which did I want? A single life; a long-term affair? Did I want an end to my marriage, and the beginning of something new? Or did I want to fight to make my marriage something worth fighting for?

So many questions, each seeking an elusive answer.

He wanted to know whether I was going to see Ben again. I don't know, I responded. What do you think? To this he gave me one of his customary considerate smiles, one I would come to know well, Dr Benn nothing if not quintessentially enigmatic in his therapy: never responding yes or no to anything I asked, but instead gently encouraging me to take responsibility for myself, and the consequences too, as if I were the one in ultimate control here, as if I were the grown-up in this situation.

I didn't return home immediately after the party in Bristol, but instead loitered around town awhile, taking a collection of Sunday newspapers with me to the station's nearest greasy spoon. My phone deliberately off, I lost myself in the problems of the wider world until the real one pulled me back again. The café owner approached, wanting the table back. 'Getting busy here, love.'

I walked home, my overnight bag bumping against my hip, and arrived shortly after midday. The house was cold, Andrew having forgotten to set the thermostat in my absence. It was silent too. I slipped my shoes off and walked quietly through the house, then upstairs to his room. His bed had been slept in but was empty, yesterday's clothes in a pile by the wardrobe, whose door was gaping open to reveal his suits. Four pairs of shoes lay neatly by the far wall underneath the window that looked out into our garden, fresh from recent rainfall. I considered for less than a second switching on my phone and calling him to learn his whereabouts, but instead, suddenly impossibly weary, lay down on his bed, the smell of him rich in my nostrils, and fell instantly asleep.

I awoke sometime later to the earthquake sensation of him gently shaking me. Andrew. I smiled up at him, confused, but he didn't smile back. I sat up, and checked the clock on his bedside table: almost four.

'I must have—'

'We need to talk.' He was standing straight, an unreadable expression on his face, his voice level and reasonable, polite even. 'Could you get dressed and come downstairs, please?' For what I imagined was about to come, I'd rather he'd have shouted. He turned and went down. I got up and went into my room to change into something soft and comforting, an old sweatshirt-and-T-shirt ensemble. In the bathroom, I splashed water on my face and brushed my teeth. I caught my reflection in the mirror and saw that the pattern from Andrew's pillow had imprinted itself on my right cheek, the skin latticed with red grooves.

Slowly, I descended the staircase, imagining it my therapist's bridge. My footsteps were silent beneath me.

He was in the living room, standing by the window, both hands in his pockets. He turned to face me, and his eyes, I noticed, were milky. He hadn't been *crying*, had he?

'I know,' was what he said.

Two words. That's all it took for everything to change.

I said nothing.

'I know,' he said again, clearing his throat, giving it volume, 'that you've been cheating on me.'

My mother once told me that when you are confronted with an inconvenient truth, feign ignorance.

'Excuse me?'

'Lucy, don't. Please.'

Still by the window, his form was obliterated by the last of the afternoon's sunlight. All I saw was silhouette. He allowed his pause to become pregnant before eventually starting to talk again. He told me that he had had his suspicions for months now. I had been distracted, aloof, miles away, sometimes literally. He'd called Jane last night when I didn't respond to one of his texts, and Jane had failed to cover for me. After that, he had dug out my laptop and started browsing.

'Do I look tired today?' he asked. 'I should do. I was up most of the night. There was a lot to read. I did call you, you know? Several times. It went straight to voicemail. You were with *him*, presumably?'

Had I turned up the thermostat earlier? It was still cold in here, and I was shivering. But it felt more like the early onset of flu; I could feel my brow breaking out in a sweat. This was disappointing, but not surprising. I had a terrible immune system, always catching cold. Post-pneumonia, I was perpetually terrified of being laid low again. I stood stock still, facing my husband across the expanse of sisal rug with cream piping and edged with baby blue cotton twill, and tried to remain outwardly calm. How dare he look at my laptop! How careless of me to leave it lying around . . . *Think, Lucy!*, I told myself. *Think!* How much had he seen? Because much of it, the incriminating stuff at least, was password-protected, and I knew Andrew enough to know that he would never be able to break it. Perhaps he had only seen some messages from one of

290

the forums, but nothing from Ben, nothing too damaging.

My first impulse was to call Dr Benn, my counsellor: *I'm on the bridge! I'm halfway over the bridge! What should I do? Tell me, please!*

Andrew was pacing the room now, hands still in pockets. I sat down on the sofa, needing something solid beneath me. He glanced over intermittently, awaiting a response. It felt like an hour since his accusation, but was probably little more than a minute. I knew that I had to fill the growing silence, and fill it quickly.

'I don't know what you are talking about,' I said.

'Lucy, I *saw* your laptop.'

'And *what* exactly did you see?'

He shook his head. He was looking, at last, angry. 'The messages. Those . . . *chats*.' He reddened. 'Full of cocks and cunts.'

A wave of relief.

'Andrew, I never wrote anything like that.'

'No, but *they* did. To *you*. And from what I saw, you responded in kind, basically.'

'Andrew, listen . . .'

I patted the space on the sofa next to me, hoping he would come and join me. Instead, he sat in the armchair opposite. I explained the language of the chatrooms, the *n*etiquette, how it all meant very little, was merely the way people expressed themselves online, and I reminded him too that it was *he* who had given me permission all those months ago.

His response was an incredulous one. '*What?*'

'You told me that, as you had your interests, your drinking and your gambling, your football, that I should have mine . . .'

He winced. 'Okay, fine – whatever. But this?' He swallowed. 'And anyway, what about *Ben?*'

I froze, and surely my face gave me away. 'Ben?'

'I encouraged you to, you know, to have some – fun. Just fun. But one of the strands . . . sounded all very lovey-dovey. With . . . with Ben.'

In my head, I scrolled through hundreds of emails. Ben and I had communicated through a private account, mostly, though it was true that we also sometimes communicated in the forum where we had first met. If Andrew had happened upon these, then he'd have found us both careful with our language, our declarations. Neither of us ever wished to reveal too much within a public forum, and so these messages were merely our overly polite way of getting into contact again after one of our infuriating hiatuses, before doing so more intimately, via private Hotmail accounts. I concluded, quickly and with relief, that whatever Andrew might have seen had been innocent. But innocent enough?

I gathered myself. Ben, I told him, was one of the nicer ones. He had been someone I had been chatting with for a few months now, and, yes, getting more intimate with, too. The relief I felt while telling him this – a confession of sorts – was overwhelming. It was hard not to cry. As I spoke I watched Andrew's face turn an even deeper red. He asked whether I'd met up with him, whether I'd slept with him, with Ben, with any of them. His eyes twitched. He swallowed. I had never seen my husband cry, and I didn't want to be responsible for making him cry now.

Here I am on the middle of the bridge, I said to myself. *Do I progress? Do I turn back? Which way?*

'No,' I told him firmly, then immediately wavered, corrected myself, and admitted that, okay, I had met a couple of people, yes, on a couple of occasions. I told him about Tyke, the wannabe jockey. The mention of his name caused Andrew to wince. He must have seen Tyke's messages, and there had been many, the majority of which had arrived *after* we had met, Tyke pleading we do so again. Andrew presumably knew this. He presumably was trying to catch me out in a lie. I told him also about having wanted to meet up with the chef, but that the chef had stood me up.

'So who were you with last night, and why did you lie to me about being at Jane's? Jane told me she hadn't heard from you in months, that you'd gone all secretive and weird. She said she didn't even realize you were friends any more.'

I ignored the sting this brought, and acknowledged, silently, that it was a reasonable question. I could have predicted it, so why didn't I have a ready answer? Why?

'I went to a party.'

'Whose?'

'. . . Somebody I met online.'

I could hear him breathing through his nostrils, long, slow, even breaths.

'Nothing happened, Andrew. It was boring, and I wish I'd never gone. I was the oldest person there by years. It was awful, embarrassing.' I'm not sure I realized, then, that I was lying here – lying to protect him and me both – but as I was saying the words, I found myself believing in them. Perhaps I wanted to believe them. 'Look, I'm sorry I lied to you, Andrew, but we've been leading separate lives for such a long time now. You are always out with your friends, and drunk – you are *always* drunk, Andrew, and I'm left here, alone and bored, and going out of my mind. I want to have a life as well, you know? And if I can't find one with you, then, well, I'll try to find one elsewhere.' It was my turn now to be on the brink of tears. 'But sadly it didn't work out as I'd hoped. I'm looking for a replacement for you, Andrew, because you are never fully in my life any more. Don't you realize that?'

He came to join me on the sofa, but not necessarily as a concession. He made the most of its expanse, him at the far end, me at the other.

'You did tell me to go out and have my fun,' I said again. 'Well, that's what I was trying to do.'

He looked distraught. When he spoke, he did so in a quiet voice. I had to strain to hear him. 'Perhaps I didn't think it through properly.'

Perhaps neither of us did.

We had the longest conversation of our marriage that night. Neither of us moved from the sofa for over five hours, not even for a toilet break, as we attempted to disseminate just where it had all started to Go Wrong for us. Occasionally we laughed, but more frequently we cried. We didn't, however, argue; a novelty. He admitted helplessly that he was a man of habit, an unreconstructed bloke who, like his father, like Dan, ultimately believed that men and women were separate and distinct beings, and that the best way to stay together long-term was by existing mostly apart. This was how it was for all the men he knew. I pointed out that most of the men he knew were separated or divorced, or married and miserable.

'But you seem to want us to do *everything* together,' he complained. He didn't want to go hill walking with me, or to the gym, the theatre, to art galleries. He wanted to live with me, to go out to dinner with me, to sleep with me (said with a sad blush), but otherwise he wanted to go to football with the lads, racing with his friends, and sit in front of the television with a takeaway.

'I don't know how to be with you the way you want me to be with you,' he said.

A lone woman walked past our window then. I found myself wishing I were her.

He turned to me. 'What do you even like about me?' he asked. A horrible, loaded question, freighted with a significance that had the power to change everything.

'What do you mean?'

'What do you like about me, Lucy?'

He wasn't going to make it any easier.

'I like . . . I like your company. I like talking to you. You're generous, you're funny. You bring, I don't know, a certain kind of energy to a lot of the things you do. I love that. We have fun together, sometimes.'

He nodded. 'That it? And what don't you like about me?'

'Andrew, we really—'

'Answer the question.'

'Oh, well, look, I don't know. Okay, no, I do. You drink too much. You gamble a lot. It's not the money, it's the time. You'd rather be amongst horses than me. You'd rather be at the football. Watching television. Sleeping.'

'And my friends. You don't like my friends. Dan.'

'No, I suppose not.'

'What else?'

'Andrew, please.'

'What else?'

'You go to bed, every night, at ten forty-five. You snore. You don't seem to do anything about your snoring, which you know drives me insane. You don't want to do anything with me. You're bored with me. *Of* me.'

'That's not true. I'm not.'

'Well it doesn't feel that way.'

'That's because . . . because, because you're a stranger to me. Half the time, Lucy, you *are*. I don't know what you're thinking any more, or what you want. Ever since the house, and after you lost your job. You've shut me out. You've become distant. And you look at me with such disappointment. You make me feel – worthless. Fat. Ugly.'

'No, that's not . . .' *Did I?*

295

'I revolt you. You shudder every time I come close. You never want . . . You never want sex.'

'Andrew, I—'

'Not with me, anyway.' He pointed to my laptop, on the floor beneath the armchair. 'But with them, oh, with *them* you do. Even if you haven't, as you claim, actually had sex with any of them, you write all that . . . *stuff*. It's disgusting, perverted. And it's sad. That's what it is: sad. How do you think that makes me feel, huh? No, seriously, Lucy. How do you think it makes me *feel*?'

It was gone midnight, and suddenly we were ravenous. We ordered pizza with extra pepperoni, which was how Andrew always used to like it in the early days of our courtship, before he had any concept of cholesterol and its mortal dangers, and it was how, I knew, Ben liked it still. We washed it down with a bottle of wine, but there was little convivial about our meal. We were eating because we were hungry, and we were drinking to blot out the pain.

By half past one we'd run out of things to say. My mouth was dry; I felt indigested. I wouldn't be sleeping tonight.

Andrew broke the silence. 'Do you want us to split up?'

I blanched. 'No. I don't know. I'm not sure. You?'

The mood had been shifting throughout the evening, from anger and bitterness to, latterly, gradual understanding and neutral ground. Andrew, I thought, had been mellowing, perhaps in forgiveness, perhaps guilt. I knew that he didn't want to be on his own, that the idea of a second divorce appalled him. So it was a shock to hear him say, 'I don't know. Perhaps.' His words fell on to me from clean out of the sky, as heavy as bricks, and suddenly I was back on my bridge and actually crossing it this time, whether I wanted to or not. The prospect of divorce was clearly more worrying to me now than it was to him.

He said, 'Think it would have been different if we'd had children?'

Before I could answer, he yawned. 'Look, sorry, but I'm exhausted. As I'm sure you've noticed, it's after ten forty-five. Work tomorrow. 'Night.'

He stood up unsteadily and left me there on the sofa, the detritus of our takeaway surrounding me, the empty bottle on its belly on the rug. I spent a redemptive half-hour tidying up, putting the boxes out for recycling, and, as soundlessly as I could, the wine and beer bottles too. I filled the dishwasher, then realized that the dishwasher itself needed cleaning. Perhaps this was something I could tackle in the morning. I looked around the kitchen and saw, for the first time, signs of wear and tear, things too long uncleaned and uncared for, ignored and over-looked. Yes, I would clean everything in the morning. A new day, a different perspective, a fresh start.

By the time I went upstairs, Andrew was asleep. He always had been the kind of husband who could fall effortlessly into unconsciousness on an argument.

But not me. In bed, I switched on my phone, craving comfort from somewhere – from, inevitably, Ben. But the anticipated buzz of a message or voicemail never came. I switched it back off again.

In the morning I awoke to the surprising sensation that I must at some stage have slept, albeit briefly and badly. I stretched, my eyeballs bruised, my skin prickling, and remembered the very edges of a dream before, a moment later, I lost it. I went to the bathroom and brushed my teeth, then walked past Andrew's room. His door was ajar; he must already have left for work. I walked into it and saw his bed empty and made, the doors to his wardrobe still wide open. But the wardrobe was empty now, his clothes gone, so too his shoes, his suitcase. I spun around on my heel, suddenly lightheaded. I needed to sit.

My husband, it seemed, had left me.

*

If ever I fantasized about this moment, it was always me leaving him, not the other way around. But in real life, my tireless enemy, it was Andrew who had pulled the rug out from under *me*. In response, I crumpled. I cried more that morning than I had done in any of my therapy sessions, great rib-racking sobs tinged with a deep-seated panic that shocked me and made me cry all the more. I muffled my tears in a pillow lest my neighbours heard me and started to worry.

Mid-morning I received a text from him: STAYING WITH DAN. WILL BE IN TOUCH. X.

I was pitifully grateful for the X, but any relief quickly turned to anger, which I directed now exclusively to Dan, he clearly the bad influence here, the man who had given Andrew the strength to do what he wouldn't have done otherwise. If Dan could do it, could leave his wife and start again, then his best friend, his old mucker, could too. Life goes on. They would probably have the time of their lives now, their midlife crises legitimized by women who had failed them. They would now live hedonistically, purely for themselves, strip clubs and ponytails and motorbikes, and never having to say they are sorry to anyone ever again.

That night, Jane called to offer support, having heard about my marital developments on what she called, archly, the 'grapevine'. I told her I didn't want to talk and hung up on her. I wanted to be angry with Jane as well, for not covering for me, but I couldn't be. There was only one person at fault here, and that was me.

I put on my coat and gloves and my boots, and wrapped my scarf around my face, and passed the afternoon sat shivering in the garden. When darkness came, I transferred myself to the living room, still dressed for the elements, where I wrote a dozen text messages to Ben, but sent none of them. The fact that he hadn't been in touch told me everything I needed to know.

By midnight, I had a realization: perhaps I could make it through this after all. And perhaps I could, and should, be alone, at least for a while.

The resolution, when I realized that this was what it was, felt good. Tainted with a most painful regret, of course, but good. I'd made a mess of my life; the last thing I wanted to do now was make even more of a mess of it. I wanted to start over again with Andrew to give us both a chance to rectify things, if he'd have me back, because wasn't that what a marriage was all about?

And Ben? Ben would become part of my history, a cherished part, admittedly, and quite possibly one of my favourite chapters, but there was no going back now.

In my mind, I wrote an email to him. About how much I loved him, but. About how much I wished we could be together, if only. About the parallel universe in which I wished I existed, where.

But I could never get to the end of the sentences, and so the email remained unwritten. But then perhaps I wouldn't need to write it. I could take the coward's way out, and let my silence do the talking instead. Because my resolve was firm.

We were over.

Then, the following night, he contacted me via Messenger.

Paranoidandroid: Are you avoiding me?

I hesitated. I thought about ignoring the message but I knew he deserved an explanation. It was now or never.

Lucy: I thought *you* were avoiding *me*.
Paranoidandroid: why would I do that?
Lucy: You tell me.

Paranoidandroid: the party?

Lucy: What about it?

Paranoidandroid: the way I behaved. ☹ I apologise.

Paranoidandroid: I was drunk, and ashamed, and I didn't contact you afterwards because . . .

Lucy: Well?

Paranoidandroid: Eh?

Lucy: You left a dot dot dot.

Paranoidandroid: Yes.

Lucy: So . . . ?

Paranoidandroid: look, this is difficult for me. Perhaps it would be better if we spoke. can I call you?

Lucy: My battery's dead, and my husband is here. Safer this way, I think.

Paranoidandroid: okay, well, the thing is, I think you are fantastic, really I do . . .

Lucy: More dot dot dots. Can we just get this over and done with, please?

I waited, convinced he hadn't gone but was rather typing out a slow response. I became anxious as the seconds ticked by, wanting desperately for his words to materialize on the screen, to have ingested them already and dealt with whatever pain they would inevitably cause. I knew what I wanted them to say, what they *had* to say, but I dreaded having to read them all the same.

Paranoidandroid: Actually, I've written it all down in an email – a kind of letter, basically, that explains everything. If I send it, will you read it?

I told him I would. My inbox chimed.

Hey you,

When I first met you online, Lucy, I wasn't in a good place. You know that. More than anyone, you know that. I was coming to the end of a relationship, my first serious one, and surprise surprise I wasn't dealing with it very well. I know that I wanted it over, but I didn't have the courage to end it myself, and when she ended up doing so for me, it devastated me. Ridiculous, I know, but still. And then I was back living with my parents, my degree over, few job prospects, no life. I'd been depressed before, it runs in the family probably, and here I was getting depressed all over again. I never went out, I didn't want to meet anybody. But I did want some kind of escape, even if it was just from the voices in my own head. I wanted somebody to lift me out of my world and into adventure. I never thought I'd find it, certainly not online, and I never thought that I'd end up finding somebody like you. Lucy, you were amazing, you helped me out of my shell. You showed me that there is life beyond the breakup of your first relationship, and that nobody has any right to wallow. You taught me that people get over things all the time. You had got over relationships, you told me, and so would I. I didn't believe you at first, but I wanted to. And now I do. And I am so grateful to you for that. You gave me confidence. In fact, you gave me so much more confidence than I ever had before, and what happened was – well, I started to feel better about myself, not just in my room in front of my laptop while my parents slept or argued down the hall in their room, but also confidence to deal with the rest of my life. After that open mic night – which you crashed so magnificently! – it began to seem likely that I might just be able to become a teacher, a good teacher, after all, and after that night, and for all sorts of reasons since, my confidence has continued to build and build.

When I invited you to the party, I wanted to show my old friends another side of me, and, I'll admit it, I also wanted to show off. I've grown up! I've moved on! I've got a girlfriend, an older woman! You, Lucy, were my potential realised. And I wanted everyone to know it. I felt so proud to be with you, even though I know that you didn't feel particularly proud, that night, to be with me. I behaved badly . . . But then what did you expect from a 23 year old! You were being judged by my friends, harshly and wrongly, and I didn't do anything about it. I wanted to hate them for it, for laughing and sniggering, but I knew that I'd probably have reacted just the same if it had been Tom or Caius who had turned up with an older woman instead. We are all tribes at the end of the day, aren't we? And we stick together in our tribes, because we're mostly too scared to break out on our own. We lack the imagination to do so as individuals.

We stick together because we stick together, and so I think what I realised the night of the party was that, in an ideal world, I would want to keep you elsewhere, to hide you away from my world and to have you all to myself. I didn't want to sully you, and what we had together. It was too precious for that. Also, if I'm honest, I didn't want my friends to think too weirdly of me because I was dating somebody old enough to be . . . well, older than me.

I actually think them seeing me with you did me a world of good. I shocked them, and I've never really shocked my friends before. I was always so predictable. But not now. It even made me popular – with girls! – girls who had previously never even noticed me . . .

Before you say anything, I know that this is no way to treat you, and so I don't for a second expect you to be patient with me here, or put up with me any more. I am in every way your inferior, and I'll prove it: if I'm entirely honest, I want you only for my plaything, my fantasy made occasionally real. I want you to book us a hotel room whenever the mood takes us – takes *me*. But that's not right. It's selfish, it's immature, and it is what it is – fantasy.

I'm glad we managed to make the fantasy real for a while, more than you can ever appreciate, but I'm also aware that if either of us allowed it to continue, we both know how it would likely end up: you hating me, and me ending up hating myself all over again. I don't want you to hate me, I don't want to contribute to the ruin of your marriage, and I also don't want to get into that self-loathing place again. I'm not strong enough for it.

I know, I know: I'm a hypocrite, I'm a wimp, I'm selfish, and I'm stupid. I think what we had together was amazing, the highlight of my confused private life to date, and I'll never forget you but . . .

Paranoidandroid: That's as far as I got. I hope . . . Actually, hang on, are you still there, or have I lost you already?

Tears stung my eyes, and spilled down my cheeks. I typed out my response slowly, one letter at a time.

Lucy: I'm still here.
Paranoidandroid: Phew, that's a relief! ☺ Look, what I think I'm trying to say in all this is that I'll never forget you, Lucy, but I think perhaps we should leave it – for now. I like to think that if I met you in five years' time, I'd ask you to fall in love with me, to be with me, to have my children. But I'm 23 years old, a baby still, and I don't really know what I'm doing. Thing is, all my friends are in much the same position, so if nothing else at least I'm in good company.

None of this, I imagine, will make you feel very good, and will probably make you hate me. I can only say that I am very very very sorry. It's not you, it's me. Seriously, it is. I don't think I'll ever get over you, and I'm not sure I particularly want to. Who, after all, wants to forget the best thing that ever happened to them?

I hope you can understand where I'm coming from. I hope you

sympathise, and if not sympathise, then I hope you pity me. But please please please don't hate me. I'd find that too difficult to bear. You don't hate me, do you? Do you?

Dot dot dot.

It was late, so late. I thought for a long while on how best to phrase my response, what to say and how to say it. I took a deep breath, wiped away the tears. And then I started typing, this time completing every sentence all the way to their full stops.

Fifteen

It is never easy to get back what you had before, and even less so when what you had has been so carelessly tainted. I'd never done it previously, gone back. Whenever a relationship had begun to flounder, I simply walked away. Often I ran, and frequently into the arms of the nearest somebody else that would have me, thereby kick-starting the whole process again, an endless taunting cycle of love, doubt, break-up and begin-again. If I'm honest about it, it wasn't always me doing the running, but sometimes the other way round.

But it gets harder to start again as you age. It does. Or at least it did for me.

The next few weeks were not good ones. I reverted into my shell, the house, and passed my days on my hands and knees, cleaning the place until it shone, then crying unreasonably when I realized I didn't want it to shine, I wanted it to sparkle. I think I might have been losing my mind. My mother must have sensed something was up, because out of the blue she began calling every day for a chat. I couldn't remember the last time she had called merely to *chat*.

'Where is Andrew?' she asked the third day we spoke.

'He's . . . he's here,' I responded non-committally.

'Can I speak with him?'

'. . . He's in the bathroom, the toilet.'

This was how our conversations would pan out, friendly questions first, then mild interrogations to follow, my mother trying to eke out a confession that Andrew wasn't really in the bathroom at all, and neither was he at home in any kind of permanent sense, that something had at last happened between us. She could hear the tears at the back of my throat, she claimed one day, and could sense too that I was becoming, not so much in what I said but the way I said it, a depressive. She clarified: 'And it takes one to know one.' I confessed nothing, and to my surprise she didn't press the issue.

It was the cruellest of months, December, Christmas looming like a threat. My mother insisted I be their guest, and though I didn't particularly want to spend Christmas Day with her, I didn't want to remain alone either. I complied. The day passed in the way it does for so many of us, the cliché of turkey and crackers and false bonhomie, an argument over dessert, and Clive helping himself to generous servings of successive postprandial brandies while my mother took her non-specific bad mood with her into the kitchen where it simmered nicely. This left the two of us at the dining-room table, alone together. Clive smiled with a generous warmth. 'Water off a duck's back, Lucy,' he said. 'It's the saying I've come to live by since meeting your mother.' He did something then that he had never done to me before, or since: extended his hands across the table, covered both of mine and squeezed. He continued. 'There is plenty you have to endure in a marriage, but it's worth it, trust me.' He had to raise his voice now because my mother was making it clear in the kitchen just how much she preferred the company of dirty plates to him. This made him smile all the more, a little drunk now, I thought. 'Even if it doesn't seem immediately obvious to anyone else. But despite it all, you know what? Your mother, she's the port in my storm.'

His port stormed back into the room a moment later,

stopping short when she saw us now standing in an embrace. I know my mother well enough to know that this affected her deeply, but with my mother the head has always ruled the heart.

'I'm not surprised you don't want to stay married,' she said to me, helping herself to the remains of Clive's brandy. It was the first time the subject of Andrew had been mentioned that day. 'And who knows, maybe I'll come to feel the same way soon enough. We could flatshare together.'

I couldn't decide whose laughter was the more manic, Clive's or my mother's.

Andrew texted shortly before the Queen's speech, Ben shortly after. HAPPY CHRISTMAS, was all the former said. HOPE UR HAVING A BETTER ONE THAN ME, said the latter, which I wanted to convince myself was actually a cry of help, an apology, and a suggestion perhaps that there was a way back for us after all. Maybe, maybe not. But then, after my third Baileys, my mother and Clive asleep together on the sofa, their heads touching, I was no longer sure if it meant anything at all, or even if I wanted it to.

I responded only to Andrew's. YOU TOO. ALL MY LOVE.

Against all better judgement – but then what forty-year-old recently separated from her husband has judgement? – and desperate to fend off the yawning black dog of seasonal depression, I elected to spend New Year's Eve at Jane's. She'd called, inviting me at the last moment, perhaps because a better offer had failed to materialize. The call came shortly after eight, truculent and businesslike, and quintessentially Jane: 'You're alone, aren't you? Me too. Come on, come over. I've lots of drink in the fridge.' She had clearly made the same calls to Lydia and Lindsay as well, because by the time I got there they were arriving too. The first five minutes were exquisitely awkward, familiar faces having become those of strangers. There was much to be said about how it was that we came to find ourselves in such a situation – single ladies together – on the eve of the new year, but words weren't needed right now. We had history, and that was enough. For the time being, we also had each other.

Over four separate takeaways, we joked about old times and old boyfriends, and we drank so very much, crowded into Jane's small living room, laughing loudly and with increasing abandon. A sudden downpour was endeavouring to spoil many people's al fresco celebrations, and we couldn't help our reaction: we were glad of it. 'May all their umbrellas break!' was one of our more memorable toasts.

Somehow we missed the midnight bells altogether and only noted the New Year about half an hour into it, the muffled sounds of sopping-wet fireworks fizzing listlessly into the black sky. We fell into a tearful collective embrace, then said fuck it, and got out the Trivial Pursuit, which we argued over, and cheated at, until two in the morning, at which point Strip Monopoly seemed a *much* more sensible idea, Jane filming our efforts on her phone and promising to post it up later on YouTube. We each of us attempted to ignore the underlying misery of the evening, masking it instead with a forceful hilarity which I was grateful we were able to maintain for so long. We drank champagne and vodka, a forgotten bottle of last year's Drambuie, some gin and Tia Maria. It was a wonderful, messy night, and we awoke well into New Year's Day feeling a new kind of wretched. My headache would last a week.

I was up first on the day itself, pulling myself into an upright position from where I had passed out several hours previously on the floor. Lindsay was snoring gently in the armchair opposite, and Jane was on the sofa, which meant that Lydia had been the only one who had made it into the bedroom. I checked, and saw a cold foot poking out underneath a mountain of duvet. I went to the toilet, then into the kitchen, and peered out of the window, pulling the blinds up to reveal a leaden, grey start to January, the clouds so low you could almost reach out and touch them.

I hunted the flat for my bag, and my phone, and eventually found both beneath Lindsay's thighs. No missed calls, but seven text messages. Each had been sent the previous night from friends, and even my mother, each wishing me a Happy New Year. Nothing from Ben, but one from Andrew. AULD LANG SYNE, it read. I checked the time it was sent: 12:01 a.m.

'We've run out of milk,' announced an unnaturally deep voice.

I turned around. Jane, without make-up, seemed ten years older than she had yesterday. But then I was hardly one to talk. I looked much the same.

Suddenly, a suffocating imperative, I craved fresh air.

'I'll go and get some,' I said.

I had planned to aim for the corner shop and then promptly return but, once outside on the pavement, my feet kept me walking. I now felt an overwhelming need simply to return *home*.

I made no New Year's resolutions. I never do. What's the point of promising yourself the impossible when failure to deliver is the perpetual conclusion? But when the phone rang on 2 January, bringing some unexpectedly good news, I did wonder whether I had in fact done so during the post-midnight chaos at Jane's, only later to have forgotten all about it. It was my old boss, wondering if I might possibly be able to handle a little freelance work. Cost-cutting, he relayed, was now bringing its own problems, those cost-effective new recruits not always capable of doing the work they had been drafted in to perform. 'Clueless twits', was what he called them. He wanted employees who knew what they were doing, he said, 'like the old days'. He wasn't able to offer me my old job back. Instead of being associate producer, I would be more associate to the associate producer. 'Labels and titles; the usual nonsense. Basically, you'll be nanny.' Nevertheless, he added quickly, the pay would be good, the freelance scale so much more generous than an employee's day rate. Four days a week to start, very likely rising to five the moment I reminded everybody upstairs how indispensable I was. A short-term contract to start with, five, possibly six months, but very likely more, and they wanted me to start right away. Could I?

And so that was how I came to be back in partial full-time employment by 3 January. A good start to 2010.

I threw myself into what was pretty much the same job I used to have, only this time in a more overseeing role, and alongside the newly promoted Catriona, who had so impressed me at that inter-departmental meeting months ago. Catriona welcomed me back, but I could see that my returning presence somewhat dented the collective confidence of the department's New World Order. She remained professionally tolerant of me, though, and I found myself grateful for that, and happy simply to be back in work.

I worked long hours, and went out for drinks afterwards, not with the new crowd but helplessly gravitating towards what was left of the old team, my former colleagues now seeming to me like late lamented friends whom I hadn't cherished enough at the time and should do so now. The days passed, and became weeks. I was rarely at home unless I was there to sleep – not consciously avoiding it, but that was precisely what I was doing. Why go home when I could remain in the world outside?

My old friend Elliot contacted me after an unlike-him silence, and I was stunned to learn that real life was happening to him as well. Estelle, his perfect wife, had recently left him, having revealed herself an adulterer too. She'd been having an affair for the past year with a single father she'd met at the crèche. It was obvious why Elliot was contacting me now: he needed not only a friend but an expert in these matters, someone to guide him through. We met for drinks and dinner, but he surprised me. I had expected him to be devastated, but he admitted that Estelle's abrupt confession of having fallen in love with someone else only made him realize that that was what he had wanted to do himself: fall in love with someone else. Everybody, in the end, does, he said. As a result, they were now being curiously grown-up – and very French – about it. Elliot had moved into a well-appointed studio flat around the corner from the family house; he continued to have breakfast with his children every morning, and picked the older daughter up from school each afternoon. There was something emboldened about him, the way his eyes trailed the waitresses in our restaurant as they moved from table to table, and I realized that perhaps it was *he* who could guide *me*, not the other way round. In similar situations to him, I had only felt deep pessimism, but here he was full of hope, looking forward to fresh sex and new love. Did I hope he wouldn't find it quite so easily, as I hadn't? A little bit, yes. But then cliché abounds in such circumstances, and misery really does love company.

Jane, Lydia and Lindsay continued to drift around my consciousness, updated phone calls and texts mostly, and often after eleven o'clock at night, all of them filling me in on their latest man escapades, their ecstatic highs, and the inevitable follow-through of catastrophic lows. We talked, vaguely, about an all-girls holiday in the summer, Barcelona, maybe, or even, if we dared, Ibiza. Were we too old for Ibiza? 'It's good to have you back, Luce,' Jane said more than once, a song in her voice.

Another month, and Martin called. His wife, Illeana, was going back to the Czech Republic and taking their daughter with her. It was up to him, she had said, whether he chose to follow or not, but his decision would not affect hers. She had grown tired of England, and would not be bringing up her child in a country that so lacked in moral fibre. 'Moral fibre?' Martin shot back at her, offended. 'Well, just look at your friends,' was how she responded. He had no immediate comeback to this.

We met up. 'What should I do?' he pleaded, tears gathering in his eyes.

'You're asking *me*?'

I took Martin's disappointment to heart, and couldn't help but see in it a reflection of my own situation. Seeing quite so much of my friends was hard work, I realized. I was grateful to have them, and their company, but I recognized that the more time I spent with them, the more lonely I grew, the more fearful for my own future.

Which is probably why, by the end of the month, I was seeing Andrew again, the pair of us drifting back to one another not so much because marriage is the tie that binds but because we were each too bruised to continue alone, and perhaps too hopeless – too *scared* – to start up with anybody else. There was history between us, we knew one another, intimately, and, I suppose, we liked one another still. And love; that too. Dan, I learned, had gone back to Scotland, his midlife crisis over and desperate to rekindle things with his wife. I asked Andrew how he had liked flatsharing with his old mate, and his reply came with deep crow's feet around the eyes, deeper than I remember them being.

'I've had better set-ups,' he smiled tiredly.

He told me that he had missed me, and that he didn't want to miss me any more. He wasn't asking to take me back, and he didn't necessarily forgive me, not entirely, but as he reminded me over a lovely dinner one night in what had been one of our favourite restaurants, he had married me for a reason and, despite recent events, the reason hadn't really changed very much.

312

He took a deep breath. 'So I thought we could perhaps, you know, try again?' My heart lifted like a teenage girl's. 'I thought perhaps we could try to have an old-fashioned marriage.'

My heart was fluttering wildly. I said, 'Old-fashioned? How so?'

'One where we could actually honour our vows.' Another tired smile. 'In sickness and in health, through thick and through thin.'

I laughed. 'I don't remember that line.'

'That was the general gist, I think.'

When he reached for my hand, I did not withdraw it.

It was strange seeing him again like this, intimate strangers re-feeling our lost way with one another, and cautious in each other's company in a manner we hadn't been before. Both of us were breakable; we knew that now. We had to be handled with care. He had lost weight, I could see, and it didn't really suit him. His was a frame that needed sustenance to it, blubber even, a blubber I loved. This, I realized, was what true romance for grown-ups was all about: not the fleeting sensation of love in youth, but a previously dead love suddenly revived and gifted a second chance. It prompted a heady sensation, like standing at the top of a tall building and sticking your head out of the window. Everything about me was all pitter-patter breathlessness. But outwardly at least I kept calm. This was, after all, a game of sorts. There were rules to follow.

He told me that he was paid up until the end of the month in the flat that he had shared with Dan, and was now living in it alone. He could extend the lease if he wanted to, if *I* wanted him to.

'I'm not sure I'm ready for you to move back in just yet,' I said, wavering.

His face fell. 'Are you still seeing your toyboy?'

I had to restrain myself, from claiming that Ben was never

313

that, could never be written off so easily, so mockingly. Even my therapist had told me so.

I composed myself. 'No. I am not. And what about you? Are *you* seeing anybody?'

'Would I have called you if I were?'

He saw me to my door that night – to *our* door – and gave me a peck on the cheek before turning and walking back down the street, then he turned right, up towards the main road. It must have been so strange for him, walking away from the house that he had helped to buy and renovate, and leaving me there. It certainly felt strange watching him go, a wrenching sensation tearing inside me. I very nearly called out to him to come back, but then one of the neighbour's cats appeared on my wall, so I stroked it instead. We pushed noses and it purred loudly. Were it not for Rummy, the hamster, I'd have invited it in, but then that was a dangerous path right there: Cat Lady. I didn't want to be Cat Lady, not yet.

To my surprise, the next time I heard from Andrew, a full week later, as if to prove that he too had understood it was now required for us to take things slow, he told me that he had extended the rental on his and Dan's place for another six months. My stomach sank. I think in my dreams I had him banging on the front door and pleading to be let back in, that he couldn't spend another night away from me. Clearly he could.

But then I was forgetting the game, its convoluted rules. Andrew was back in the marital home within six weeks, the pull between us now so crushingly inevitable that it wasn't worth the effort of denying it any longer. (As it turned out, he had not wasted his money on the lease. Dan did manage to get back with his ex-wife, but the marriage would buckle for a second, and final, time shortly after, and he was installed back in the flat by the end of the month. He found another job, and also another girlfriend, this one Romanian and young enough to be really very young indeed.)

So Andrew and I were together again, the hump on the road successfully negotiated and now behind us. A happy ending? Or merely an inevitable one? It may just turn out to be only a temporary one, Dan winning back his old flatmate in the long-run. We shall have to see.

It was interesting how quickly I found myself again after so comprehensively losing all sense of identity. I felt like I'd been given my life back, a second chance, and my initial response was evangelical zeal, every little detail about the two of us together suddenly rare and special and worth obsessing over, cherishing. Many times I found it hard to believe so much of the last eighteen months had happened at all. How foolish I had been, how reckless, and how thoughtless, too. Did I really believe that happiness lay within a computer screen, much less with a man so much younger than myself? Regrettably, I did, yes. I really did. But not any more.

For the first few weeks of our reunion, Andrew and I were a courting couple all over again. We went out to eat most nights, we drank a lot of wine, and pretty soon he had put on all the weight he had lost during our separation. I too ascended help-lessly, but curiously contentedly, from a size 10 to 12. We began to have sex again, awkwardly at first – fleeting impotency (him), faked orgasms (me) – before we settled back into a certain familiar rhythm. It was pretty good, consistently satisfactory. Afterwards, we would fall asleep in one another's arms, a pharma-ceutical strip on the roof of his mouth and another across the bridge of his nose successfully stemming his snoring. I found I loved his body beside mine, the warmth we generated between us. I hadn't felt this good, this protected, since, well – since Ben.

Ben. I hadn't heard from him again, and I suppose I was relieved not to have. True, I wouldn't have considered it the end of the world had he emailed or texted to say that he had made a mistake, that he couldn't live without me, but he didn't. He had disappeared from my life. In forbidding myself to track him online, I was already forgetting his face, his eyes, his smile.

Now back in the marital bed, each morning my husband and I would wake together, breakfast together, brush our teeth side by side and see one another off, Andrew bound for the train, me the bus, a parting kiss that left a trace of him on my lips and left me sated with happiness and, more, relief. People would watch our exchange, I kidded myself, with envy: *There goes the perfect married couple. If only we were as happy as that* . . .

I knew of course that this was merely a honeymoon period, an unsustainable utopia, and that, ultimately, old habits, and old routines, die hard. And so, after a month, but perhaps maybe as many as six weeks, when the novelty of our reunion became more settled, an established comfortable reality, and work became more stressful for both of us, our syrupy romance downgraded to a steady potboiler status. The muddled bureaucracy at work was exhausting me. I was tired and grumpy; I needed sleep. Andrew, too, was increasingly distracted by work, and the football season was nearing its climax, demanding his attention. He complained about the pharmaceutical strip in his mouth, and the one on his nose, and began deliberately to forget to affix either each night, which led to a quick resumption of his snoring, which in turn led to separate bedrooms once more. After breakfast in the morning, he would frequently forget to brush his teeth altogether, and was out the door while I was still upstairs pulling on my tights. It seemed like a crude waste of money to go out and eat every night, and so we didn't. We ate in, in front of the TV, which removed the need to share with one another our respective day's events. Sometimes we would finish the night with perfunctory sex in either of our bedrooms, but

Andrew's approach was by now noticeably lacklustre. He blamed his age, the natural wane of his sex drive, and he hoped I understood. But how could I when mine was still confusingly sky-rocketing, my hormones still scrambling inside me? We ended most evenings communally enough, me accompanying him upstairs at his usual witching hour, a chaste peck on the cheek outside our respective rooms and a whispered goodnight, a robotic routine I felt we could perpetuate now for ever, until the end of our days.

Occasionally, I still went out with friends – though not Jane so much; I sensed she was disappointed I'd taken such a reductive step back – and Andrew was always on standby to come and pick me up afterwards, just as a father would have done, as my therapist would no doubt have suggested – and did. My weekly appointments were now, as far as I was concerned, set in stone, my therapist helping me to find at least some kind of clarity in all this. He still never directly answered my questions, but instead gently steered me towards what I thought was best for my life. And if *I* didn't know what was best for my life, who did?

My marriage was going well. It was. There was more mutual respect between us now; we tolerated one another more, and swallowed arguments where once we would have been quick to vent them. And if our sex life petered out altogether, then that, I reasoned, was true of many long marriages. We weren't that different from anybody else. We were normal, ordinary, and functional, but also middle-aged before our time, and treading endless water. This was not a nice thought, one that visited me at night, and so I dwelt on it sparingly, trying to snuff it out altogether.

Ignorance is bliss, after all.

'It's Royal Ascot in a couple of weeks. Fancy going?'

Summer. The garden was in bloom, partly nature's doing,

partly my own. When I wasn't out in the garden nurturing another of my new interests (I had also recently undertaken a course in beginners' French, as well as Pilates), I was still doing four days' work a week, and enduring it the way anyone does with work: grudgingly, and with a list of growing grievances. Andrew's own job had had yet further developments, sinister ones. There was talk now of comprehensive restructuring efforts, which would comprise new staff, many from overseas, the likely upshot of which would be to lay off some of the older lags, Andrew among them. To my swallowed horror, he was rather hoping this would come to pass, not just for the generous pay-off, but because he had started talking recently of early retirement. He'd decided nothing yet, but was looking into facilities-management consultancy work, and also developing his golf habit, which he and Dan had recently discovered and which now competed with the horses for his enthusiasm. He had put on more weight over the spring, and was contented in a quiet and settled sort of way I had not previously seen in him. A month before, we'd been discussing summer holidays. I was leaning towards France, he, a narrowboat on the Norfolk Broads.

'Two weeks at five miles per hour,' he beamed. 'What's not to love?'

He brought up the possibility of Royal Ascot during dinner in front of the television one night. I turned to look at him and was greeted by his inane, mostly lovable grin. He told me it might be fun. We could buy new clothes and dress up properly, and enjoy a champagne lunch, a flutter or two. 'Our last chance to splash the cash before they put me out to pasture.' He roared with laughter.

He needled me about it over the next couple of days in the way a child does their parent when she wants to visit the circus, the funfair, or to stay up late past bedtime. Please please please, oh please. My old self would have sneered and refused, but not the new me. I said yes.

We looked ridiculous, he in top hat and tails, me in aquamarine silk and a hat-and-veil combination that spoke of a fashion designer's identity crisis. We couldn't face the bus to the train station and so took a cab, our driver chuckling to himself as he checked us out repeatedly in his rear-view mirror. But we blended in surprisingly well alongside hundreds of other Ascot-goers at the station, all congregating together like an endangered species across a hostile veld. I imagined huntsmen gathering at the perimeter, guns drawn, mulling over which multicoloured head would look best on their wall.

Our carriage was full of the tang of generously applied perfume, and the atmosphere was that of a party, the men jocular and masculine, the women flamingo pink and peacock proud, all of us talking and joking, exchanging fashion tips and racing forecasts.

We arrived at the ground and promptly found the VIP section, Andrew having bagged us tickets via a colleague, and we took our positions at a table which overlooked the entire course. We watched the first couple of races go by as mere spectators, but Andrew could hold off no longer and took me with excitable roughness by the hand to the betting window where, tongue protruding between his teeth, he frowned over the betting slips of the next seven races, bringing the full weight of his ticking mind to bear. I merely marvelled over the non-sensical names: Tinkerbell Operative, Forceful Faster, Poppy Delight III.

I began inevitably, and quickly, to flag, incapable of maintaining my mask of enthusiasm any longer. One of my horses came in second, another fell. My hat was itchy, and I wanted to sit somewhere quiet. We were no longer at our table, but rather in the scrum of the crowd, Andrew having gravitated towards some men with whom he could shake fists and jostle in a way that couldn't end well for his top hat.

I felt a tap on my shoulder and turned to see a vaguely familiar face. Ruddy and round and lined like a turnip, the kind of face that made you think of uncles at Christmas time. 'You belong to Andrew, don't you?' he demanded with what I hoped was irony.

I nodded obliquely, then pointed him out.

'Fabulous! Fabulous!'

He then stumbled away and into the melee. A woman appeared at my side next, and again I was confronted by someone familiar.

'It's Lucy, isn't it?' she said, and suddenly it came to me: Sally, one of the Racing Widows I'd met what must have been two whole years ago now. She was smiling. 'Come,' she said. 'Come and join us.'

I followed her towards a large corner table, around which I recognized several other of the Racing Widows – Kay and Jean, and other women whose names I couldn't immediately recall, and Lorraine, too. I remembered Lorraine, the woman who had confessed last time to regularly dating escorts ('*so* much cheaper in the long run'). They greeted me as an old friend, and I was immediately consumed into an ongoing conversation about boring husbands and feckless boyfriends, which prompted in me a wave of déjà vu. We were naughty schoolgirls transformed into the bodies of grown-up women, and this time at least, two years on, I didn't feel quite the naïve fledgling, but eager now to match their stories of heartache and disappointment, and also of reckless adventure.

After all, I had talked about this to no one – no one, that is, except my therapist (and they were thrilled to know I had a shrink) – and I wanted to compare notes, to tell these women everything. As I talked, they leaned in conspiratorially, lapping up my confessions as they did the champagne, my very own pantomime crowd replete with trembling oohs and aahs, gripping me by the arm and frequently scuttling over to hug me close to their bosoms.

'Well done!'

'Good girl!'

'*How* young was he, did you say?'

'You lucky bitch. However did you do it?'

'Can I have his number?'

They were surprisingly sanguine when I told them how easy it was for Andrew and I to get back together ('You didn't really think he was ever going to leave you for good, did you?') and seemed genuinely dejected that my affair was now over. Foolishly, I started crying. Half a dozen handkerchiefs were swiftly proffered.

'Welcome to the club,' they said, toasting my inauguration with champagne.

'If you've managed all that in the last couple of years alone, then just imagine what you'll have for us this time next year,' laughed Lorraine. I shook my head in response, and held up my hand. 'No, no,' I assured them. 'Not any more; once is enough for me, I'm afraid. I'm really not cut out for all this, not like you.' I winced. 'No offence. I just mean I want a quiet life now.' I composed myself, and cleared my throat. 'I've started gardening, learning French, Pilates.'

It was as if I had said something funny, a joke. The Racing Widows, all of them, leaned back and shrieked. Scanning their faces, it was hard to tell them apart. I could only imagine them here, together, a bruising collective, and I wondered what kind of people they were individually, when apart. Quieter, surely. Less indomitable and not so sure of themselves. Breakable, too.

They were still laughing, and I blushed deep. Without really knowing why, I laughed too.

'You'll learn,' said Sally.

By the end of the afternoon, Andrew and the other husbands returned to us. A couple had won big and insisted on treating us all to dinner at a nearby restaurant. It was late when we reached the Jullandar Shere, but we ate and drank with the kind of momentum that encouraged them to stay open later still, anticipating a massive bar bill and a generous tip. We were like a school party that had got out of hand, the boys making fun of the girls, the girls responding with catty remarks, and all of us shouting over everybody else, wanting to be heard. In the middle of it all I realized that perhaps this was what life for the over-forties was like: an increasing division between the sexes confused by moments of solidarity and communality. That night I wanted to be nowhere else but there, amongst people who weren't friends really, not in the proper sense, but compatriots nevertheless. I felt powerfully bonded to them all, my true peers. Perhaps I would come to these things more often now, and become a Racing Widow myself. Why not? If life had taught me anything in the past year, it was that it was still full of surprises.

After an enormous cheese platter – a rather French finale to an otherwise very Indian meal – the men went outside to the car park to smoke cigars, leaving the women sat around the chaos of our table. Two waiters were dispatched to clean up, a pair of beautiful young Goan men with sculpted noses and shy eyes, who responded to our coarse catcalls and come-ons by blushing violently and retreating quickly.

Kay and Jean insisted Lorraine show us her new iPad, which she now removed from her Louis Vuitton handbag, this otherwise comfortably antiquated middle-aged woman unexpectedly au fait with modern technology. She registered the surprise in my eyebrows, and giggled. 'Needs must.' Making sure the men were still puffing away outside, we gathered around her while, with nimble fingers, she scrolled through countless apps. On to the screen bloomed a dating site I was unfamiliar with. It specialized, I read, in 'women of a certain vintage who prefer fizz to plonk'.

'I average a couple of dates a month through this,' she told me.

'Show us the one you've lined up next,' said Jean.

Lorraine touched the screen again, her pink fingernail clacking on the perspex, and an image came to life, a handsome man in his mid-thirties with smoky eyes and a square jaw. 'He's Arabic,' Lorraine said breathlessly. I scanned his personal information, hoping to find out whether this really was a dating site, or else merely an escort service, but the print was too small and Lorraine's fingers too quick. She tapped at the screen again.

'I'm meeting him next week,' she said. 'I can ask him to bring a friend, if you like. What do you think?'

The question was directed at me. The Widows egged me on, as if my reply represented the final part of my initiation into their club. More waiters approached, to remove the tablecloths now, but saw us huddled together and serious. They retreated.

It was late; I had had a lot to drink. I was tired, and confused. I wasn't sure about this, wasn't sure I wanted what they wanted. I shrugged.

Lorraine spoke again. 'A double date, you, me, him and his friend.'

There was no pleading in her eyes – she didn't *need* me to accompany her – but rather the suggestion of a challenge. My mettle was being tested, my answer judged significant. It would do me the world of good, Kay said, would help me forget Ben, accept Andrew, and make the best of my life. But I prevaricated. Did I really want to become a serial adulterer? And if not, was it somehow anti-feminist of me, the little woman at home in defeatist acceptance of her lot in life?

I looked up and into their faces, one by one. I wanted to please my new friends, be complicit with them, but also remain true to myself, whatever that truth might be.

I smiled, melancholic. 'Another time, perhaps?'

Lorraine nodded briskly, once. 'Sure. Of course.'

The men poured back in through the doors, bringing with them their trails of smoke. Andrew, cheeks beetroot red, reclaimed his seat alongside me, a possessive hand on my thigh. His top hat had long been lost to the night, his tie was askew, shirt stained, the lenses of his glasses full of smudges. 'Having fun?' he wanted to know.

I was a woman of a certain age, I had made my choices in life, and now I was living with the consequences.

'Having fun?' Andrew had wanted to know the night before. I had answered him diplomatically, wanting only to please him.

But was I? In fits and spurts, I suppose, yes I was, though some days more than others. What I did know categorically was that I was lucky still to be married at all, and that I wanted the luck to continue. But that niggling boredom that had driven me into this mess in the first place had not quite gone away. And though I was no longer driven by that same reckless abandon, a reckless-abandon-shaped hole was still waiting impatiently for me to fill it with something else.

As Andrew had done with his drinking – cut down on my account, reserving it these days mostly for special occasions only, or else as a flagrant disregard for my feelings whenever we argued – so I had done with my online activities. It had been months since I had been online. I was frequently aware of those months in increments of weeks, days and hours.

Every addiction requires a replacement, a viable alternative, and so I directed my persistent needs and cravings into those other forums instead, the ones filled with similar accidental adulterers either wishing they could retrace their steps, or else wanting to go further still. There was a lot of hard-won wisdom aired here, alongside bitter regret and even threats of vengeful recriminations. I read the posts, hundreds and hundreds of them from all over the world, the way one would an airport thriller, perpetually hungry for the next instalment, with its cliffhangers, its shocking denouements.

These were my people now, and I couldn't help but take – not pleasure exactly, but comfort, certainly, that I was not the only one struggling. Sometimes, whiling away the hours on these message boards brought me a greater sense of comfort than I could find anywhere else. I relished the peeking into other people's troubled lives, and occasionally I would enter into one-to-one conversations, eager to compare and contrast our respective war wounds.

But this morning, after the races, after Andrew's 'Having fun?', when my thoughts were filled helplessly with longing once again, with Ben, Ben who was lost to me now – and where was he, and did he think of me, and did he miss me as much as I him? – I went to the forum again, not to read but rather to post my whole story up on the general message board, to lay it bare from beginning to end, suddenly experiencing an overwhelming need to confess all. I knew from my therapist sessions that certain episodes in our lives were always so much easier to make sense of, and gain closure from, when freed from the over-activity of our minds. And so, a cup of steaming hot coffee by my side, I began to type.

Immediately I was forced to stop due to a careless oversight: Andrew, stumbling down the stairs, late for work and grumbling that I hadn't woken him.

He looked every bit as bad as I felt. 'Christ, I'm late,' he said, pecking my cheek, before swigging from my coffee cup, reaching for a slice of bread and posting it, unbuttered, into his mouth, then heading for the front door, breadcrumbs trailing in his wake.

Returning to the forum, I began typing again, and couldn't stop. I wrote it all out, the reasons for my going online in the first place, and what I found when I got there. I wrote about all the advice I had read along the way, how much of it I had foolishly disregarded, and how ultimately it had helped me to here and now, out the other side, sanity and security still almost intact. But I admitted that it was hard, so hard that I continued to pine for what I had left behind, and that sometimes, on days like today, I felt the overwhelming urge to once again follow my compulsions wherever they may lead, irrespective of the ensuing fallout and the further hurt they would surely cause.

'But,' I typed, 'I mustn't, I shouldn't, I won't.

'Will I?'

My hangover asserted itself powerfully. I made another coffee, some toast, then sat back in my silent kitchen. It was a Friday, my day off. The sun was streaming in through the window, affording everything a blinding brightness that challenged my tired eyes. One of the neighbourhood cats was on the outside window ledge gazing impassively in at me, blinking out a message I ignored. My handbag was where I had left it the night before, in the middle of the table, on its side, buckle open, contents spilled forward. I emptied it all out now, the travel-cards, tubes of lipstick, chocolate-bar wrappers, chewing gum, coins, endless till receipts. The cat, no longer impassive, scraped forlornly at the window, asking to be let in as I sifted through it all and quickly found, as I knew I would, the piece of A4 paper that had been folded and folded into a small, neat rectangle. I opened it. 'In Every Sunflower', the title read, in Ben's meticulous, easy-to-read handwriting, so appropriate, I thought now, for writing on blackboards, his future students hanging on his every chalk mark. It was his poem from the open mic night. I read it again, poring over every word. I still didn't understand it, and still it made me cry.

I reached for my phone and tapped in his number, which I still knew by heart, and always would. My thumb hovered over the green CALL button. I mustn't, I shouldn't, I won't.

Will I?

I heard, then, a soft ping. An email. I placed my phone back carefully on the table, Ben's number still lit up, and reached for my laptop. I'd had a response to my post already. The name she gave was 'Lori', and she said she was writing from California. I looked up at the wall clock. Eight o'clock here, which meant midnight on America's West Coast.

> Your post reached me just in time, as if I willed it to before doing something I would surely later regret. I find myself in pretty much the same kind of situation you write about, and I have to say that reading about your experiences has made me cry and smile at the same time.
>
> Like you, I've been married a few years to a basically good guy. We love each other, we're good friends. But it often seems to me like we've gone from fun and happy to settled and middle-aged in the space of a few short years. He wants kids, I'm not ready. He wants to spend nights in front of the TV, I want adventure still. I mean, you're only young once, right? And I'm still 'only' 38, and no grey hairs yet!
>
> Anyway, couple months back, I started to have a little innocent fun with this guy online. I don't know his real name, and he doesn't know mine, and we don't talk about personal things too much, but we click like I've never clicked with anyone before. He makes me laugh, he makes my day, and sometimes he lifts my soul – and I've not even met him . . . yet. But he's been pressing for a date recently, and I was coming dangerously close to saying yes.

My sweet husband doesn't have an argumentative bone in his body, so I've been going out of my way these past few weeks to deliberately start fights. My thinking was this: I thought it would make it easier to set up my little date with this guy if I could fall spectacularly out with my husband first. How nasty am I?!

But my sweet husband wasn't playing ball. He thought I was stressed because of pressures at work, and that I needed even more of his TLC, Goddammit!

Until tonight, that is. Tonight I was REALLY unreasonable. I was cruel, and I said hurtful things, and he snapped. He shouted back at me, and it turned ugly. 'Yay!' I thought, selfishly. 'At last!' I threw things, and I slammed doors, not quite believing that I was doing it – I felt like an actress! – but it worked. He's in the spare room now, asleep. And I'm in our bedroom, brooding. It's lonely in here . . .

I thought I would feel right now that I'd gotten my permission at last, that I could make contact with my guy, and we could meet soon – tonight, even. But guess what? I was terrified! Full of doubt.

And so I came onto the forum – looking for . . . what, really? I confess that I don't know. Support, encouragement? Somebody to help me make sense of all this?

And then I saw your post. I read it like 10 times straight thru. Afterwards, I didn't feel so much like calling my guy. Maybe now I never will. Who knows?!

So, anyway, I just wanted to say that you may have saved my marriage! Of course, you may have just condemned me to an eternity of marriage hell as well (☺) but I don't think so. We'll see.

What I wanted to say to you most of all, is thank you. Thank you for sharing. I will always be grateful to you. Keep strong yourself.

Your friend,

Lori

I closed my laptop. Tears streamed from my eyes, and I sat there, at my kitchen table, knees drawn up to my chest, and let them come. I picked up my phone, touched the screen again, and there was his number, waiting. My thumbnail, I saw, needed filing. It had a tiny tear in the middle. It would catch on my clothes and annoy me if I didn't do something about it.

I put the phone down and went upstairs. My search for the clipper took a good quarter-hour, but I was in no particular hurry. I eventually found it by the side of the bath, its tiny jaws filled with Andrew's nails, two or three clippings curling and yellowed. I ran it under the tap, watching my husband's bodily cast-offs swirl lazily down the plughole.

My nail, once I'd finished with it, was a perfect semicircle, clean and smooth, shiny with good health. I went into my bedroom and got dressed, checked myself in the full-length mirror and felt happy enough with what I saw staring back. I smoothed myself down, pulled my stomach in and my shoulders back. And then I went downstairs to start the day proper, and to resume my life.